# COMMON SENSE AND REASON AGAIN

"John Bassett McCleary follows a long-time family characteristic of upending the status quo. His grandfather, James Madison Bassett, was the driving force in exposing the corporate fraud of one of the "Big Four" railroad barons, Collis P. Huntington. And John's father, W. K. Bassett, initiated the field workers union in Hawaii,providing protection and benefits for the laborers against the fruit canning company owners. John has led the effort of multiple generations to question authority and persons in power.

"McCleary's writings continue a journalistic tradition, for he is the heir to a family of penmen titans—owners, publishers, editors, reporters for the publications *The Golden Era, Oakland Tribune, Los Angeles Herald, Oakland Enquirer, San Francisco Chronicle, Pacific Commercial Advertiser*, the *Honolulu Times, Boston Herald, Providence Bulletin*, the magazine Controversy, *Pacific Weekly* and the *Carmel Cymbal*."

*Douglas Schmitz*
Author, historian, Bassett family biographer

_KENTON ÷ SCOUT_

# COMMON SENSE
# and REASON
# AGAIN

**Comments On The Flaws of Our
Government and Society in General
With Concise Remarks on
Capitalism and Religion**

*written by*
*John Bassett McCleary*

*edited by*
*Joan Jeffers McCleary*

SLOW LIMBO
PUBLISHING

**COMMON SENSE AND REASON AGAIN**

Slow Limbo Publishing

ISBN: 0-9668687-3-9

Other books by John Bassett McCleary

**The People's Book**

Celestial Arts, 1972

**Monterey Peninsula People**

ISBN 0-9668687-0-6

Slow Limbo Productions, 1998

**The Hippie Dictionary**

ISBN 1-58008-355-2

Ten Speed Press, Crown Press/Random House, 2002 revised 2004

**Mother's Heart, Father's Mind**

ISBN 0-9668687-4-6

For more information about this book or John McCleary's other works, please see: hippiedictionary.com or commonsenseagain.net

*Common Sense and Reason Again* is *the second book in The Hippie Trilogy:*

*The Hippie Dictionary*

*Common Sense and Reason Again*

*Mother's Heart, Father's Mind*

DEDICATED TO

The people who have spoken out unheard.
Those who are afraid to speak out.
And to
John and Richard Miller, who spoke out all their lives
and demanded to be heard;
you know which Millers you are among all the Millers!

With guidance from Thomas Paine

John McCleary

# CHAPTERS AND CONTENTS

THOMAS PAINE
Common Sense [1776]

"In the following pages I offer nothing more than simple
facts, plain arguments, and common sense; and have no other
preliminaries to settle with the reader, than that he will divest himself
of prejudice and prepossession, and suffer his reason and his feelings
to determine for themselves; that he will put on, or rather that he will
not put off the true character of a man, and generously enlarge his
views beyond the present day."

# INTRODUCTION

Perhaps the sentiments contained in the following pages, are not yet sufficiently fashionable to procure them general favor; a long habit of not thinking a thing wrong, gives it a superficial appearance of being right, and raises at first a formidable outcry in defense of custom. But tumult soon subsides. Time makes more converts than reason.

As a long and violent abuse of power is generally the means of calling the right of it in question, (and in matters too which might never have been thought of, had not the sufferers been aggravated into the inquiry,) and as the king of England hath undertaken in his own right, to support the parliament in what he calls theirs, and as the good people of this country are grievously oppressed by the combination, they have an undoubted privilege to inquire into the pretensions of both, and equally to reject the usurpations of either.

In the following sheets, the author hath studiously avoided every thing which is personal among ourselves. Compliments as well as censure to individuals make no part thereof. The wise and the worthy need not the triumph of a pamphlet; and those whose sentiments are injudicious or unfriendly, will cease of themselves, unless too much pains is bestowed upon their conversion.

The cause of America is, in a great measure, the cause of all mankind. Many circumstances have, and will arise, which are not local, but universal, and through which the principles of all lovers of mankind are affected, and in the event of which, their affections are interested. The laying a country desolate with fire and sword, declaring war against the natural rights of all mankind, and extirpating the defenders thereof from the face of the earth, is the concern of every man to whom nature hath given the power of feeling; of which class, regardless of party censure, is the ...

AUTHOR [Thomas Paine}
Philadelphia, Feb. 14, 1776.

Thomas Paine wrote in Common Sense,

JOHN MCCLEARY
Common Sense and Reason Again [2020]

## INTRODUCTION

There are immoral minorities, but no immoral majorities. Most people are moral and that is why democracy is the best form of government. In order to save our world, we must, at times, be disturbingly frank, painfully truthful.

I want to focus on the male ego, greed and insecurity. These are the reasons for most of the world's problems.

Our world can be a family, a tribe, town, state or country and then our planet. And our family, tribe, town, state, country and world are not, personally, ours alone. There are other family members and other occupants of "our" world. We are all just in these groups and places for a while with others. Your country is other peoples' world, other peoples' family. If you think you are the center of the universe, you are not alone; everyone thinks they are the center of everything. It is only the greedy and arrogant who make a big deal out of it. In order to be a good family member, you must respect the other "family" members in our world.

Patriotism, nationalism and ethnic pride are important to give us a foundation in our history, but global democracy exists to prepare for and insure for our good future. If you have no living family, children or spouse, you might, I say, might, have a justification for not caring about our environment, peace and freedom, after you die, but I am sure you will not be going to heaven, nirvana or Club Med wherever you think death should take you.

Don't confuse the difference between a revolutionary war and a war of economics and expansion. Don't confuse the difference between a weapon of defense and a weapon of aggression and expansion.

In 1776, Thomas Paine's little book, *Common Sense*, helped usher in a totally new form of government, a democratic and representational form of government whereby the common people were given the opportunity to speak their mind by voting for a representative who would gather with other representatives from the other Colonies to propose, hash out, vote and agree on the laws to govern the then 13 states of the United States of America. His little book was the catalyst that bound together the Colonists of America in 1776 and gave them a voice to speak out against the tyranny of English rule. It was the start of a revolution.

The tyrants that Thomas Paine wrote against were put aside. We gained our independence and started a great nation. In the process, our Declaration of Independence, Constitution and Bill of Rights were written.

These documents are arguably the greatest pronouncements for the freedom of mankind ever created. It is obvious also that they were written by people of great intellectual capacity.

Now my small book is here to tell you the tyrants have returned. With new faces and in new guises, the people who chased us from the Old Country and hounded us in the New World have re-emerged. All the advantages our Founding Fathers created for "the huddled masses longing to be free" have been slowly wiped away or watered down by the wealthy elite and their political friends.

We colonists were all aliens and the Native Americans could call us illegal aliens, but we came to save our lives and make a new life just as other new aliens do today. To treat new aliens as criminals is hypocrisy of the worst kind; sending people away, back to where they came from to endure poverty and death is immoral, and especially if you are doing it for your own financial gain. Do you have Native American blood in your body, or is it just upon your hands?

If the native population of North America in the 17th century had been able to kick us back into the sea, the world would be a different place. But I am not here to speculate; I am here to promote a benevolent future. Our dreams shouldn't be of a tragic past; we should be dreaming of a beautiful future.

I believe, as a majority of the "thinking people" in this country do, that the United States of America is in big trouble today. The main problem is capitalism and conservative ideology stealing away the American dream from the majority of citizens. And the second problem is failure of the silent majority to recognize the crimes of capitalists. I am equating capitalism to what we, in 1776, were fighting against, the King and the feudal system of England.

The worst problem in the United States of America today is neither crime, poverty, illegal aliens, nor terrorism. It is corporate greed and excesses and the ignorance that allows it to exist.

A large portion of our population believes that intellectual exploration is somehow dangerous or sinful. They have been convinced of this by a small, wealthy ruling class of people in this country who have a lot to lose if the majority population ever figures out what is really causing the troubles in this world. And yet the human brain is what made humans the strong and vital species we are. Without intellectual exploration the saber-toothed tigers and mastodons would rule the world today.

It was the feudal system, not religion, that forced most American colonists and immigrants to leave the old countries. You know, the feudal system where a few people owned everything and the rest of us were indentured to them to work, to make money, so we could give the money back to them for our necessities and "rent!" It is a well-organized and subtle form of slavery.

Does that sound like capitalism to you? Yes, because capitalism is the new feudal system!

This little book contains suggestions on how to bring back the American dream. Many of these ideas are "revolutionary" in the way that Thomas Jefferson meant it to be, meaning that they are non-violent, yet unconventional and ground-breaking. A true and righteous revolution is an uprising of the majority of people to equalize happiness and prosperity. Revolution does not have to be painful and violent.

Because of my life, where I've been and what I've done, I have an opinion on many things! But I have facts and truth to support what I say. Don't knee-jerk a rebuttal, please read and think; it may be important for our continued existence.

Herein you will also find suggestions about how to fix the mess in which we find our democracy. If you do not read this book, then you will have no basis on which to agree or disagree with me, for there are many totally unique concepts and viewpoints within. Everyone has room to learn, even you, even me.

Lying is more time-consuming than the truth!

Lying is more destructive than the truth!

Lying gives you only a small amount of solution or satisfaction, and then a world of hurt!

The truth will give you a lifetime of solutions and satisfaction!

I try to date when I wrote things. I will at times use a date stamp on some of these ideas and writings that look like this 2003/2020, designating when I first wrote them and when I edited them for this publication. I may also emphasize some things I think important with boldface type or italic! And I like poetic quotes.

Also, I have several friends, family members, alter egos and created personalities whom I quote or use to illustrate what I am saying. They are Dudley Griffin, JOB, Jesus, and Ug, Mug and Thug. Dudley Griffin and JOB are still alive and feeding me insights today. Ug, Mug and Thug are fictitious people from 400,000 years ago. Ug is a female, Mug and Thug are males.

## In this book—Issues to be discussed:

**Tax Structure**: the old "taxation without representation" adding the question of "taxation without benefits," which is the growing problem today.

**Advertising Industries:** false representation of products.

**Monopoly:** the temptation to steal from the public if you own a whole industry.

**Planned Obsolescence:** using poor quality workmanship and materials in order to sell more products at higher profits.

**Saving the Planet:** poor government and industry conservation and preservation policies.

**Stock Market:** the possibility of phasing out the market or at least ending the Ponzi scheme aspect of it.

**Military and War:** the possibility of scaling down our military and rethinking the value of war to the citizens of the world.

**Representational Form of Government**: consider phasing it out, yet keeping democracy, of course, by instituting retinal scanning electronic voting for all issues that concern you. **OVE: One Vote Everyone**.

Without Thomas Paine's political intellectual exploration, our country and its democracy and freedom would never exist. I am hoping that this little re-creation and homage to his book will help preserve democracy and freedom for future generations.

What I will be doing is preaching, educating, advocating and condemning. And I swear on my mother's righteousness and beauty that everything I write is the truth as far as I could research it.

All of these things are connected by one emotion of the human being-- self preservation.

All of these things are connected by one element of human nature-- the male ego!

**Government**

**Democracy**

**Voting**

**Representational Form of Government**

**Tax Structure**

**Capitalism**

**Free Enterprise**

**Advertising Industry**

**Planned Obsolescence**

**Monopoly**

**Stock Market**

I am just here to help cure ignorance.

Author.

Monterey, California, April 18, 2020.

# VOICES OF COMMON SENSE

*"Freedom of speech does not give you the freedom to lie."*
*JBMc 9.13.09*

*"You can't exercise common sense unless you have the common knowledge."*
*Dudley Griffin 5.10.10*

*"The history of man is not a blueprint for mankind's evolution; it is a list of our mistakes."*
*JBMc 9.13.13*

*"Diplomacy is the only thing that separates us humans from being wild animals trying to eat each other!" JBMc 10.30.17*

*"If journalists published only what people approved of, there would be very little printed."*
*Paraphrased from Benjamin Franklin*

*"Those who will not allow peaceful revolution are making violent revolution inevitable."*
John Fitzgerald Kennedy

*"Find out who the liars are and banish them; find the thieves and banish them; the greedy, banish them also, 'cause if you don't, you and all of the good people will suffer forever!"*
Dudley Griffin, 11.5.18

*"We are now dealing with things that are not written down anywhere." JBMc 2003*

*"We are now dealing with things that are written down here only." JBMc 2020*

*"Conservatives, fundamentalist religious people, you want to control everybody else's life because you don't have any control of your life." JOB 4/20/2020*

*"People of power and influence, please don't mistreat us, the people, because we might then have to rebel. We don't want to rebel, it is not in our nature to be nasty, like your nature is to mistreat us."*
*Dudley Griffin 1/8/2020*

*"People of power, read history to find out what will happen if you continue to mistreat us. Even Caesar, King George III, Napoleon and Hitler found out… too late!"*
*Dudley Griffin 1/8/2020*

*"God, you have several choices:*
*You can let us go on and kill ourselves!*
*You can let us go on struggling day to day to physically and emotionally live in this chaos! Or you can let us reach our potential and become perfect!"*
*JOB, 4/5/20*

*"Mankind, you have several possible choices: You can let us go on and kill ourselves! You can continue to struggle day to day to physically and emotionally survive! Or you can get together with your brothers and sisters to strive to reach your potential and become perfect!"*
*JOB, 4/5/20*

*"Pride is the first sin because it begets all others." JBMc 2/1/2*
*"In the eyes of God, nonviolence raises you above those people of violence!"*
*JOB, as told to him by God*

I introduce to you three people from prehistory who have been recreated and reborn over and over from then until now: Ug, Mug and Thug,

**UG** was driven to save the world.
**MUG** was driven to get by in the world.
**THUG** was driven to own the world.

Come on people of the United States, we can do it; we are the melting pot of people, the conglomeration of the whole world. If we demand cooperation among the people of this world we can change all our lives to be a cooperative effort. We can create a perfect world, in spite of the greedy and egotistic selfish few. It is only 1% that we have to put in their place, so that the world will work.

Working people don't always know who pays their salaries, it is not the companies they work for that do so, it is the other people, like themselves, who buy the food and products who really pay for everything.

We have too many disreputable big box stores, to many car manufactures, too many air carriers, too many gas companies. What we don't have is enough reputable schools, hospitals, or home town stores. Let's stop worrying about the corporations' survival or the rich peoples net quarter bottom line and start worrying about the real people and their future and the future of their children.

This coronavirus has shown people for who and what the really are! Some people are worried about the death and the human suffering brought about by the virus, and some are worried about the capitalist world and not being able to buy a new Porsche later this year.

# COMMON SENSE AND REASON AGAIN

# CHAPTER 1

## The Argument Against Kings And Capitalism

Our Founding Fathers chose democracy and free enterprise (not capitalism) to be the political and economic foundation for this country. They did so as a deterrent against discontent and rebellion of the masses, and because they knew it was for The People, the most people. They knew, maybe only instinctively, that if the people are given the ability to form their own destiny, they will be happy and not need to revolt violently.

As you know, if you read our history, the word and the activity "capitalism" has been around only two hundred years, whereas this country has been here for 244 years. Capitalism is the new feudal system, the same feudal system most of us left the "old country" to get away from! Some left for religious purposes, but most left for economic freedom.

In much of Europe in 1776, most everything was owned by a small percentage of the population: royalty, major and minor nobility, landed gentry and "The Church." It was much the same in 1620 when the Pilgrims came to America.

The Pilgrims came on the first boat, *The Mayflower*, in 1620 for freedom of religion, free land and opportunity, and the feudal lords sent their accountants and lawyers on the second boat, *The Fortune*, one year later. The feudal lords have been trying to take everything back ever since. Capitalism is against anything free.

Communism, socialism, free-enterprise and capitalism are the four primary economic terms we us for the spectrum of our world economies. I am a free-enterprise socialist, not a capitalist or communist. I believe that free enterprise, combined with a social safety net system, is the perfect majority-satisfying democratic economy. I have lived in villages in Greece with that same economy, and my ancestors lived in villages here in America with that as the basic economy.

Nobody ever died of starvation or neglect in a tribal village. Most families and small towns are communes. Socialism is a democratic form of economy. It is congenial, and you can be sure that many more people will be happy in a democratic form of economy. Greedy people don't agree with majority happiness.

Many social systems were created at the beginning of our democracy. Benjamin Franklin devised the free fire department and free library systems. Thomas Jefferson thought higher education should be offered to deserving people without money in their family. These two men are still today considered two of the most intelligent people in mankind's history. They knew that educating the masses was good for the people and the nation.

What's wrong with socialism? Are you ashamed of being nice to people in need? Every village or small town in the world runs on a socialistic morality. Are we going to let greedy people destroy mankind for the sake of their egos? Yes, "ego" that is one of the major flaws of mankind. Ego elevates self, developing into selfishness and then greed.

We, as a democracy, should not have capitalism as our economic foundation. It is a shaky platform for the workingman and not a level playing field for anyone, except those people who already have wealth.

Without dictators messing it up, communism would be socialism and free enterprise together.

**Socialism** is a democratic economic system!

**Free Enterprise** is a democratic economic system!

**Fascisms** is a dictatorial economic system!

**Capitalism** is a dictatorial economic system!

A free enterprise and socialist economy allows everyone capable of competing to do so, and it supplies a safety net for those who cannot. Without a safety net, many people will slip into poverty, which is bad for society. A poor man is capable of desperate actions; it may even be said he is required and destined to steal for the survival of his family and self. A healthy society is one where everyone is content with his or her life and opportunities.

Competition is good for development of the mind and body. If it is done with love and rationality it will advance you and society into a good future. If it is done with greed and hate it will destroy our world.

Socialism is, if you know your Bible, the actual Christian way. Christ tended to the poor, aged and sick. Now we just put people who can't compete in dog-eat-dog capitalism into the modern poor house; prisons or institutions.

I believe in a rational economic food chain, like the animal and natural kingdom's food chain. Human economic sustenance should start from the bottom. All nutrition in the animal kingdom travels up from the smallest creatures through the chain until it eventually reaches the top predators. Actually, it flows best when it flows both ways. The large die and feed the small, and the small feed the large again. Everyone touches the food and/or money. This makes for a happier society, everyone receiving the food they need. It's natural, it's democratic, it's socialistic and it is the opposite of trickle-down.

I realize that this book contains new ways to look at things we already thought we knew as factual and established. Don't just close your mind to new things because they are different; look at their value in this changing world. We must learn new social and economical actions just as we have learned how to deal with the computer, cell phones and virtual reality.

To save our country's integrity and validity as a democracy, there are several things that we as voters must do.

Lobby for politicians and vote for candidates who would be open minded to:

1. Reinstitute monopoly and usury laws.
2. Scrap the trickle-down economy, it doesn't work for anyone except the rich.
3. Stop tax breaks for advertising, and increase breaks for real R&D into areas of quality and conservation.
4. The government should offer carbon credits and give tax breaks for keeping people employed. Government should reward good behavior, not bad.
5. Censure and scale back the stock market. The stock market should give new and good companies a chance to research and develop new products to benefit and advance mankind and our environment.
6. Control election contributions to make us a democracy again.
7. Get rid of the electoral collage to make us a democracy again.

We need intellectuals making our fiscal and economic decisions, not MBAs and lawyers. Intellectuals and academics make decisions based on facts gleaned from research and study and will most likely make non-personal and non-partisan decisions regardless of who benefits. No one who will disproportionately benefit from a political decision on economics should have a say in the laws. Let's have women making decisions for women. Wow, that would be unique!

The one thing that makes us human beings is our society. If we do not fit in or add something to society, then we are an outcast, and if we are an outcast then we fail as a human being.

Governments are not really our society; they are just representative of society. People are society.

As our Founding Fathers showed us, it is possible to be a revolutionary and still be a valuable member of society. If the government does not add to the welfare of society, then it should be changed, as Jefferson wrote.

When the King was in power, he kept a tight reign on those who opposed him. When they came to power, they, of course, would do the same to him.

Again:
> *"Those who will not allow peaceful revolution are making violent revolution inevitable."*
> John Fitzgerald Kennedy

Although it has not been publicized widely or spoken of much, one of the underlying reasons for our Founding Fathers choosing a democracy for the government of the United States was that it is a benevolent pacifier for the masses. All other forms of government are dictatorial or autocratic, and they eventually ferment revolution, unrest and social and economic upheaval.

The difference between a government and a totalitarian dictatorship is that a dictatorship deals with dissent; a true government listens to it.

On July 9, 1776, the Declaration of Independence was read to General Washington's Army of the Continent on the commons in New York City. That day, common mankind learned that freedom was its birthright.

CHAPTER 2

## The Personality of America

"Democracy means freedom."

America has two personalities. It is democratic, tolerant, peace-loving and generous. It is also self-centered, arrogant, violent and greedy.

Which of these two would you like to be known as? Which of these two do you think is better for America?

Our founding fathers were by far the most insightful government leaders this world has ever known. Our Constitution and Bill of Rights are the best foundations for a peaceful, and profitable population on this earth. But we are not following the leadership of great men right now.

The formative idea of democracy is that whatever is best for the majority of the people will be better for everyone in the long run. Greedy people say, "To hell with that! I'm getting everything I want, and let everyone else suffer the consequences." That is poor fiscal planning for this country and the world.

That mentality was perhaps acceptable when we lived in a kill-or-be-killed jungle. Now cooperation among people is the more responsible and more profitable path.

Most people are trying to improve themselves economically. To do so, they might start by improving themselves socially.

The Perfection Chart

Learn to like people.
Learn the work ethic.
Learn to be tolerant of all others.
Achieve a reasonable economic stability.
Maintain a sexual control.
Find some sort of spirituality.
Achieve a giving spirit.
Achieve a volunteer attitude.

# CHAPTER 3

# Government

Until the Constitution and Bill of Rights of the United States of America were written, all other governments before were created as ways to control people and resources under the power of a few leaders or kings. The idea of American Democracy was a unique and inspired concept.

Giving the populace control over their own lives and a role in their own governing was genius, not merely as a benevolent concept, but as a practical solution to the continual conflicts and wars that had raged for millennia over man's basic desire to be free. Here was the true answer to human rebellion. Give mankind no reason to rebel. Give human beings their freedom.

Sadly, the natural evolution of mankind will always slowly slip toward economic and military dictatorship. This is true because the strongest and greediest will always gravitate to the top of government because of their desire for power and money. Without a population-friendly government using laws that protect the poor and weak, both business and government will eventually exploit the poor and weak.

Observing the problems of all other forms of government before 1776, our Founding Fathers created in our Constitution and Bill of Rights a balance of freedom and democracy. They also included reasonable restraints and checks and balances for the government, all based on legal and moral responsibility.

In order to keep faith with our Founding Fathers and to protect our perfect majority-run form of government, we need to preserve our democratic election process and ensure a free and diverse news and information media. We also have to be sure that our judges adhere to the laws of the land and common sense rather than the influences of partisan politics, religious doctrine, superstitions or economic pressures.

Remember the four levels of a democratic government. Executive, legislative, judicial and the free press.

The true genius behind the creation of our economy and government was the way our founding fathers designed it by joining opposites together to form a mutually reliant union. Our founders instinctively knew that to create a country that would last, they needed the cooperation of both the liberal working class and the conservative business class. They realized that the dominance of either class would continually create revolution or anarchy, over and over again, as history had proven.

People need to know they have some control of their future. If they are given no opportunity to ease their struggle or to improve themselves, they will rebel.

Knowing the basic instinct of human beings, the drive for individuality and freedom, democracy was chosen as the form of government to give everyone an investment in their future. The promise of free enterprise, and yet the checks and balances to protect the working class, were designed to make it possible for anyone of any birth to prosper financially and ascend to leadership.

Incentive to maintain the Union for the benefit of yourself and the benefit of all others, that is the glue that created the American Dream. The writers and framers of our Declaration of Independence and Constitution were employing an astute knowledge of basic human nature to create a nation that would work together to maintain itself.

These men were creating a work of art for the future of mankind, and they knew it. They were not just reacting to the first visceral dimension of self-preservation; they were considering the destiny of human beings.

Our founders knew that as long as there was a monarchy, feudal system, dictatorship or economic tyranny hanging over the population, there would always be social unrest. No one would be able to find true peace and comfort. Even those who thought they were in control, even the tyrants, could have no tranquility. History had already proven that over and over again.

Our founders realized that humans needed to govern themselves in order to be satisfied and at peace. The human being is different from most other animals, which accept their fate in nature. Humans will always lash out to gain control of their own destiny. With ideas that transcended their own lifetime, the framers of our Constitution conceived a form of self-government, which, if followed through to its ultimate, would lead humankind into paradise, self-satisfaction and peace. Don't laugh; That was their dream!

Franklin, Jefferson, Hamilton, Madison and Adams astutely realized that an independent man was not automatically an undisciplined or unscrupulous man. These deep thinkers knew that freedom and security were the ways to unbind man from his selfish fears of personal preservation and to help him progress toward unity, cooperation and preservation of a nation's high ideals. The United States was born of the ideal of freedom.

But the dream has been unraveling slowly ever since the business class forgot the basic truth that to maintain a harmonious and tranquil society, the working class must feel free and must believe that it has a true opportunity to prosper from its labors. At this point in time capitalism has shattered those dreams.

*Thomas Paine:*

"But as the same constitution which gives the commons a power to check the king by withholding the supplies, gives afterwards the king a power to check the commons, by empowering him to reject their other bills; it again supposes that the king is wiser than those whom it has already supposed to be wiser than him. A mere absurdity!"

Because of a long and violent abuse of power, capitalism has finally revealed itself as an oppressor of the people of this country, and thus it has given us the excuse and the opportunity to reject it. The problem is that capitalism has been helped and allowed to reach this level of corruption by our own government, which was originally created to halt this kind of abuse.

Separation of Church and State has been an important element of our Democracy since the beginning. Now it is a necessity that we separate Business and State.

Our incredibly intelligent Founding Fathers realized that religious faith suspends all adherences to reality and common sense. They knew intellectually that a government based on democracy and tolerance toward diversity could not survive being influenced by the selfishness and bigotry inherent in most organized religions.

Our founders insisted on separation of Church and State. What they didn't expect were the problems that would arise with the association of Business and State.

They knew that religion created selfishness and bigotry. They forgot that business, and the greed it contains, also breeds selfishness and bigotry. Both religion and business have an insidious habit of producing an unnatural desire for power within people.

The two major reasons for immigrating to the Americas were to escape religious intolerance, and to break away from economic dominance, feudalism and enforced poverty. Our Founding Fathers stipulated that religion must not have influence over our government and our lives. They made one mistake. They should also have banned greedy business people from places of power in our government.

The oppression that threatened Thomas Paine's America was ended by our War of Independence and the writing of our Constitution. However, slowly but surely over the last 200 years, a new threat to freedom and justice has been growing. Capitalism has taken the place of the King of England and its Parliament. The colonists rebelled against King George; it is time for us to rebel against capitalism.

Throughout the past 200 years many laws protecting the majority from unscrupulous business practices and laws promoting unscrupulous business practices have been enacted, debated, revised, reversed and dismantled. Slowly but surely, through legal, congressional and judicial changes to our laws, the balance of power has finally shifted over in favor of those who indulge in unscrupulous business practices.

We are not the same free enterprise democracy we once were. Today when a businessman says, "I did nothing illegal!," he may technically be speaking the truth. His actions may not be illegal, due to changes in our system, but are they ethical or moral? And do they follow the letter of the law and Constitution as created by our forefathers? Often the answer is no!

Our present government in America is run by businessmen, for the benefit of businessmen. Where does that leave all the rest of us who are not so economically competitive and who are concerned primarily with leading a good, clean life of liberty and the pursuit of simple happiness?

Some of you older folks and middle-class citizens may not understand my discomfort with the economic politics of our present government. You may say to me that our government has served you well, and you may be partly right. If you have a nest egg that was not wiped out by the last stock market treachery or loan industry shenanigans, you might just live out the rest of your lives in relative comfort.

But judging by what is happening now, the question is how will your children and your children's children live? And what about those in this country less fortunate than you?

Today, in 2003/2020, the American people face the same struggles against basically the same threat they did in 1776 when Thomas Paine's *Common Sense* was first published.

When Paine wrote *Common Sense*, this country was a colony of England. American colonists were being used as an economic resource for the needs of King George III and the English business class.

Today, again, Americans are being treated no better than serfs by a business and industrial class that considers this country to be its own private bank account. I contend that today, capitalism and those who support and empower it pose as much of a threat to the American people as did England and its King in 1776.

Washington is allowing and even enabling capitalists to enslave us. Our own government has become our own worst enemy.

In 1776 the colonists were being taxed without having representation in the government and without receiving benefits from the tax revenue. Although they had left England and other countries of Europe to escape the tyranny of its feudal system, they found they were still controlled by the economic greed of a possessive master.

Again today, we face that same situation. Although we pay taxes, the infrastructure of our country is falling apart. Schools, libraries, roads, welfare for elderly and health care are on a long list of deficient social systems which our politicians and industrial leaders are ignoring. Those who run our government are willing to pay billions of dollars to protect their oil interests in the Middle East, but children in this country don't eat breakfast or don't have books and pencils to obtain an education, and our elderly have to decide whether to eat or buy medicine.

Within the last few years in particular, it has become difficult to distinguish between our government and our industries. Our government, which was created to ensure our security, and the business community, which was created to produce the commodities for our comfort, have, it seems, banded together to make our lives miserable. It is time to consider separating corporations and government.

Our government was constructed under strict democratic laws. Capitalism is anything but democratic. In a democracy the rules are supposed to flow from the people to the heads of state who administer them. In capitalism, the rules come from the heads of the corporations and down to the workers who must follow them.

For the majority of people in America, the American dream is further away than it has been for the last 100 years. Today we are unrepresented and unsupported by the infrastructure of a government we ourselves originally created to help us maintain our freedom to pursue happiness.

By this date in 2020 the government, which we thought would forever protect the majority of us from economic tyrants, has turned against democracy and is now systematically dismantling the checks and balances that controlled economic tyranny.

We should not allow businessmen and lawyers to run our lives anymore. They have proven untrustworthy. They have wrapped us up so tightly in red tape and laws that we can no longer breathe freely. They say that these rules and pronouncements are for our own good, but you know better. It all somehow makes more money for them, and it allows them to keep better track of us and our money.

By nature, most businessmen, accountants and lawyers are into control. We must consider letting intellectuals make the rules of society. Who do you want running your government, someone who is hooked on money and control or someone who is in search of facts and truth?

Who do you think wrote the Declaration of Independence, Constitution and Bill of Rights? The CEOs of large corporations, or intellectuals, freethinkers, educators and scientists?

Businessmen are interested only in their own well-being. They want to control you and me. It is easier for them to capitalize on a stationary object. Thinking, moving, evolving people make them nervous. It's too hard for a capitalist to figure out what to sell to a moving target.

We have lived with our laws for so long. For this reason we take them for granted. Some of our laws are wrong for this day and age, and, just the same, some of the freedoms we take for granted infringe on the rights of others in our society of today.

Some activities in which we indulge daily are not really freedoms granted to us, but just bad habits somehow condoned through mistakes in our culture. These must be rethought by people who consider thinking as an end, rather than a means to profit.

The freedom to lie was not granted to us by the freedom of speech. The freedom to be greedy was not granted to us by the freedom to pursue happiness. The freedom to indulge in capitalist activities of lying, cheating and stealing was not granted to us in the Constitution or Bill of Rights.

And yet some people think it is the American way of life to be selfish. These people think it is OK to destroy someone else economically, simply because they think they are a better competitor and because they believe greed is our birthright as Americans.

Our forefathers would disagree, and today liberal intellectuals also disagree that America was meant to be a nation of greed and corruption. What do you believe?

Government is a necessary evil. There is a definite need for government, but not as some think... to control the people! No, government is necessary to control the people who are trying to control the people.

The majority of folks in this country can live their entire lives without harming anyone and without even considering it. But around 15% of the population seems to exhibit antisocial, psychopathic or greedy tendencies. These are the persons for whom governments are needed.

*Thomas Paine in Common Sense:*

"Some writers have so confounded society with government, as to leave little or no distinction between them; whereas they are not only different, but have different origins. Society is produced by our wants, and government by our wickedness; the former promotes our happiness positively by uniting our affections, the latter negatively by restraining our vices. The one encourages intercourse, the other creates distinctions. The first is a patron, the last a punisher."

When I speak today of government, I speak of a democracy, of the people, for the people and by the people. This is the only rational use of the word government. Since 1776, all other types of administrations of countries are really just some form of dictatorship.

The creation of governing bodies is a natural progression in human societies. In prehistoric times when the world was sparsely populated, our ancestors lived in family units, then clans, tribes, villages, cities and states. Then we progressed into forming counties.

With the increase in population, we joined into larger groups for mutual benefit. And with each coming together, laws and governments were created as needed by the strongest, most dominant people of each group.

It would be nice to believe that these governments were all created to protect society and control the behavior of those who would take advantage of others. But quite often governments were created to facilitate taking advantage of others by those who governed.

For controlling the petty criminals and individual killers, the laws and government have functioned quite well, but it has always been the thieves in government itself and those they support in business who kill and steal much more with a pen. They are the ones who have wreaked the most havoc upon society.

This then is what prompted our Declaration of Independence. This is why the United States of America came about and why our Constitution, Bill of Rights, Congress and Supreme Court were created. To control the people who take advantage of humankind is the primary reason for a democratic government.

In a true democracy those who oppose government are obviously undemocratic. But in a true democracy it is possible for those who do not really believe in democracy to join the governing process and make it work for them.

Within the last 150 years the checks and balances protecting us against the corporate criminals and killers have been subverted, eroded and changed. The middle class and poor have become more vulnerable each year. We have now almost completely lost our American right to Life, Liberty and the Pursuit of Happiness.

Our own government is slowly going back on its promises to us. Our own government is dismantling itself and taking the American Dream away with it.

The issue is that a proper government, one founded on the ideals of democracy, should in all things be democratic. Laws that a democratic government makes and upholds must, by nature, be democratic. They should be written and enforced with equality, but utmost, and here is the most difficult part, they must always benefit the majority.

It is often difficult to live in a democracy and yet have individual ambitions. Some people feel they have the right to circumvent the rules of a democracy for their own benefit. They think they are better than everyone else. This is the basic nature of a true capitalist.

These giants of industry rebel against controls on their own activities, and yet they support a multitude of restrictions on the common man. These conservative businessmen eventually gain power, and money through their actions, circumventing the rules of government, and if they gain enough power they eventually exert pressure, lobby or buy support to change the laws to benefit them even more. The laws enacted in 1886 and 1978 here in America giving corporations human status caused the worst damage to our democracy.

It is difficult to be in the minority, but in a reasonable society it is best for the whole of society that all rules be democratically created and enforced. Yet some people think that money or position should put them above government and its laws. And because these people are the wealthy and privileged, they have gained more power and control of our government.

And so we find ourselves in a situation where our laws are no longer written or enforced equitably. The poor and middle class are treated as second-class citizens. Often they are poor or middle class only because of the laws that discriminate against their opportunity to advance.

*"Why have we done this to ourselves?*
*If humans had been like bees or ants or whales,*
*we would all be living in a perfect world today."*
Dudley Griffin 2020

17

*"Is cooperation so difficult, considering that it would bring us all peace and happiness?"*
*JBMc*

*Thomas Paine wrote:*

"Society in every state is a blessing, but government even in its best state is but a necessary evil; in its worst state an intolerable one; for when we suffer, or are exposed to the same miseries by a government, which we might expect in a country without government, our calamities is heightened by reflecting that we furnish the means by which we suffer."

Some people will say that it is unpatriotic or even treasonous to speak out against our own government in this way. But the government is not itself patriotic if it does not work diligently to protect the ideals upon which this country was founded.

We, as members of a democratic country, are taught to believe that the government is composed of our own ideals and desires. But as you know, the fact is that the person in the White House today was not actually elected by a majority of the population of this country. The other candidate got one-half million more votes, and there are other irregularities in the 2016 election that make it even less democratic.

Most of the early colonists came to America to flee from some form of economic or religious oppression. The feudal system in Europe created an environment in which the majority of the population was economically trapped. Without the ability to own land or achieve education, people were unable to improve their lives.

We find ourselves in the same situation today. Most of the people who govern us and most of the people who control them are not really concerned about the well-being of the majority population. They are otherwise occupied making it possible for themselves and a small number of their friends to gain more wealth. They would not be considered very good Americans by the fathers of our country. They are breaking all the rules of democracy and free enterprise, and they are doing it right before our blind or uncaring eyes.

These wealthy politicians and businessmen are continually telling us that helping them make and keep more money will eventually give us economic security. Well, has it ever?

No, we are all in more debt than ever. We may have lots of stuff, but we are working so hard that we have less time to enjoy it. And we have less security than ever before.

It may upset you to think that a person who calls himself an American is saying that our leaders are un-American. Yet the most patriotic thing I can do is to tell you that there are people leading our country today who don't really believe in democracy for all; they believe in democracy for whom they choose.

In a dictatorship it is unpatriotic to speak out. In a democracy it is unpatriotic to be silent! Speak out when you see something wrong, and soon there will be no wrong!


*Paine wrote:*

"Here then is the origin and rise of government; namely, a mode rendered necessary by the inability of moral virtue to govern the world; here too is the design and end of government, viz., Freedom and security. And however our eyes may be dazzled with snow, or our ears deceived by sound; however prejudice may warp our wills, or interest darken our understanding, the simple voice of nature and of reason will say, it is right. I draw my idea of the form of government from a principle in nature, which no art can overturn, viz., that the more simple any thing is, the less liable it is to be disordered, and the easier repaired when disordered ...

"Absolute governments (though the disgrace of human nature) have this advantage with them, that they are simple; if the people suffer, they know the head from which their suffering springs, know likewise the remedy, and are not bewildered by a variety of causes and cures. But the constitution of England is so exceedingly complex, that the nation may suffer for years together without being able to discover in which part the fault lies, some will say in one and some in another, and every political physician will advise a different medicine."

*"Does money always win the day.? Maybe, but hopefully it will not win in the final solution! When mankind has eventually reached the point of anarchy and the breakdown of water and food disbursement, will our deep nature of human feelings arise and save us?"*
Dudley Griffin 2020

The problems in this country today stem from our own government's cohabitation with business and industry. It is the classic "Sleeping with the Enemy" scenario.

Our democratic/republic form of government was designed to be the lawgiver and police force to protect the majority of people from the greed of thieves and businessmen (terms that are often synonymous). Yet today the business community runs our government. My definition of govern: to protect and allow normal human activities within the boundaries of morality ... not to control, but to allow rational human actions.

Is a criminal going to support laws to put himself in jail? Is a businessman going to pass laws to make it harder for him to make more money? Is it any wonder that industries are being deregulated? Even in a democratic society, there are those who do not want full disclosure. They fight the creation of controls and laws on their actions, even if their actions are against a compatible social order.

A statement you hear from these borderline Americans is, "I am not breaking any laws!" That turns my stomach, because they are technically not "breaking" any legal laws, but they are shattering the first human moral code that has been with us since we sat around the first fire. They are breaking the Golden Rule.

In a country run by majority rule, a person who wants less government is probably someone who is doing something of which the majority would not approve. Is all of this fair to the majority of people who are just trying to pay the rent and feed their families?

Another concern is that our government has gotten too big and impersonal. Big would be OK if government remembered who it was working for. Washington is self-perpetuating, continually creating new functions for itself, and often without regard for how its actions affect the people it was created to serve.

At this point our government is Ouroboros, the snake that eats its own tail and will eventually consume itself. It is so big, so self-important, so concerned with its head that it forgets it has a tail, which is part of itself and important to its existence. And therefore our government, under the guidance of the business community, is consuming its own tail, which is the people who make up this country--the people who make the products and pay the bills!

We are supposed to be a democratic/free enterprise country, which means that we are governed by the will of the people and that all of the people are to be allowed to work and live freely as they wish. In such a country the government functions merely as a policing force to ensure that that environment continues to exist for its population.

This form of government was created by our Founding Fathers as a benevolent organization. It is Of, By and For the People, and therefore, it is supposed to be a continual reminder to the population that we are all in this together and that we must all play by the same rules in order for it to work.

*"... though we have been wise enough to shut and lock a door against absolute monarchy, we at the same time have been foolish enough to put the crown in possession of the key."* Paine

*"... though we have been wise enough to create a democracy, we at the same time have been foolish enough to put the greedy in possession of the key."* JBMc

Somewhere in this book, some of you are going to say; "This guy is a fucking idealist! He is fighting the nature of mankind, and it will never happen." But I say, "It is all up to you if our history has a happy or a sad ending. I am only the messenger!"

# CHAPTER 4

## Democracy

*"One of the most important things that we must improve in our democracy is public confidence and public involvement."* DG

There are powers within our government itself right now that are trying to dismantle this perfect idea. Lesser men than our Forefathers are now trying to control the masses, thinking that is the way to hold the union together. This is counterproductive. It only creates unrest among a people who are used to freedom ... no, a people who demand Freedom!

Our government today is running this country for business, not for people. Democracy was always for the people.

Perhaps the true terrorists in America are the capitalists.

The present leadership does not realize that it is un-American in its actions. They think it is the purpose of government to control the population. Our Founding Fathers knew that setting people free was the purpose of this new form of government and that it would one day make the world free.

How are we going to sell democracy to other countries when democracy is not alive and well in our own country? Our government in recent years has not been promoting democracy to other countries; it has been promoting capitalism.

Sure, if you give the leader of some country a lot of money, he will embrace capitalism, and he may even give lip service to democracy. But most of the people in these countries to which we are selling capitalism and democracy never see or benefit from the democracy and definitely not from the capitalism.

Often, our foreign aid is supporting dictatorships and suppressing democracy and free enterprise. It sounds a lot like what is going on right here in our own country.

Our present "fathers" are not visionaries as were the framers of our Constitution and country. Present leaders say, "What is good for business is good for the nation." They are not saying, "What is good for the people is good for the nation."

What should we be patriotic toward? I think that a country is a combination of the physical place, the land and its beauty and resources, and its personality, which would be its people.

It is not always true that what is good for business is good for the people or the country. Often, nowadays, the business community is busiest screwing the people and polluting the land.

What is treason in a democracy? Treason in a democracy is not speaking out against the government when you should. Treason in a democracy is to allow the government to oppress its people and spoil its land.

*"There are laws that enslave men and laws that set them free! No one said it would be easy. Then again, no one told us it would be this hard!" Attributed to King Arthur of The Round Table, about the first forms of democracy in Europe, including the Magna Carta.*

There is nothing more complex than the concept of being given democracy and then told at the same time that everyone else possesses that same democracy. On top of that, everyone else's democracy, collectively, is more important than yours!

That's equality, dammit, but it doesn't always make sense to an individual. A person's self-interest often gets in the way.

Democracy for one and all ... at the same time ... equal amounts for all...but you have to wait in line. That's a cooperative society.

Many people can't understand it, and some can't abide by it. It takes a mind that thinks in several dimensions. It takes a person who has evolved into true humanity.

Democracy, first conceived in ancient Greece and finally brought to flickering life in America in 1776, is the answer to all man's psychological and technical conflicts, but it is also his most confusing tribulation. In the form of The Golden Rule, democracy is the basis for our highest aspirations of religion and even higher ideals of the spirit and soul.

To "do unto others as you would have others do unto you" is the hardest of our goals, and yet it is the strongest drive of the human inner psyche. It is the answer to our truly becoming stewards of this earth, fathers of all creatures, one with God.

Yes, democracy and the Golden Rule are one and the same if you have the dimensions of thought to grasp it. And you do if you try.

In Mother Nature's jungle of survival of the fittest, it is hard to have compassion for your food or for the creature who looks upon you as food. But man has risen above that, or so he should have. Now we are the fittest, and the only predator we have is ourselves.

We now have room for the compassion and morality that lies hidden in all of us. We don't need to compete to live. We can create. Or can we?

No, there are still those among us who have not put aside the jungle competition, the greed, the predatory nature of lesser animals. They are called capitalists, for lack of a better expletive.

Our Founding Fathers knew that, as long as there was a feudal system or economic tyranny hanging over us, there would always be social unrest. No one would be able to find true peace and freedom. Democracy and the ability to control tyrants with the majority rule was the only answer to creating the ideal government.

Other animals have self-preservation as their life's goal. Humankind has other dimensions--creative desires, curiosity, moral exploration. We need to be free of the troubles of economic pressures and undue competition to accomplish these. And this is where democracy and freedom should play their part.

The selfishness of a few is keeping democracy from working as it should to create utopia. People who think democracy should work for them, but not for others, are slowly destroying the dream our founders started.

Capitalism is the largest threat to democracy. Democracy is the largest threat to economic and political oppression. If you want democracy for yourself and for all others, you must work toward controlling the out-of-control capitalism in this country and world.

As long as anyone in this world has the power to dictate to and oppress other people, then you too are in danger of being treated in that same manner. As long as you look the other way and let others be oppressed, the possibility exists that some day others will look away from your oppression.

But, it ain't easy giving everyone the same freedom you expect. Freedom for you and democracy for all is the strange dichotomy of our form of government. It is not easy, but it is workable and it is much better than constant conflict.

It works only if people can live without selfishness. Self-preservation is OK, but not economic selfishness.

When talking about human cooperation, freedom or selfishness, the automobile driving scenario always comes to mind. Automobile protocol, etiquette and laws are potentially one of humankind's most valuable successes. Basically, it is one of the few things of which society can be rightfully proud.

*"It seems like everybody is driving only for themselves nowadays! It used to be that we paid attention to others; it is so much safer that way!"* 1/3/20 Dudley Griffin

One of the most obvious and poignant automobile comparisons

to real life is the parking scenario. They paint those white lines for a reason! If everyone were properly socialized and considerate of others, we would all park between the lines, and then when we came looking for a parking place, someone would not be parked in the middle of two spaces. You most likely have pulled up to find someone else encroaching on the space you need, so how could you be so selfish as to do it to someone else?

Parking outside the lines may not be a devastating sin in the pantheon of transgressions, but it may be an indication of selfishness, rebellion or unhappiness. My next query is whether or not the offenders have got it all wrong. Following the rules and making other people's lives easy and happy may be a better way to act if you are displeased with your own life. It may actually make you feel like a worthy human being.

Another example of how important car cooperation is in this world relates to harmony in society. Have you ever been in a long line of cars trying to get through an intersection traffic light when the cars ahead of you are not keeping up with the flow of traffic by allowing three or five car lengths between them and the traffic ahead? It's slow traffic; keeping half a car length between would not be dangerous at that speed, but they lag. So you and two other cars don't make it through because of a selfish slacker. So when you're up there, remember the frustration you had when someone else slacked off, and keep up with traffic. It is courtesy and self-control that will stop road rage. I personally drive with concern for those behind me almost as much as those in front of me. Look at your speed and in your rearview mirror every ten seconds!

When you are driving, it is the most important thing you are doing, not talking, the radio or the phone. Death is as close as two seconds away.

When you are driving a car, lives depend on it and also the whole vibe of the world around you matters. Soon at this rate of automobile greed and stupidity, road rage will begin to kill more people than heart attacks, smoking and suicide.

We do not live in this world alone, so we must physically and emotionally communicate with other people. Receiving bad vibes from someone you have inconvenienced is not a good way to improve your own life. We would all have a better life if everyone around us was happy and secure. Helping others helps ourselves.

> *"There is a reason that the Democrats are named such. It is because they believe in democracy."*
> Dudley Griffin 2014.

# CHAPTER 5

## Voting

*"Never vote with your ego, maybe for who you think will benefit your financial situation, or if your life depends on it, but always vote with your intelligence. Education is your best salvation"*
Dudley Griffin

In a democracy, the most important thing that you should not be free to do, is to not vote! You can't complain about anything concerning this country and your rights and freedoms unless you vote and register your desires to the government. If all eligible people voted as they should, maybe then this place would be a true majority-ruled democracy, and we would all live righteously ever after.

But just voting is not enough to make you a true patriotic American. To do so you have to have respect for the process of democratically electing representatives. You must not lie, cheat and steal to elect whom you want. If you really care about the United States of America, you know that, more important than your choice, is that the choice of America must be made by an honest, democratic process.

There are people in high places who do not know or care that they automatically lose their patriot's status when they cheat to elect whom they want! They can't call themselves true Americans; they can't call themselves Christian, and they are people without a country or a moral guiding force. Forsaking America, turning their back on Christian morals, these people are pariahs. The problem is that when insecure, selfish and greedy people control the information and the voting system, then democracy is lost to the rest of us.

If we are to keep our representative form of government or to get back to a pure democratic republic, we must reform our electoral process.

If this country is to remain a democracy, we must pass strict election reforms. First, the electoral college must be tweaked, censured or abandoned. It can be done with every true American's approval. Any group of sensible people can come up with it. Second, valid political parties must be restricted to the same budgets. An independent panel of intellectuals can easily determine how that money is collected and dispersed. If we can't get these democratically driven laws passed by our representatives, maybe they need to be fired (voted out), and we will do all the deciding ourselves.

We need election reform. Here we are in a democracy, and we can't all agree that every person who contributes to this country and its economy should have a vote, and that the person most people want is (in a democracy) the person right for the job (in a democracy). It is almost as if we cannot understand the concept of "freedom for all." You get freedom, but you have to give everyone else his or her freedom.

Do you know what democracy means? It means you have a voice in the kind of world in which you live. It does not mean you have the last word, nor does it mean you have no word. It means you can guide the system that guides your life. Some people like the freedom that democracy gives them yet, they are not willing to abide by the limitations of one vote per person.

Many of you think that if you support capitalists and vote their representatives into government, it will bring you closer to being one of them and having their kind of money. But be informed; a capitalist will not reach down to pull you up. To them, you are competition. There are only a limited number of stalls in the corporate bathroom.

No, this is not just a script written for a movie; this is real life!

Not "reality" media, or fantasy media, walking dead or a Kardashian's fake drama! Real people are suffering and dying because people like you are in a media lalal-and and don't have enough common sense to vote for good people who want to see everybody healthy and happy, not just the powerful and rich happy and richer!

This is not a free country. As long as we cannot elect our president with the majority of votes, we are a dictatorship!

Everybody who thinks America is better than this should speak out about the undemocratic election that has just been forced on all of us.

Even the supporters of our current president are diminished by this travesty of un-democratic politics. How do you think his supporters would be reacting right now if the circumstances were reversed? And it could happen! Next time their candidate might just win the popular vote and lose the election, although that has never happened to the Republicans. How would they like that? Would they feel violated as I do today? To win a bogus election actually makes you anti-American, and your celebration would definitely be the action of an unpatriotic, undemocratic and immoral person. So now how do you feel? Are you willing to win under any circumstances? That makes you un-Christian and unpatriotic! Or maybe you are not smart enough to see that.

There have been only five US presidents elected by a minority vote, including the current one. They were four Republicans and one, J.Q. Adams, who was a Democrat/Republican before the present political designation of Republicans.

Five presidents elected even though they lost the popular vote?
Again, John Quincy Adams, 1824 as a Democrat/Republican
Rutherford B. Hayes, 1876 as a Republican
Benjamin Harrison, 1888 as a Republican
George W. Bush, 2000 as a Republican
D.T. 2016 as a Republican

The Republicans have stolen four presidential elections because of their abilities to fraudulently gerrymander the population votes. Are you proud now, you lying, cheating, un-patriotic Republicans?

So the Republicans really know how to <u>steal</u> the presidency and subvert the democratic process! Well, Republicans, are you proud of yourselves? Can you still call yourselves patriots when you go against the wishes of our Constitution and the will of our Founding Fathers? No, you can apply fake news to any truth you want, yet you are still being unpatriotic at the highest level!

The current president and his supporters who revel in this election have made this country a shameful place with which to be associated.

Voters, don't just believe in what you want to be true.

Look at the political history of your candidates and the history of their parties' actions.

Don't just hear what you want to hear! Let's have a peaceful revolution, as Adams, Franklin, Jefferson, Madison, Patrick Henry and Washington envisioned. Vote, vote fairly, and adhere to the democratic rule.

In creating the perfect government for the people, the process must be a completely non-corrupt democratic majority choice! Our "leaders" must be elected by a foolproof, and majority and democratic way. And our elected leaders must adhere to non-corrupt democratic actions. This may be impossible for some candidates to handle. They may feel in their egos that they are of no importance as only representatives. If they can't handle being a facilitator and want to be a dictator, they must be let go. We may have to find a new way to vote on our lives. Retinal recognition voting, One Vote Everyone!

*"The numbers prove that you will never become a capitalist, but if you stop voting for capitalists, you can become a solid member of the middle class American dream."*

DG 4/24/20

# CHAPTER 6

## Representational Form of Government

*"But as it is more than probable that we shall never be without a Congress, every well-wisher to good order, must own, that the mode for choosing members of that body, deserves consideration. And I put it as a question to those, who make a study of mankind, whether representation and election is not too great a power for one and the same body of men to possess?"*

I am now proposing that we at this point in democracy disband our representational form of government, and then everyone gets to vote on every decision that affects their lives.

One of the most important things that we must reform in our democratic republic is our democratic republic itself. This indirect democracy, which we first established as a new country, was a step forward, and it was logistically necessary under the circumstances.

In 1776, with a population of approximately 2,500,000 people and the desire to be a democracy, a dilemma arose. How do we get all of those people into one building for one big town meeting?

We settled on a democratic republic, a democracy with elected representatives to express our will and choose our direction accordingly. Well, sometimes it works, and sometimes it fails.

What with campaign contributions and paid lobbyists, the system has become more like a capitalistic Republic. Our system is now of the money, by the money and for the money.

To get back to a pure democratic republic, if we want to keep such a dinosaur, we must reform our electoral process.

You must admit that the 2000 election was a turning point in this country, but not in the way you might think. It will go down in history as a moment of infamy, just as other major political tragedies of this county, The Civil War, Lincoln's and Kennedy's assassinations, Watergate and the Iran-Contra scandal.

The 2000 election may have been the last straw for the morality and common sense of the American people. A backlash against the anti-democratic results is building.

The facts that surround the 2000 election are frightening to anyone who values democracy and freedom of speech. That election should be shocking and abhorrent to any true American, even those who are pleased with the results.

Anyone who is not repulsed by the circumstances of the 2000 election is forsaking the freedoms and democracy that are the foundation of this country. Democracy was taken away from the people of America that day. And any time democracy is taken from one faction of our society, it means that democracy could just as easily be taken from all others as well.

If this country is to remain a democracy, we must pass strict election reforms. First, valid political parties must be restricted to the same electioneering and advertising budgets. How that money is collected and dispersed could easily be determined by an independent panel of intellectuals. No conservatives with connections to the business community should apply.

Second, elected officials should be forced to take polls on issues from their constituents and then be expected to vote accordingly. Private interest lobbying must be drastically curtailed.

If you don't think these suggestions are valid, then you are in the wrong country. You would be more comfortable in Communist Russia or Nazi Germany. It's *"Love It or Leave It,"* back at you!

Noblesse oblige is a well-respected and yet seldom used French term meaning that a responsible representative or boss of people is not supposed to take advantage of those people by abusing his or her power. The Oxford English Dictionary states, *"noble ancestry constrains to honorable behavior: privilege entails responsibility."* Homer in the Iliad wrote, *"Behold our deeds transcending our commands."* Of course, right now we have people in our own government who are breaking this time-honored responsibility.

I believe that if all the people concerned with a particular subject could meet in one room and discuss with some rules and constraints, the issues would be democratically decided. But because physically that would be impossible, we must find another foolproof way to chose our government, our rules and laws.

*A few other changes that should be made to make America a true democracy:*

- If we must have an electoral college, we should lobby them to vote with the majority voters to place properly and duly elected candidate in their states!
- Every good American should lobby their elected officials to get the electoral college disbanded.
- Elected representatives should be required to vote with the wishes of the majority of their constituents which would be polled, or have their vote canceled!
- If we disband the Congress, the members could keep their jobs until they died or retired at three-quarters salary, and they could keep their retirement benefits!
- The Supreme Court should have a term limit of eight-to-ten years and have to take a break until the next election. New judges every election would have overlapping terms.

CHAPTER 7

# OVE:
## One Vote Each

Our Founding Fathers chose a democracy for the United States because it encourages the public by giving them control of their own destiny. All other forms of government are dictatorial or autocratic, and they eventually ferment revolution and social and economic upheaval.

In 1776, our democratic government had to be representational, because they couldn't get all two-and-a-half million people into one room. Never mind the time lapse and travel inconvenience.

I propose that America consider phasing out our representative form of government! Yes, end our representative government!

There will be a time shortly where we can look into an eye recognition, retinal sensor, say "One Hundred Dollars," and the money will come out of the dispenser! The bank will know your balance and you cannot overdraw. Most importantly for you and them is that the recognition will be flawless!

There is no reason this system cannot be used to vote on those things that concern our lives and the lives of our children's children.

Dissolving Congress may be the only way to save democracy, this country and this world. When elected or appointed representatives of a democracy turn into agents of an economic or political dictatorship, those representatives must be reprimanded, and if they do not return to democracy, they must be removed from power by democratic forces. The vote <u>must</u> be a democratic election, lest we act in the same immoral way they do. Vote with an informed finger or eye print. Vote with a mind that takes into consideration the rights of other people.

I am sure this will not be popular with all the current elected representatives and the masses of Washington, D.C., employees, but they can be repurposed and shuffled into positions in our government which actually help protect the people of this country. Please bear with me, listen and think about the possibilities of this idea.

The difference between a "government" and a totalitarian dictatorship is that a dictatorship <u>deals</u> with dissent. A "true government" listens to dissent of its people and rectifies the democratic and reasonable complaints.

The one thing that makes us human beings is our society. Governments are not really our society; they are just representatives of society. People are our society and people are the country.

Is mankind capable of governing itself? Jefferson questioned this, but he had faith and hope.

As our Founding Fathers were revolutionaries, it is possible to be a revolutionary and still be a valuable member of society. Sadly, they had to resort to violence, but they tried to avoid it.

Again I quote:

*"Those who will not allow peaceful revolution are making violent revolution inevitable."*
John Fitzgerald Kennedy


Remember, in all of this, that if you believe in democracy and demand freedom for yourself, then you must give it to all others or you are living a lie. It is possible to be a patriot without being a fanatic. I want freedom for myself, yet I want it for everyone else. I love my country, but I can still be critical of my government.

*"If the government does not add to the welfare of society, then it should be changed,"*
as Jefferson wrote.

Without intellectual thinking today, our country and its democracy and freedom will soon disappear. You have to work very hard to be ignorant in this world of today. With all the media and information available to us in this time, you have to stick your head very deeply in the sand not to see who is screwing you. And if you continue to elect those people who support the corporations that are screwing you, then you are not ignorant anymore; you become stupid.

# CHAPTER 8

## Taxes

In a democratic, majority-ruled country, taxes must be equal for everybody for the amount of benefit they receive from being in this country, city or state. Duh!

But taxes, before American democracy, used to be demanded with no representation or no benefit to the the taxed. Your land owner, chief or king got the money for their own use. Don't blame King George III for following his family tradition. But then, many in the British Isles left to get away from that. OK, we are now facing the same thing again.

We are now facing the same thing except we don't have anywhere to immigrate in order to get away from this American form of the feudal system.

*"Tax cuts and welfare for the rich"* is not a bumper sticker or placard; it is the truth!

What Republican capitalists don't tell you and what they don't want you to know is that when they cut taxes, it automatically means you lose benefits. The benefits of living in a benevolent, people-concerned, people-friendly, people-oriented society. Such as reasonably priced, education, roads, medical health, and fire and police protection.

When times become necessary to find money to continue the functions of this country, roads, bridges, dams, levees, education, Medicare, welfare for people who actually need it, rich people normally don't raise taxes on themselves, so they have to freeze or cut taxes for themselves and let you poor and middle class people pay the necessary short fall.

Free, good schools for all, libraries, Social Security and Medicare this is the democracy that the founders and visionaries envisioned. You lose all those things that make living in America beneficial to the lower and middle class. You lose the ability to compete with the Republican conservative capitalists.

And this is just what conservatives and capitalists want. They don't want an educated population because an educated population is competition to them. They don't want an educated population because they can't lie to an educated population.

There is an income level, which can be computed, that is the dividing line between those who benefit from a tax cut and those who suffer from it. It is much higher than you think. (Meaning fewer people benefit, than are hurt from a particular tax cut) The braking point is probably somewhere around $300,000 per year discretionary income. That means it is money they don't have to work for, or have to spend to live. (These numbers change on a regular basis; it could easily be much more today.) Anyone making under that amount is hurting themselves if they vote Republican.

The software industry has wasted more money on advertising and received less for it than any industry before or since. Of course, it was all a tax write-off and a stock market scam! With the right plan, many of these online companies that had good ideas could have stayed in business and made more money, and actually helped people in the process!

*"The "real people" need to be given reparations for what the stock market has stolen from us and done to us!"* DG 4/18/20

# CHAPTER 9

## Free Enterprise

Capitalism is not Free Enterprise
and
Socialism is not Communism
and therefore
Free Enterprise is not Capitalism
and
Communism is not Socialism

Our Founding Fathers chose democracy and free enterprise (not capitalism) to form this country as a hedge against rebellion of the masses. If the people are given the ability to form their own destiny, they will not revolt.

I am a free-enterprise/socialist, not a capitalist or communist. I believe that free enterprise combined with a socialist safety net system, is the perfect economy. Free enterprise, not capitalism, is what our Founding fathers chose for this country. After all, they were rebelling against a feudal system in England. Capitalism is the new feudalism.

Many social systems were created at the beginning of our democracy. Benjamin Franklin devised the free (socialized) library system and free fire department system. What's wrong with socialism? Every village or small town in the world runs on a socialistic morality. Are we going to let greed destroy mankind and the world along with us?

Socialism is a democratic economic system. Free enterprise is a democratic economic system. Capitalism is a dictatorial economic system! A free-enterprise and socialism economy allows the freedom to be enterprising for those who can compete in the system, and provides a safety net for those who cannot. It is the moral and actually, if you read your Bible, the Christian way. Currently, we just put people who can't compete in dog-eat-dog capitalism into prisons or institutions.

I believe in a rational economic food chain. As with the food chain of the animal and natural kingdoms, human economic sustenance should start from the bottom. All nutrition in the animal kingdoms travels up from the smallest creatures through the chain until it eventually reaches the top predators. This makes for a happier society, everyone receiving the food that they need. It's natural, it's democratic, it's socialistic, and it is the opposite of trickle-down.

Socialism, free enterprise and democracy could solve all the problems of the world if the capitalists, fascists and religious fanatics could stop being violent, bigoted, greedy and insecure. All the problems of the world could end if people would realize that they, themselves, could be, the poor, the disadvantaged and the minority.

We are not talking about communism. Socialism is benevolent communism, just as free enterprise is benevolent capitalism.

*"People of power and influence, We 'the people' are here to do the work you are not willing to do, so you can work to be powerful and to make the money you desire to deserve for your work. So give us the money we deserve for making you powerful! P.S. please, how can you believe that you are an intelligent, culturally aware person and still not know that eventually you will be found out as a liar, cheat and, well, dumb person for being such an asshole?"*
Dudley Griffin 1/8/2020

CHAPTER 10

## Advertising (Advertising Industry)

*"Christ, if you want advertising, create advertising channels,*
*as many as you like. If I want advertising I'll turn to one.'"*
Mr. California

We know that mankind rewrites history, yet we sometimes do it before the history happens. People think that this is going to happen, because these things are going on. Then a few radicals come along, Diogenes, Christ, Mohamed, Buddha, Ben Franklin, Thomas Jefferson, Washington, Abraham Lincoln, F.D.R, Doctor Martin Luther King Jr, Bob Dylan and Joan Baez, and they say, "this is not right," so let's change the direction of mankind toward a more perfect conclusion.

Just like my other suggestion, such as that we individually vote by retinal scan, that we disband the stock exchange and do away with our representational form of government, I know that what I am going to propose to you right here will sound like a crazy scheme or an unattainable dream considering the competitive nature of the business world right now. It is not a frivolous suggestion. It is a possible way to make our economic world a kinder, gentler palace and to slow down in our rush to make <u>more</u> money, thus using up all of the world's natural resources, which are limited and getting scarcer.

Many industries have had to scale down or have disappeared because of changing times--the dirigible, eight-track tapes, hard rubber tires, the Edsel. Human progress is pragmatic, when some thing's are not useful any more, useless or bad for mankind, the smart thing has been to change them.

I am suggesting that we as a voting public, and living in a country of democracy and extreme intelligence, should start thinking about making our economic and industrial world work better for everybody. This, of course, in homage to the Constitution and Bill of Rights of this country, whose framers envisioned peace, sustenance and freedom for all.

We the people should start by convincing the advertising industry to rethink the use of all their powerful creativity and that they suggest to the corporate world to consider thinking about selling the quality and creativity and utility of their products rather than just the glitz. The glitz is the unnecessary part of products, and it ends up being the wasteful part. Give me a hammer that does the job; it doesn't have to look cool or cute, and it won't unnaturally fall apart.

Advertising agencies are in the business to lie. This industry should change its morality and start stimulating sales by advocating quality and creativity in the product, not the just the <u>presentation</u> of the product.

I think we as a society should encourage advertising agencies to become members of a consumer advocacy industry. This industry will be assigned the task of informing the people the true value of, and how good, a product or service is, and which product or service would be best for the individual's needs.

Why don't companies stop doing advertising and instead use those monies and energies for R&D and into finding more eco-friendly ways to produce their products? The world would love you.

As we know, the stock market and advertising industries are mutually supportive partners in the   for the sake of sales.

The advertising industry is one of the major threats to our free enterprise system, our clean water and breathable air. Yes, that institution, which many people believe to be one of our culture's most American and most valuable industries, is actually our biggest enemy. That is, if you believe in democracy, and life and breath.

Sure, advertising is good for capitalism, but, as I continue to emphasize, capitalism is not the champion of democracy that many people think it is. Capitalism separates the money from the masses, gives complete power to a few and drives the common man, like you and me, into a lifetime of continuous labor. And if you don't know that by now, you have succumbed to the propaganda that the advertising industry has pumped into your eyes and ears for your entire lifetime.

What advertising actually does is lie to you about how good life is, or how much better it could be, if you possessed more of the company's stuff. With smoke and mirrors, and damn good psychological hypnosis, capitalist advertising convinces you that you are inferior until you own their bright, shiny objects, at which time you become just like them--rich, beautiful and self-confident.

This author once worked in advertising. One of my jobs was hiring models for TV commercials. In Hollywood. Choosing from the pool of beautiful people available, the young couple selected to represent the upper middle-class, cool people of the world, was often a girl who couldn't make it in the movies, became a junkie and a prostitute on the weekends, and a boy who was a homosexual.

No disapproval of the gay life, but this couple was a lie. What they had and how they lived was a fabrication to sell you some sugar water in a bottle. We created the Joneses who had everything from actors who had nothing, and told you that you must be just like them or you would never be part of the in crowd.

The advertising industry fabricates the value of products and services that you don't need in the first place. This then causes you to waste your money on these things that are manufactured by using up and polluting the air, water and resources, which we and all other creatures need to survive on the earth.

Contrary to what some people think, lying, cheating and stealing are not democratically ordained freedoms. In fact, capitalist theft and deception are actually un-American. The right to make phony advertising claims is not protected by our freedom of speech rights. Actually, that kind of activity is rapidly destroying our freedom of speech by making a mockery of the truth. And it is also enslaving us in materialism at the same time.

Well-crafted lies by advertising agencies are part of what is wrong with this country, and they are contributing to the disintegration of the moral and ethical fiber of this otherwise proud nation. Freedom of speech functions properly only if there is an agreement that the truth, or at least the truth as one knows it, is employed by all parties in the discussion. The moment that lies and deception are used, freedom of speech becomes useless. We are back to communication anarchy, and our culture suffers.

Is this what our beautiful America has come to? A country driven by greed, where deception is the common practice in business, and morality is reserved for Sunday?

Advertising as we know it must be altered or our society will become the domain of cheaters, and our earth will dry up and be unable to sustain life.

How do we do this without destroying the livelihood of hundreds of thousands of otherwise good people? There are solutions for both the environment, our free-enterprise system and for the advertising industry, but we must listen to intellectuals to find them. Here is a beginning:

In a perfect world, ad agencies would be changed slowly to become product and services research, and consumer report companies. This is how it works:

A portion of all companies' income would go to former ad agencies to conduct product tests, report the results and rate all products. Every company would be treated equally regardless of size or importance.

Companies could still advertise their products and pay ad agencies to create ad campaigns. But companies could not make unsubstantiated clams, and they must, in their own advertising, name all other companies who have a better product rating then their own. This means that if a company has a better product, it would be mentioned in other companies' ads. This one would surely cause some consternation in the dog-eat-dog world of corporations. But we don't need a lot of dogs eating each other in a reasonable society.

This, of course, would force companies to make better products. Even companies with no advertising budget would be tested and rated in other companies' ads, which could help them to become more profitable. Eventually, only companies that were willing to produce better products would survive.

What better way to entice companies into producing better products than to reward them economically? Tax cuts?

A company's value would no longer be based on how much money they could throw into advertising on an otherwise poor product, but they would rise or fall, as it should be, on the value of their product.

Instead of creating a system that would slowly produce poorer products and services, we could build a society that rewards good work and better products. Pay people for being good; don't pay them for being bad!

Does this make common sense to you? Why are we not functioning this way already? Because left-brained, accountant-type people have been making the rules in government and business for too long. Give liberal intellectuals the opportunity to write the laws and make policy, and eventually everyone, even rich people, will be better off.

One of the major problems with present-day advertising is the amount of product packaging created and the natural resources it wastes. This is an area in which intellectuals and the creative community can help. The possibilities for improving and saving our future are numerous if this society will listen to the intellectual's voice.

Liberal intellectuals do not want to do away with jobs and people's businesses. We want them to be more efficient, fair and, in the end, more profitable for all. We do not want to do away with capitalists and corporations. We just want them to play by more democratic and reasonable rules.

*"There are a very few things more valuable than freedom! The rich man who has always had it, and the poor man who has never had it have very little to compare with each other's position. Oh, God I would love to see their positions reversed!"*
Dudley Griffin, 2/17/20

# CHAPTER 11

## Planned Obsolescence (Built-in Obsolescence)

"America used to be known for its integrity and American products for their quality."

Intentionally using inferior materials and/or skills to build a product to sell to others, so that it will fail, and they will have to come back and buy another one soon. Sounds pretty nefarious, sneaky, low-down and immoral, doesn't it? Well, that is what the American capitalist manufacturing industry does on a regular basis.

There should be laws against it, and people should have to go to jail if they participate in such practices. But, since the offenders are often the same people who make the laws directly or indirectly, there are very few workable laws and no penalties on our books for stealing from people in this way.

Companies manufacturing products should step up and build the best damn product they can, and then pay money into the consumer advocacy agency to "help" the people get what is best for them. Planned obsolescence should be criminalized and penalized with jail time and stiff economic penalties.

For "the people," technology is highly overrated for their needs. We could survive and not have to work so hard if this technology were not being forced and pushed upon us. We always end up paying for the mistakes of technology, but then the powerful people get paid even for their mistakes in the technology we buy from them!

Ug, Mug and Thug were walking around on the earth 400,000 years ago. Ug, a female, was a feminist; Mug was a man with a spiritual and creative mind, and Thug a taker of other peoples' ideas.

Thug was a capitalist who raped Ug and stole ideas from Mug. Thug had sat in the back of the cave and watched Ug and Mug invent, create and make all kinds of things to make the cave more comfortable and safe for the whole tribe. One day Thug patented all of the things Ug and Mug had created: the fire, a log to sit on, wall paintings, and the bowl to hold food and water. Then Thug started charging all the tribe members, as well as Ug and Mug, for using all these inventions. He was the first accountant/capitalist!.

# CHAPTER 12

## Monopoly

Ever since Monopoly became a board game played in most American households, the seriousness and consequences of real monopoly have been lost on the general public. The dangers of allowing one company or one person to control the source of production of a necessity or the total control of an essential service has been obscured by the introduction of a fun little game.

Monopoly is no laughing matter. The game has succeeded in taking peoples' minds off the destructive aspects of cutthroat competition, and it has diverted our attention from real tangible problems in our society created by monopolistic practices in business.

This is how it works: two companies make the same product. Because of their businesslike competition, the companies are forced to maintain a reasonable level of product quality and price.

Improvements to the product are developed by each company in an effort to gain a better share of the market, just as prices are kept at a reasonable level, affording a profit, while at the same time keeping the item at a price the public can justify.

But once one company gets an unfair economic advantage, it can afford to spend more money on advertising and thus capture more of the public's attention, further outpacing other companies until it has the whole market. The advance has had little to do with quality of producet and all to do with advertising. Of course, the fact that advertising is a tax deductible business expense makes it profitable and exciting, since you can lie about your product tax-free.

Pretty soon, the competition is out of business or unable to compete, and the monopoly company can do even more of what it wants. Once such a company is able to capture the business, the price of products usually goes up and/or the quality goes down.

A monopoly of any product or service is bad for the majority of the population. It is bad for our culture, and it is leading to wage slavery and an eventual fascist dictatorship.

The irony of the popularity of the game of Monopoly and how it promotes greed and insensitive combative competition is that the first person to invent the concept of that game about capitalism was actually opposed to the business practices of monopolies and the existence of capitalism and its anti-democracy activities.

*Monopoly...Supply Side...Consumer Side...Economy-Driven Market*

Basically for thousands of years' human economy was driven by the person who wanted or needed to exchange for or buy something! That's called consumer-side economy, and it worked to keep the money flowing properly. If our present capitalists were around then, they would have been the people who were just stealing the things.

Now, for the last three to five hundred years, with the feudal and capitalist society and the help of advertising and government complacency, we are mostly in a supply-side economy.

Supply-side economics is driven by someone who wants to sell something and therefore creates a desire or need for it by advertising a product or creating a need through product failure, attrition or, as sometimes is the case, planned obsolescence.

Supply side economics is just a way to give industry a free hand in creating what they want the public to buy, and then getting advertising agencies to convince the public that the product is what they need .

*Monopoly Laws...Usury Laws...Bill of Rights*

We have to stop allowing the criminals to make the laws. All laws and government programs should be written and created by liberal intellectuals, just as the framers of our country were when they conceived of America's Declaration of Independence, Constitution and Bill of Rights. All laws should be written to benefit the majority of the population. Ya think? We are a country based on freedom and democracy!

The thought that right now there are people in our government who want to add amendments to our Bill of Rights that are not democratic or beneficial to the majority sickens me. Most liberals do not have hidden economic interest in the outcome of the laws that deal with industry, tax and labor issues.

I believe any drastic economic changes can and should be made in a way that no one, rich or poor, is negatively impacted. It is even possible to censure and restrict corporations and capitalists' activities without inhibiting their lawful activities or hindering their democratic and free-enterprise rights.

# CHAPTER 13

## Stock Market

*"Some people are in love with the dollar sign. $, the monks used it. It is found on every keyboard, from the time keyboards were put on linotype machines and typewriters. Cell phones today have one, along with the happy faces, the sad faces and da da da..."*
Dudley Griffin, 2020

The stock market needs an overhaul and a downsizing. The original intent in creating the stock market was to provide money for companies to research and develop new products and services. It was not intended to provide profits for the companies' owners, officers and executives. The market was meant to be a means, not the end in itself.

The stock exchange became corrupted when it became more important as a source of income for the stockbrokers and investors than as a stimulus creating new and better products for the economy. That is when this country started on its way toward becoming a paper, or shadow, economy rather than an economy based on the industry of its people.

We must change the concept of the stock market back to its original intent. Originally "going public" was a way for new companies or companies with a new product to "borrow" money to use in research and development to get new products out in the marketplace.

This process was intended to stimulate our country's economy in several ways at the same time. First, to give companies fresh funding to spend in the marketplace to develop new, useful products to sell and then to give dividends (profits) to the investors for them to spend in the marketplace.

The first glitch in this process arose when some people discovered that they could make a profit by buying and selling stocks rather then waiting for the dividends. At this point, the whole concept of the stock market changed into a large government-sanctioned and legalized pyramid scheme.

At this point, "the market" itself became a business. In other words, there were people devoted solely to buying and selling stocks ... and making a lot of money from the process. Of course, this siphons off some of the money in commissions, which should have been, or was intended to be, invested into the product or services.

I know there are investors, the professionals, who don't care where their investment is spent as long as it brings them back a profit. The amateur investors might as well bet on jumping frogs. Even the mutual funds are loosing money right now. How does that all fit with our president's claims that he has helped our economy?

Another major problem with this present stock market system is that the "loan" from investors is not guaranteed or secured by anything except the prospect that a new product is profitable. This gave some people the license to steal, because if they cook the books, which they do, they can show a loss and never have to pay any dividends.

This brings up the last big scheme that the market has spawned--corporate CEO salaries. Stock market invested money is supposed to be spent on valid research and development only. It should not be used for CEO salaries or such things as advertising, new office furniture or trips to the Bahamas.

If a company is public or on the Stock Exchange, the CEO salaries should be regulated to match the profits of the business. Another step in the right direction would be to put a cap on corporate profits. We have a minimum wage. It makes sense to balance that by having a maximum wage, based on someone's value to the society.

The bugaboo is advertising, which is tax deductible, and used to inflate the value of the product, even if it is the same old product ... painted pink or in a new box.

Who created the present economic system anyway? You say, "Rich people did!" Oh, I see! Two maybe five, perhaps seven percent of the population established this system for the whole culture. How stupid of us! I'm sorry, but it has been proven time and time again, businessmen cannot be trusted to be fair.

We should start thinking about letting intellectuals make the rules for the stock market. Big business isn't a democracy; how can we expect corporate CEOs to govern the stock market democratically? Intellectuals should make all the economic decisions in government and in the stock market. Businessmen can administer them, but only if we watch them closely.

All of my suggestions for eliminating certain institutions, businesses or actions may have an impact on the people involved in them, but I am not a wicked, deluded, or greedy man wanting to take away a person's livelihood or self-esteem. I am mostly trying to change the industries to function so that they will impact fewer people negatively. This is called pragmatism, common sense and benevolence. It is also called adhering to the idea, ideals and spirit of the Construction of the United States of America. Business people of our country have to remember that the wonderful idea of democracy is more important than their own ideas for success and status.

Oh, and by the way, don't get your ego too involved in anything you do. You will eventually fail because of that one mistake!

# CHAPTER 14

## This Is Not Supposed to Be a Capitalist Country

*It is Barely a Democratic Country Right Now!*

*"The only problems we have in this world are greed, insecurity,*
*and the male ego!"*
JOB 4/9/20

Not since the Vietnam War era has our country been in such cultural turmoil. It is not just because of the war then and the war now being waged. It is mostly because of the atmosphere and personality of our government and its politics in this country right now.

Our freedoms and the freedom of all mankind forever are in jeopardy.

The disenfranchised of Europe and the world came to America to get away from economic and religious tyranny, but it has followed them here and multiplied to boot. Don't let anyone tell you otherwise, but capitalism and self-perpetuating religion are the world's most devastating problems. And now we in America have no other continent to which we can immigrate.

Basically, right now in 2020 America has no government. Many of the people who are in our "government" today are just lining their own pockets or conducting international vendettas in the name of the American people. We are back to taxation without representation.

These are the ten worst problems facing this country and all human society:

Greed

Pollution

Greed

Overpopulation

Greed

Religious intolerance

Greed

Ethnic intolerance

Greed

and Selfishness

Greed is at least half of the problem facing this world, and it is what creates or allows the other problems.

This country was never meant to be a bigoted country; it was meant to be an escape from bigotry.

This country was never meant to be a greedy country; it was meant to be an escape from greed.

Those were the two things which brought most people to America.

The colonies and later the United States was never meant to be a capitalist country. We left the Old World to get away from the feudal system, which was what capitalism was called before it moved to America.

The first colonists and immigrants to this country were actually more socialists than anything. Original Christianity and, for that matter, most other religions are based on socialism. Take care of the children, widows and elderly.

The Pilgrims would not have survived if they were not socialistic. As a matter of fact, greed and profit-taking was what destroyed many of the first colonies. And here is where the male ego failed many attempts at colonization. Competition for status, land or profit spoiled plans that required cooperating in this new land.

Greed and capitalistic attitudes are responsible for most of the problems in America today. Capitalism, as practiced in America, is not a democratic form of economy. Our Founding Fathers did not and would not have agreed upon such a selfish economy for their union of, by and for the people.

Capitalism as we know it is only about 100-150 years old. The United States of America is over 220 years old.

Capitalism developed from the free-enterprise system, yet it is not the true democratic economic system that was envisioned and adopted for the United States by our founders. Free enterprise is the rightful, just and fair economic system for a democracy, and that is what was chosen for our country.

Free enterprise means a level playing field for everyone. A chance for each and every person to be enterprising and prosper in cooperation with everyone else who is free to be enterprising and prosperous.

Capitalists do not believe in free enterprise; they believe in monopoly, where they and only they have the power and right to be prosperous. And capitalists have been slowly eroding all the checks and balances that our Founding Fathers created to make prosperity possible for everyone.

We are letting them do this by voting for capitalists, conservatives and Republicans to run our government. What we need are free-enterprise Democrats with an appreciation of socialist programs that will protect those people who can't compete in such a vicious environment as our world has become.

And then we need to get rid of greedy, competitive people. And since I am not in favor of shooting people, I feel that they should be reeducated.

But, I am afraid it is almost impossible to reverse the process after a person has become a capitalist pig. So we have to address and repair the social situations that cause a person to become greedy and excessively competitive. And that means educating the young, teaching that greed is bad behavior and making it a crime.

A respectable, moral society requires and demands following the Golden Rule. Selfish people have to be forced, if need be, to cooperate with everybody else on this small planet! This planet is getting smaller, and that is why we have to take drastic means.

This book is dedicated to the effort to abolish greed. We must stop it in this world, or it will be the downfall of mankind and the destruction of our planet.

The primary difficulty is that those who are in power now are benefiting from greed and capitalism. And because of their vested interest in the culture of money, they are concerned only about their own comfort and lifetime. They are not in the least worried about the world after they die. They are not even concerned about the life expectancy of their own children and children's children!

Stop voting for capitalists, whether Republicans or Democrats. Vote for someone who cares about America and its people, all of its people.

*"In my deep worst mind, I sometimes wish that God would strike dead those people who lie, cheat, steal, impoverish, unrightfully imprison, or kill other human beings, but then I realize, that I would be immoral, and hideous just as they are for even thinking those things.*
*But I can hope they get what they deserve. What if they suffer for the rest of their life and eternity with the knowledge that they are scum, hated by God and everyone?"*

# CHAPTER 15

## Separation of Business and State

*Paine in Common Sense:*
"However strange it may appear to some, or however unwilling they may be to think so, matters not, but many strong and striking reasons may be given, to show, that nothing can settle our affairs so expeditiously as an open and determined declaration for independence."

Today the separation of business and state is even more important than the separation of church and state. To have businessmen running our government is even more problematic than having church leaders doing so.

It is like employing a wolf to guard the sheep when we allow corporate CEOs to run a free-enterprise system and a democratic government. The definition of a corporation could easily be "economic dictatorship," and most businessmen are not really so keen on free enterprise. They much prefer a monopoly. Are these the right people to govern a free-enterprise democracy?

One of the most important requirements of the government of a democratic society is to protect the majority population from the few greedy people with an inclination to take advantage of them. In America at this point in time, we have the wolves running the sheep's pen. Our government is protecting the economic predators and watching as they devour the poor and silent majority.

It should not take much brain power to realize that corporate heads make bad administrators of a democracy. Corporate business is a dictatorship, so do we honestly believe that these people are going to be able to put aside their natural instincts of greed and not take advantage of the situation?

We of America are in as much danger today as we were in 1776, and this country is in as much peril of dissolution as it was during the Civil War. And, as during the Civil War, the threat to our country is not from outside, but from within.

In fact, the threat to this country is from the highest levels of our own government, those whom we originally believed to be our father figures. In the 1700s it was our king. Now, in 2020, it is the power structure commonly called government, the military/industrial complex.

We are being lied to, cheated and stolen from, by the military/industrial, capitalist, and conservative powers in this country. Our freedoms are being eroded at an alarming rate. More damage has been done to the freedoms of the American Constitution and Bill of Rights by this current Washington regime than has ever been done by any foreign government.

If we do not watch our own government and/or the people who run it, they are capable of dismantling it and our Constitution, purely for the economic benefit of a few people of their own choice. When certain situations occur, as they did on 9/11, it is possible for the people who are in control of our government to evoke patriotic emotions and thereby force the change of fundamental laws which in essence destroy the basic freedoms upon which this country was created. We must not let this happen again.

Dismantling the checks and balances of our government will lead to a totalitarian dictatorship. We must defend with our lives the democratic voting process. If we allow selfish and self-centered people to steal power in this country, they will turn the government into a mechanism of self-promotion.

As in the 1770s, a large percentage of the American public today is either uninformed or complacent about the economic danger they face. Again, as in the past, it is necessary for political intellectuals of this country to awaken the public to their peril. Thomas Paine, John Adams, Thomas Jefferson, James Madison, Alexander Hamilton and Benjamin Franklin were more than just businessmen or politicians; they were intellectuals more than self-serving individuals.

The problem with our world today is that accountants and lawyers run the place. The reason our society is in so much turmoil, why there is so much war, poverty, crime and greed, is because the accountants are in charge instead of sociologists, educators and intellectuals.

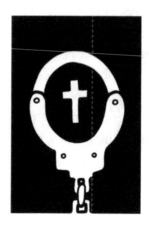

CHAPTER 16

## Separation of Church and State

More words have been thrown around about the separation of church and state than any other political subject. My comment is that, if one religious party runs the government and they persecute or pass laws against another religious party, then when that other religious party comes to power, they will persecute the other religions. War, war, on a biblical level! What would Jesus think?

The need for air, water, food, then the hormonal need to procreate, and after that the desire to have a deity to protect you. You can't take any of these essentials away from human beings, or you are going to have a fight. But the real conflicts and wars arise when people of different depth of religion and need decide that theirs is the only deity. And then they bump into people who think that theirs is the only deity, and they both start judging, proselytizing and persecuting. Well, you can see where that is heading, and it is here right now!

I know that God, any God, would not approve of these conflicts, because if you know the history of God, it has always been omnipotent, omnipresent and omniscient, meaning God does not believe in bigotry or condone forcing someone to change their beliefs. God, as

I know it, gives you choices, and then you must deal with the consequence of your actions. But only God and Mother Nature have those resources, powers and perogative.

The most human joy is in the company of other people, and more so if they know things and teach you and you know things and teach them.

*"Be diplomatic; don't let your bigotry separate you from tranquility of life."* JOB

Ug, Mug and Thug were walking around on the earth 400,000 years ago. Ug, a female, was a feminist, Mug was a man with a spiritual and creative mind, and Thug was a capitalist who raped Ug and stole ideas from Mug. Thug had tried Christianity but rejected it and experimented with homosexuality. When Thug was finally caught in his hypocrisy of being hypocritical and a deviant and perverted (no condemnation to homosexuality, which is not a choice, but a physical, emotional and social orientation/lifestyle), Thug asked God for forgiveness and then went back to doing what he dammed well pleased anyway.

We left the old countries to escape economic and religious oppression. If the capitalists and the religious nuts destroy this continent, then those of us looking for freedom and peace will have no place left to go. This place, America, is the last continent that was "almost available" to which we could escape.

# CHAPTER 17

## Capitalism and Capitalists

*"You do not like dirty hands, but you would have nothing with-*
*out <u>our</u> dirty hands."*
John 2.4.02

*"Insecurity is often dissolved by vanity. Vanity must be*
*bankrolled by greed. Greed begets selfishness. Selfishness*
*forsakeseven family."*
John 2.19.06

*"Capitalism is to Free Enterprise what Greed is to Ambition"*
John 3.5.17

Many people admire rich people because they want to be rich themselves. "He is rich; he must be doing something right." No, he is rich; he must be doing something wrong! People fear and support the wealthy because they want to be like them, but most people don't have the immoral personality to be that rich, and the rich are not going to teach them how to compete or take over their preferred parking spaces.

Capitalists are always fixing prices! Quote me! And they are always cutting costs, and cheapening materials. Quote me! It is endemic to profit-driven industry.

There is nothing wrong with making a profit. It is how you got that profit and what you do with it, that is the problem. Having a nest egg is what everybody wants, but greedy people seem to want so much more. Taking care of your family and providing for them after you are gone is a worthy endeavor, but trying to impress people with your wealth is a mental problem.

Almost every business on the Stock Exchange is cutting, cheating, deviating and downright stealing from the public and from the government. Quote me!

Capitalism is the creator of monopoly, not the game, but the larcenous practice of controlling prices and salaries, which happens when one company controls the whole market in any one place.

Sony, the corporation once sued a noodle soup shop named Sony to stop the owner from using the name Sony, which was his family name.

Capitalism is the new feudal system! Feudalism and feudal tyrants are the reason most colonists and immigrants left the old country to find a new home in America. The problem is that the tyrants and feudal lords, in search of new people to subjugate and land to conquer, arrived on the second boat to America.

Capitalism is not a democratic form of economy. Why do we allow it in America? Most Americans do not know that free enterprise, not capitalism, was the economic foundation upon which our Founding Fathers built this country. Capitalism as we know it, the name and the attitude, is maybe only 200 years old in this country. Free enterprise is a level playing field for all. Capitalism benefits those who are already wealthy and, the proponents are continually changing the rules so that they are even more advantaged.

If you're not fed up with this planned-obsolescence economy today, then you must be one of the thieves involved in it.

Capitalists care only about themselves and their own kind. And, believe me, you could never be their kind, even if you wanted to. They won't let you! There are a limited number of martini glasses in the executive dining room.

In order to be a true capitalist, you have to have hundreds of thousands, millions or billions of dollars invested, which you never touch, which is earning millions of dollars for you to play with. You also would most likely have had to lie, cheat and steal to get there. Are you willing to do that to be rich? Well good luck for your trip to heaven or prison.

Don't be fooled with all of the philanthropy; they have more money than they can use. It's a tax write-off. The poor and middle class actually, historically, give a larger percentage of their incomes to charity.

You must realize that you are only hurting yourself when voting for a capitalist or his political ally. They will not reach down to help you up, because then you would become their competition.

Materialism is the common man's worst enemy. The fabric of human society began to tear the moment the first person went to work for someone else. It is now realized by all those who have a brain, that the hippies were right all along ... on everything!

Most of you folks out there will listen to a stockbroker who makes half a million a year by influencing your decisions, but you won't listen to a liberal, intellectual, tree-hugger who doesn't make a dime from your choices. Which one of these two people really has your best interests at heart?

*"Anyone who spends his time and makes his money scheming, scamming and skimming off the physical labor of others is more like a criminal than a businessman."* John 8.9.05

Again I say that many Americans <u>incorrectly</u> believe capitalism is the economic system upon which this country was born. This country was actually formed with the ideals of free enterprise as its economic foundation, not capitalism. There is a big difference between capitalism and free enterprise.

Free enterprise is the concept of a level playing field on which all people are free to be enterprising. Conversely, capitalism, as it has developed into today, is a system in which the wealthy and powerful do everything within their means, legally or illegally, to make it difficult or impossible for other "moral businessmen" to compete in the marketplace or survive in business.

Selfishness, pride and ego will be the death of mankind; though, if womankind had the power, it would not happen so quickly.

Somewhere about here some of you may be thinking: This guy is a dammed idealist; he is trying to correct the nature of mankind. You may believe it will never happen. You may like my ideas, but doubt the possibilities of us ever achieving them. Don't underestimate the power of the human brain; we can overcome our mistakes.

In the history of life on earth and of human history, there have been many positive reversals in fate and direction of humankind: The destruction of dinosaurs, the discovery of metal, the Dark Ages into the Renaissance, the printing press, the compass, astral navigation and the Declaration of Independence. Changes, both natural and through human science and culture, have saved humankind from destruction before.

Human life expectancy could possibly be lower right now than it has ever been, and if we don't step into a progressive, ecological and humanitarian state of mind, we will perish. Yet, I believe humans are today, in depth, more intelligent than we have ever been before. Yet, I also believe that it is a toss up if we are going to be intelligent enough to save ourselves.

Let's control our own fate, start being responsible and respectable creatures and do what is necessary to save our wonderful dream of America.

A capitalist actually does not believe in free enterprise; a capitalist believes in a monopoly. He believes in complete freedom for himself, but restrictions and disadvantages for others. A true capitalist is actually un-American and unpatriotic. A capitalist playing the game of Monopoly would have crooked dice, marked cards, sleight of hand and magnets involved.

Capitalists enjoy the benefits of free enterprise but do not play by its simple rules. They deny others the freedoms that they, themselves, demand. The "golden rule" of free enterprise is that you must afford and defend the rights of everyone else to be enterprising, too. "Do business unto others as you would have others do business unto you."

Capitalists proclaim their American patriotism, yet they are really unpatriotic insurgents in America who come from the feudalism of another time and other countries. They have pulled the dollar bill over the eyes of the middle class who admire and support them.

There is nothing wrong with capitalism that wouldn't be solved by a measure of humility, gratitude and generosity. Of course, these are all traits considered by most normal humans to be desirable, yet they are dismissed as weaknesses by a greedy person.

This book is not a condemnation of all capitalists or all those who believe in the capitalist system. However it is definitely a condemnation of all of you ambitious people who are selfish and greedy and don't give a damn about the rest of us.

For the purposes of clarity, in this book I am using the word capitalist in its most negative definition. Maybe a more descriptive term would be "Capitalist Pig."

In my previous book, *The Hippie Dictionary: A Cultural Encyclopedia of the 1960s and 1970s*, I defined capitalist pig as "a greedy person; someone who violates other people's freedoms and civil rights in the pursuit of riches." Sounds familiar, doesn't it?

Our forefathers created this country's strength and validity by promoting cooperation between the separate classes of labor and business. If we allow either of these classes to dominate, then our democratic dream will die.

The problem is that one class, the business or capitalist class, is more ambitious than the working class. They have a different gene, the greed gene.

The capitalist class marches to its own drum beat, a beat which is so loud and dominant that it changes the cadence of everyone else around them. They are approximately only 7 to 10% of the population, and yet they disproportionately affect the remaining 90% of us. Money and power are their life's blood.

Capitalism as we know it didn't have a name at the time of our independence, but if it had, it would have been called speculation, wage slavery and feudalism. These are not activities our Founding Fathers had in mind for their democratic economy.

Speculation was the loaning of money at high interest or the buying of property with the speculation that it would appreciate in value. Wage slavery was the practice of paying such low wages that a whole society was impoverished to the point that it could not improve itself or move on to better circumstances. Feudalism is when wealthy "lords" own all the property upon which the "serfs" live, work and farm, thus controlling all means of economic advancement. Sounds like what is happening in the US today, doesn't it?

Feudalism was one of the primary reasons American colonists and immigrants left the "old country." Taxation without representation, the lack of religious freedom and feudalism were the causes of the American Revolution.

Slowly but surely, wage slavery and feudalism have worked their way back into our lives. Plus, now we have no limitations on loan and credit interest. It all amounts to insidious capitalism, and capitalism is synonymous with deceit in business, the oppression of workers and now the destruction of our environment for profits.

This may seem to be unkind to the term capitalism, but that is because of what it has become. There is a respectable side to capitalism.

The original definition of a capitalist is someone who makes their living from the investments of their capital. Capital means basically "assets," which usually are not spent or depleted, but are the stable "foundation" of a person's wealth. This all comes originally from the word capital, which is part of an architectural column, the top element of the column upon which the roof sits.

In the strictest sense, the kindest definition of a capitalist is a person who does not actually need to work to maintain their lifestyle. They have set the wheels in motion with investments, decisions and power, and now other people make the money for them.

Capitalism can be a valuable economic tool. Every retired person living on their Social Security or a company retirement plan is a capitalist in the sense that they are receiving the interest from their invested earnings and savings.

Capitalism, the act of making money on one's invested capital, is not wrong. But how it has evolved and how it is employed by some people has made it the most damaging force in our world today.

As a way of living, in and of itself, capitalism is not bad; in fact, it is commendable as long as it is conducted within certain moral boundaries. But, many people who reach that level of economic success do so with a complete lack of moral conscience. And as it is written, "power corrupts," and similarly wealth corrupts and makes a person want more wealth and the power it brings.

To be rich is acceptable, but to lie, cheat and steal to get rich and stay rich is immoral, and that is where the term capitalist got its present negative definition.

The original definition of capitalism has a place in our economic system. The present negative form of capitalism has no place in any democratic or free society.

The word capitalism evokes two distinctly different emotions throughout the world today. It means a greedy, immoral, machine without conscience. It also means success, affluence and a life worth striving for. It is often thought of in both these ways at the same time.

Not everyone who is wealthy is a capitalist in the original sense nor in the negative way. Not every businessman lies, cheats and steals for their money. Also, not everyone who acts in the negative capitalist manner is rich. There are those people who are poor or who are poor businessmen, yet they still lie, cheat and steal in the role model of capitalist pig. Our current "president 2020" is one!

*"Capitalist pig is the hippie counterculture term, meaning a greedy person, someone who violates other people's freedoms and civil rights in the pursuit of riches. Just as everybody who is poor is not a criminal, everyone in a three-piece suit is not a respectable businessman; they may be a thief."* JMc

Many people who act with the arrogance and greed of a capitalist are not actually capitalists, but that doesn't matter. It is how a person acts that matters. If you try hard enough, you can be a capitalist pig and still be in the poorhouse.

Most people who want to be a capitalist will never really become one in the pure sense of the word. There is room at the top for only a small number. The capitalists know this, and they are not going to help you take away their spot.

Most people who think it would be nice to be a capitalist would not be willing or morally able to do what is necessary to be a capitalist in the harshest sense of the definition. Most people are too nice or not ambitious enough to lie, cheat and steal to get to the top.

There is nothing wrong with being financially ambitious. Ambition is what makes mankind as creative and productive as we are. But ambition to the point of selfishness and greed is counter-productive. At this point in the history of mankind, our greed is killing our society and our world.

Capitalism is now suppressing the American dream by making it difficult for ambitious individuals, who also happen to be moral businessmen, to compete. Today, it seems one has to cheat to succeed, and this is actually making basically good people into liars, thieves and cheats. Our current president 2020 is the bad example that many folks are following right now. He has made corruption seem acceptable. He is a predator and many folks are just following his lead. He is a facilitator for hate, bigotry and greed.

The people who support, like, or "love" our current president do so only because he is the only person who is a bigger cheat or idiot than they are, so they have somebody to look up to, or down on, depending on their own levels of insecurity.

With capitalism, the American dream is attainable to only a small percentage of people, those who are willing to play the games of deception. With pure free enterprise everyone has the opportunity to achieve the American Dream.

Capitalism is destructive in two major ways, socially and environmentally. Socially, through the oppression of employees, capitalism has created a world of poverty, crime and despair. By paying sub-survival wages, refusing to provide proper health care and scrimping on retirement benefits, the business community is creating a society of trapped and unhappy people.

By polluting our environment and depleting our natural resources, capitalism is now rapidly killing our planet, which will eventually kill all of us and most life. Capitalists are destroying both our society and our world for the sake of money. Shame on them!

Many Americans assume it is unpatriotic to speak out against capitalism. Actually the opposite is true; it is unpatriotic to be a capitalist. This country was formed with the ideals of free enterprise as its economic foundation, not capitalism. Capitalism is another totalitarian form of economy just like communism, and they both have the same dictatorial philosophy: "Make the oppressed masses work for a few chosen people."

Capitalism and communism are very similar in what they do to the people involved in them. The powerful people become greedy, the regular people get worked to death, intellectuals are ignored or persecuted and the weak and tired are jailed and discarded.

At one time General Motors could have been mistaken for a communist dictatorship, and the Soviet Union viewed as one of the largest capitalistic corporations in the world. One is no better than the other. Capitalism and communism should both join the list of human experiments that failed and were rejected.

Capitalism is closer to the bad aspects of communism than it is to the good parts of democracy. Capitalism is based on business ethics which require totalitarian rule and therefore are undemocratic.

Capitalists do everything within their power to restrict the competition of others. They do it illegally or through "legal" means by creating new laws that give themselves the advantage. This is also un-American activity.

Capitalism is only part of our economic system, but it has become the most dominant and the most destructive part. It divides people into categories, and that alone is very undemocratic. It creates the important people and the unimportant people.

Democracy is actually an annoyance to a capitalist, just as unions are, just as education is. Since we are supposed to be a democratic society and since capitalism is not a democratic form of economy, then why is capitalism our predominant economic system, and why are we letting capitalist CEOs run our government?

Don't get me wrong. I would never even suggest outlawing capitalism. It has a place in our economy, and those people who function properly and well in capitalism have a place in our society.

Capitalism fuels economic growth and capitalist-type people, with their drive to succeed, have a tendency to get things done. The problem is to keep the achievements within the boundaries of positive growth. Ambition is one thing, but greed is another.

Destructive growth fueled by greed is not progress. In a world bordering on overpopulation, with environmental pollution and diminishing resources, we should think closely about what we call progress. If only the rich benefit from progress, shouldn't it really be called something else like environmental robbery, or stealing from the unborn?!

With poverty and malnutrition as a fact of life, even in the land of the free and home of the brave, then we must consider how successful mankind really is. Are we doing the right things with this world we have been given? Are we taking care of our own? Capitalism is not really an improvement for the majority of people!

Capitalists make money on the money they invest. A capitalist, technically, does not work to make money; he works to protect his investments. The nature of capitalism is dehumanizing in that the investor is not involved in healthy, normal human work and accomplishments, he is concerned merely with the numbers, the bottom line.

Many people in the middle class of America look up to capitalists and dream of being capitalists one day. That is why they support the vision they have of capitalism. The truth of the matter is that few people will ever become capitalists. Capitalists will not reach down to help you up, so stop voting for them and throwing money at them. I estimate that I proportionately give more money and time to people and causes in need than Bill Gates does. And many people poorer than I am do the same and more.

If you really want to become wealthy, you are better off voting for a person with middle class or even socialistic ideals, than capitalist ideals. A socialist will share, a capitalist will compete with you. A capitalist will not help you become rich, because then you may want their limo driver or their spot at the golf club.

One of the economic and cultural travesties of our legal system was when civil courts and the US Supreme Court decided that corporations had the same rights as human beings in 1886 and then in the 1970s.

The combination of the electoral college and our representational government (republic) have made for a flawed system where corruption is easy for the people who bend the laws and then say, "Well, what I am doing is not illegal." No, maybe not, but it is a bastardization of the original Bill of Rights and standing decisions or laws of the Supreme Court.

A hundred or so years ago this country decreed that a corporation had the rights of an individual person. It is ironic that, as large companies acquired personalities, the people who owned and ran them began their decline deeper into inhumane behavior. Money and privilege have always fostered arrogance, but that one governmental act gave corporate individuals the permission to hide behind their conglomerates and become even less responsible for their inhumane actions. It also allowed them to donate to political campaigns amounts of money that paid for lies and altered truth and in the 2016 elections blocked voters.

Corporations now act as humans, yet they are neither liable nor prosecutable in the same way as an individual. And at the same time the people who make the decisions to involve the corporation in illegal activity are not liable because they are embedded in the corporate structure and therefore are not considered as individuals.

This twist of technicalities makes for several destructive tendencies in our society. Large corporations, because of their increasing powers, are becoming less personal toward their employees and customers, less concerned about the product they create, and less respectful of the government and its rules they are supposed to follow.

The CEOs and company management who are protected by the corporate camouflage and impersonality are also getting bolder in their self-importance. Power corrupts, and when people believe they are part of a huge entity that is immune from retribution, they become in their own minds almost godlike. They are above the law.

Oh, and by the way, if you want to know, really know, more about the law and morality, watch the *Perry Mason* TV shows.

Winning a monetary settlement from a corporation for illegal activity is not really punishing the true culprit. The money usually comes out of worker's wages and causes product quality reduction. The CEOs seldom suffer monetary loss or incarceration. Jail time and economic loss for CEOs would be an appropriate penalty, sort of like the same suffering as those of the people they have harmed or cheated.

All of the power being given to larger and larger conglomerates is also creating monopolies, which are fundamentally bad for our society economically and creatively. Our stuff is being made by fewer and fewer companies, and these companies take advantage of this to cheapen the quality and raise the price. That alone is a possible formula for the destruction of our culture.

Today, in 2020 the coronavirus pandemic and how it is being handled by Washington, by large industries and the corporate medical community, is an example of how those entities have distanced themselves from the struggles of the majority of people. At the same time some companies are showing their concern for the middle and lower economic population and they are to be commended and patronized.

As in 1776, we are today again dealing with tyrants who wish to monopolize money, control our thoughts and suppress our freedoms. These people are functioning under the same faults of human nature that have plagued mankind for most of our history--competition and greed.

Usually, this heightened level of competition and greed are caused by some form of personal insecurity. Insecurity is one of the major motivations for competition, desire for domination and greed. To build self-assurance, mankind uses money and status. Greed begets money, which creates status that heals insecurity.

Psychology 1A in any junior college or university will tell you that most of man's insecurity originally comes from sexual fears and imagined social inadequacies. As Freud tells us, sex and money are related.

Many rich and poor men alike have one major thing in common, a belief that money improves sex appeal, and that even appearing to have money works just as well.

One of the most damaging elements of our society today is the sublimation of money for normal good, clean sex. Our advertising industry has worked hard to fool us into thinking that possessions and the ability to buy them are a sign of sexual prowess.

Many men have bought into this idea that a man's image of his own sexual strength can cure his insecurity. So men use sex, real or imaginary, to build self-assurance. Sexual self-image can be obtained by either having more sex or by looking successful so everyone else thinks you are having sex.

Sex, power and greed start to get all confused in people's minds, and since sex is supposed to be bad, then power and greed start to take the place of sexuality. Some men find power to be an acceptable exchange for sex. Even though they still secretly and hypocritically indulge in sex, on the surface they use materialism and power to indicate their sexual value. TV preachers do this.

These people have been taught by their religion or social group that sex is a sin, and although they may have been coerced into acting ashamed of sex, they are still compelled by mother nature to perform sexually. Often their frustrations are inflicted on others in the form of economic competition and capitalistic greed.

Why is it that in almost every book written, every movie, TV show, and sermon spoken they proclaim that greed, corruption, lying, cheating and stealing are sins ridiculed and despised?! Yet in our society we continue to support, elect and look up to the one class of people who do the most of this, those insecure, gratification-seeking capitalists! Why do people envy them and want to be just like them?

Many people overlook the negative aspects of greed because the money and power seem to be such a worthwhile trade-off. There are a lot of average, respectable folks who fantasize about having money and power like capitalists do, yet they do not realize the changes they would have to go through to attain that level of greed.

To become a true capitalist requires putting aside many foundations of human society. Most destructive of all, it necessitates suspending one's morality, or becoming hypocritical about morals. Could you sleep at night knowing that your actions had economically ruined the lives of others, or caused others to be enslaved or killed?

Could you look into your own children's eyes knowing that your greed had destroyed families, created domestic violence and suicide? Wealthy and unscrupulous people are somehow able to detach themselves from the pain they cause others.

People who are possessed by money and power are able to justify their actions and live what they call normal lives. But most truly respectable Americans could never live that hypocrisy.

We must stop respecting people with money, just because they have money. They are rich, not for being good, but for doing bad.

Is that the way it should be? A country based on riches ill-gained and a population so enamored by the wealth and power that they continue to let the rich screw them?

It is ludicrous for people to defend all the sins of capitalism, merely on the justification that it keeps the economy growing. If you understand human existence, business and commerce, you will realize that economy does not need to grow. All our economy really needs to do is to supply the needs of the people and that is best done by a steady natural function. Give people what they need and the opportunity to have some things they want, and then the economy will progress. Only greedy people can fuck it all up.

Capitalists may need some tax breaks to do more research and development to create new products. Yes, but we don't need any new gadgets to spend money on and to deplete our natural resources. Our rich are getting richer from corporate welfare, while our country's bridges, roads, schools and libraries are disintegrating.

Capitalism is only valuable to the world if it keeps human needs fulfilled and the economy growing enough to help pay for the infrastructure of society.

Capitalists and conservatives are always complaining about the welfare mothers and the "criminal element," and yet by their own actions they are creating both these situations. A higher minimum wage and better education would help to solve many of the problems in our society. Prison does not solve crime; education solves crime. Abstinence does not solve unwanted pregnancies; birth control and education do. Abstinence is unsustainable. God made us do it. We as humans with brains have to save ourselves from a deadly overpopulation by choosing birth control.

But, then capitalists do not want such education because it would deprive them of a large poor and ignorant class of almost slave laborers. And then they also wouldn't have other people to look down on and ridicule.

The excessive desire for money creates many negative situations in our society. Greed, distrust and aggression are a vicious circle that go hand in hand.

A greedy person thinks that everyone else is greedy. That is how they themselves are; that is all they know, so of course they think everyone else must be the same. As Freud explained to us in his theory of projection, a person will often project his own faults and personality traits onto other people.

Since a greedy person thinks everyone else is greedy, they will react against that greed. And the best defense in the economic world is an offensive move, so they lie, cheat and steal because they think they must do so first in order to survive. This has a snowball effect, and a self-perpetuating mechanism. A person or a corporation financially attacks another, and they become offensive themselves, attacking back, and soon we have bidding wars and takeover battles and a downright unhealthy atmosphere for normal human beings.

It is also a basic insecurity problem. These people feel it is necessary to be on top of the heap, and they are distrustful of competition. They are just a bundle of conflicting mental problems.

This, of course, is how the greedy have come to run the world. Those of us who are not as needy or aggressive are at a disadvantage. The 10% who are greedy and aggressive are standing over the 90% who are just trying to live reasonable and benevolent lives.

The vicious circle of greed creates a distrust in fellow man, which in turn produces aggression in our country. Road rage is becoming more prevalent, produced partly by more cars of course, but also by the attitude of self-entitlement that is allowed and displayed by the actions of our current president. In the the eyes of most of the world, our president is the poster boy of entitled greed, arrogance, aggression, bigotry and social division.

Have you seen a <u>truthful</u> historic-outline of our current president's background and economic history? It is appalling, but you will never be allowed to see it by him! If you ever see the <u>truthful</u> man, it will be shown to us by his indebted enemies.

If you want to talk about the socio-economic, political problems of this country right now, I would be happy to!

Capitalists are very unpleasant personalities to be around. Have you ever tried to function in a corporate environment? It is worse than the jungle. The cycle of greed, competition, distrust and aggression is so hideous that many people with good, trustworthy personalities can't stand to be associated with the business world. Have you ever watched the TV series *Mad Men*? I was in the advertising industry and the memories of that polluted society made it impossible for me to watch that show.

This negative environment causes stress, ulcers and heart attacks. And it is accelerating our world into a shallow, materialistic and insensitive society. Add to that the disastrous fact that greed and materialism are depleting our natural environment, using up our world's resources and killing the earth.

We can't let conservatives and capitalists continue to destroy our world and theirs. We must now fight to save our world and to save the capitalists from their own insensitivity.

The silent middle class majority has been told for so long that capitalism, conservative politics and trickle-down economics are the American way of life. This is a lie created by people who make a lot of money by keeping the silent majority silent.

And why does the average man allow the capitalists to continue playing these games of greed, dominance and destruction? Some say it is because the silent majority is also deaf and blind to the deceit and crime of the conservative capitalist, but that is not true! We see and hear the truth, even though the news media tries to hide it; we see it in life, in movies; we read it in books and feel it at our workplaces.

Everyone knows how corrupt the rich and powerful are. So why do we put up with it?

Some people accept it because they envy the rich and powerful, and they want to be just like them. Some allow it because they think this is the way it is supposed to be. Some think it is the American way to lie and cheat for money and power.

But most other folks do not speak out because they are afraid. They are frightened of being alone in their dissent, and they do not condemn the rich and corrupt because they think their small voice will not matter or be heard.

Most capitalists "pigs" are conservatives as well. They suffer from the same insecurity as conservatives. That is why they became capitalists. To beat other people. To feel better than other people! As conservatives, they are incapable or afraid of confronting a person on a one-to-one basis as humans, so they steal the other man or woman's tools and oppress or suppress them through corporate or legal power. Dominance is a rush to all people, but sometimes you beat someone who is better than you are. Does that make you happy?

But remember, we are many, and they are few. They are only powerful and greedy because we allow them to be. Stop supporting them!!! Tell them, "I ain't your whore no more!"

There are many people out there who secretly and silently think the same way as you do. This is still a democracy. Vote out of office all those who support capitalism and the domination of your lives.

We must fight capitalist selfishness with all our hearts and souls. Greed is the most inhumane force within mankind. It is the anti-Christ.

Self-importance and avarice separate mankind from perfection. Greed and selfishness give some people the illusion that they are better than others, and therefore it disrupts communication between their spirits. We will never be buddha-like, god-like or christ-like until we appreciate the spirit of others.

Ug, Mug and Thug were walking around on the earth 400,000 years ago. Ug, a female, was a feminist, Mug was a man with a spiritual and creative mind, and Thug was a person who wanted more for himself. In fact, if he thought about it, he actually wanted everything that everyone else had. So Thug invented money, well Ug had already experimented with money and rejected it as exclusive and socially problematic, but Thug appropriated the idea and began exchanging and taking little shells for everything he acquired or supplied. Well eventually Thug had almost all the shells that exited in the area, and began have others get more for him. The little shells didn't have any real use, you couldn't eat them or build a house of them, but, Thug began giving the shells to women he wanted something from to wear around their necks, and to men he wanted to work for him. Thug was the first conniving capitalist

In this day with this predatory economy that we live under, a man should be judged on how hard he works for his money to feed his family, and not on how much money he has accumulated in the bank!

*"People have devoted their bodies to their life's commitment. Women give birth to twelve children, men break their backs and health in coal mines, writers strive to accelerate their minds, astronauts seek the moon and stars!" Dudley Griffin*

# CHAPTER 18

# The Medical and Pharmaceutical Industry, Meds and Drugs

## *Hypocrisy or Hippocratic Oath*

I have to be respectful of the medical profession because three of the most amazing human beings I have ever know were doctors. The last one died in the 1980s.

There are so many personal stories of how wonderful doctors have been to people—life-saving, care-giving, fee-canceling. I myself was birthed free of charge by the recommendation of a family doctor.

But then, by now so many of us have seen or heard the horror stories of malpractice, misdiagnosing and misprescribing. Of course, I know that the medical profession is no better prepared for the human body than auto mechanics are for a spaceship, but practice makes perfect.

Don't lie to us cattle and say it won't hurt or cost a lot of money. Please don't hurry my endoscopy so you can rack up twelve procedures today.

I know the derivation of the doctor's office term "patient," It means a person who has to sit for a long time with last year's magazines and not complain.

"Doctor, please don't be thinking of your back nine while I'm exposing my backside to you. "

2019: We are a lot better at keeping people alive longer today, but we are not better at giving them a better **quality of life**; in fact it is getting worse!

### *Pharmaceutical Industry, Meds and Drugs*

If a pharmaceutical product is made for 73 cents in the USA or Europe and sold for $4 in Mexico, Holland or Morocco and then for $10 back in the USA or Europe, what do you call that? Could it be illegal or immoral or both? Whether it is a life-saving medication or a mind altering pill makes no difference to legality or morality. They are both convictions to hell and/or to jail for the seller.

The pharmaceutical companies know that legally they could never sell all the drugs they are selling into illegal traffic. Do you want me to explain the world courts to you or the definition of immorality? Pharmaprofiteer corporations are selling pills to known drug pushers.

*"The definition of subsistence living can be positive or negative. The positive definition, is to work at your own pace at what you want or need to do in order to live free. The negative definition is living to work!"*
Sartre and Dudley Griffin

The capitalist Christian leadership in America has a fundamental dislike for people who seek pleasure without paying *them* for it. The Christian work ethic opposes subsistence living or directionless leisure and capitalism opposes free fun and cheap thrills.

Drugs, particularly psychedelic drugs, are considered subversive and immoral by capitalists and Christians because they know they cannot keep control of the minds of people who use them. Psychedelics tend to disillusion you with hypocrisy, bigotry, organized religion and non-democratic governments. People began to look more closely for the truth. As mind-expanders, they expand your mind.

Respectable doctors and respectable hospitals historically prescribe or give mood-altering and pain- relieving drugs to people all the time. These are things that are known to be helpful, yet dangerous if not given with instructions. Doctors and hospitals are not always infallible; it behooves our society to promote rational medical education to people. Some people will abuse things; we cannot always protect people from themselves. But often, most often, it is ignorance and peer pressure that get people in trouble with "drugs," alcohol included.

The hippies were the guinea pigs; society should be listening to what we have to say right now. Drugs can be like any tool devised by mankind. They can cut both ways. Drugs, like tools, can expand your horizons or cut off your hands.

The "do-as-I-sayers" are threatened by people who want to live-and-let-live. Back in the 50s when the cool people wanted to set people free, we sang and smoked in crash pads and coffee houses. And the sub-cultures or countercultures who indulged in such drugs were considered inferior and therefore to be mistrusted and feared. But they were the college students the young visionaries and artists that this present generation now relies on so much for their intellect, leadership and for breaking down doors.

Although moral reasons are often preached by the capitalist Christians for their opposition to euphoric or psychedelic drugs it is also for economic reasons. It is difficult to enslave a person in a low-paying job if that person experiments with drugs that expand his mind to think about life and values.

The war on "illegal" drugs in this country is a capitalist scam. It is a smokescreen to keep the public's mind off more critical problems. It is propaganda to marginalize, dehumanize, harass and institutionalize people that conservatives consider counterculture, second-class citizens and beneath their own status.

The number of drug deaths now in the US in a typical year is:
Tobacco, about 390,000
Alcohol, about 80,000

Opioid pills, prescription or illicit, possibly 67,000
Secondhand tobacco smoke, around 50,000
Cocaine, 2,200
Heroin, 2,000
Aspirin kills about 2,000 persons a year in the US
and marijuana kills 0
Psychedelics kill some people by accident, their own accident.

There has never been a recorded death due to marijuana at any time in US history. Yet just as with wine, you could drown in a vat of marijuana leaves.

All illegal drugs combined kill about 4,500 people per year, which is around one percent of the number killed by alcohol and tobacco. Tobacco kills more people each year than all of the people killed by all of the illegal drugs in the last century. (These figures were taken from NIDA Research Monographs.)

What do these statistics tell you about our drug laws? What is the priority that makes our society judge one drug legal and another illegal? Money! It is obvious that economics is more important to capitalists than moral issues, such as the death of the consumers.

The figures on deaths "caused" by individuals who are under the influence of illegal drugs are difficult to prove or record, but the consensus is that those statistics would not drastically change the overall percentages.

The conservative element would have you believe that it is a "moral" issue, that these drugs are "bad." Bad for whom? Bad says who? Are they mentioned in the Bible? Does the Bible say that alcohol is OK, but marijuana is evil? No, it doesn't!

Don't you think that the drug that kills the most people should be considered the most evil drug? That would be tobacco!

How many tobacco executives have been taken off the streets today by the war on drugs? Come on folks let's get our perspectives straight. What is our biggest criminal problem in this country today, street drug crime or capitalist crime?

The fact is that capitalist crime actually causes most street crime. Poverty is, to a large extent, caused by capitalist economic oppression. A poor man is likely to steal to survive, turn to illegal activities to make a living or use drugs to escape the pressures of poverty. Poverty, wage slavery and excessive indebtedness are usually caused by someone else's greed.

Drugs are a perfect way to control the masses. They are a good economic and behavioral prison for the poor and oppressed. Someone who is strung out on opiates, speed or cocaine is not in any mental or physical shape to complain or rebel against their oppressors.

Capitalists and conservatives couldn't find an above-ground way to make money on "street drugs," so they made them illegal. They knew that "Christian indignation" would make it difficult to legitimize marijuana. There were other circumstances that would make it difficult to control its sale as they have alcohol and tobacco. Strangely, they have found many other ways to profit from drugs by keeping them illegal.

Some people just can't handle drugs. They should be told this as soon as possible by their doctors and friends and their friends should help them to stop. It would help if the pharmaceutical companies didn't keep promoting and producing more drugs than the public can rationally consume.

Laws against drug takers are stupid and do not really address the problem. Laws (government) and morality (church) should address the culture of poverty and hopelessness and how the blame for that stems from the actions of the lords of pharmaceutical companies and capitalism.

Disclaimer: I do not advocate excesses of anything. Drugs can mean, coffee, alcohol, nicotine, Nyquil, diet pills, many prescribed medications, THC, psychedelics, cocaine, and some legal herbal teas. "Use your drugs; don't let them use you!"

## CHAPTER 19

## Power: What Is This Need Man Has For Power?

We have heard it over and over "Power corrupts," and it does. But, even worse, it attracts people to want it, and it attracts people to other people who have it.

To maintain a democracy and to retain our freedom, we must never let any one ideology get so much power that it can control public dissent, the media and the voting process.

The conservative, capitalist, military/industrial complex is very close to that right now. If we let them continue, we will lose our democracy and freedom.

It is essential for a society to scrutinize its leaders and reject those who govern only for power. There is the good and the bad of power. But power corrupts even those with good intentions, and that is why the checks and balances of our government are essential.

It is dangerous to allow any one ideology to control all aspects of the government because, no matter how well-intentioned power is at first, complete power does corrupt. Power is most often sought by people in an effort to hide or combat their own insecurities; these people are susceptible to temptations.

Power in and of itself is not bad. Just as with a gun; what you do with it determines whether it is bad. And just as with weapons, it is not advisable to have too much of it in the wrong hands.

Power that is allowed to go to a person's head will eventually separate them from others. It will blind them to the pain and suffering of other people. Corrupt, selfish power definitely makes a person a poor administrator for a democratic government.

Excessive power often creates the feeling of invincibility, the feeling that one has a mandate to change the rules. The basic human nature of selfishness somehow always comes to the surface with power, and that is why, in their great wisdom, our Founding Fathers gave us our three-tiered system of government, executive (the president), congress (elected representatives), judicial (the Supreme Court) and plus one, that of the free press (the media).

It is disheartening to realize that there are a lot of people in this country who want freedom for themselves and don't want others to have it. That is un-American and unpatriotic!

Power has its place in certain aspects of our economy. An ego or heightened ambition pushes people to achieve goals, which can stimulate the economy. But, if left unchecked, these personalities will gobble up everything, leaving nothing for the majority of people who are not so greedy.

This commercial class of people is important to our society's existence. But this group of people, the capitalists, has become so powerful and arrogant as to think that they are actually the most important people in this society.

These people should never be allowed to run a government, especially a government that is supposedly a democracy. The problem is that some people think money and power put them above government and its laws. And, because these people are the wealthy and privileged, they have gained more power and control of our government.

And so we find ourselves in a situation where our laws are no longer written or enforced equitably. The poor and middle class are treated as second-class citizens. Often, they are poor or middle class only because of the laws that discriminate against their advancement.

We have forgotten the lessons learned from Watergate. Misguided self-importance and misplaced loyalties can corrupt patriotism into a totalitarian regime.

During Watergate, our last great threat to democracy, the departments of our government, our Constitution and a free press worked together to save this country from slipping back into a world of tyranny. Today we again need to re-establish the freedoms upon which this country was formed.

Why do many people of the poor and middle class in this country have such admiration for capitalist power? We know that their power and money were achieved primarily by hurting someone else, maybe even you. Is our own desire for money and power blinding us, urging us to support them, and, by doing so, giving, them even more power over us?

We must stop respecting people with money and power just because they have it. You might say, "He has power. He must be doing something right!" No, very often, "He has power. He must be doing something wrong!"

We must fight against corrupt power in the voting booth and in the market place. Do not vote for people who use their power to make the rich richer and poor poorer. When shopping, buy only goods and services that make sense to the environment.

Much has been said about some men's lust for money and power. The money can be understood, because it brings material goods and comfort. But what is this passion for the "power" that excessive money brings? Yes, "excessive money." There is such a thing as too much money. It is an illness.

The power that money brings is not the real reward most greedy men desire. What they are really after is the "glory" that power brings. Power itself is not a bad thing. It is what a person uses it for that matters. If it is only for self-glory, then it is misused.

Glory is man's most sinful desire, because glory is reserved only for God. Whenever a man lusts for glory and does not treat it with its due respect, that man is waiting for a fall that will last for eternity. I'm not being funny, spiritual or poetic. This is almost my only religious proclamation.

Arrogant rich people are the worst people in the world! They cause more death, pain and suffering than any rapist, heroin dealer or 7-11 robber. The 9-11 hijackers killed only 3,500 people, but most international corporation CEOs kill many, many more in a year. This is not arrogance from a left wing radical. This is the truth. Look at the facts, and it is indisputable.

What is wrong with all of us that we will sit back and let those people do this to us?

These people should be consigned to the junk heap of history! Yet some regular people idolize them and want to be capitalists, but, as they should know, the rich will never help you to get rich unless they get richer. To the rich, everyone is a competitor. They will not help you get rich because there is only enough room in the executive restroom for a limited number of egos and a limited number of urinals.

To get them to leave us alone and stop stealing from us, we may have to pay them off, for that is all they understand--money. At least if we negotiated a golden handshake, we would have a voice in the pro-cess. They will fight because they are not rational where money and power are concerned. We will have to negotiate, educate and convict them of their moral social, environmental and economic sins.

We may have to give them an island or a small continent where they can lie, cheat and steal from each other and leave us alone. They can have their golf courses, condos and mansions, private islands and fake tans, but we cannot take away all their power, because power is more important to a capitalist than even money. But we cannot let them have the power to govern anymore, because they will abuse it again, and then we will be back to this economic anarchy.

Almost always, when a person lies, cheats or steals, they get caught. Why then do people continue to do these things?

1. They are stupid.
2. They are desperate for something: money, love or fame.
3. They don't know what law and morality is!
4. Or they may know that law and morality exist, but their personality wants instant gratification!

*"I don't get no jollies off of proving you wrong; I get my jollies from helping you to be right, and learning together what is right!"*
Dudley Griffin 2020

CHAPTER 20

## **Freethinkers or Money-thinkers**

*"The whole world is going in the wrong direction right now. Money is more important than family, more valuable than ethics, more sought after than beauty or honor."*
Jesus Christ 35 BC and 2020

Freethinkers are liberals; money thinkers are conservatives! Freethinkers don't want to choose your life for you. Money thinkers want to choose your every move so that they can control the money and things you buy. Someone else controlling your money puts you in a flypaper sticky, cultural trap.

Who do you want watching your life? It is time to make a decision! If you don't make it now, it will be too late. You will be stuck with the conservative dictatorship whether you like it or not.

Freethinkers and liberals have an unwarranted reputation for being smartasses or arrogant. Only a few people accuse them of this-- people who are not as intelligent as they are, and capitalists who have an economic greed to protect and want to discredit liberals so the public won't hear the truth from liberals.

Definitions of:
- Intelligent: high IQ.
- Smart: someone you don't want counting your change.

- Ignorant: someone who doesn't have the facts or ignores the facts.
- Stupid: someone who continues to ignore the facts even when they are available to them and impact them negatively.

Ignorance is your worst enemy. The only reason mankind has reached its lofty position is intellect. The reason that humankind will destroy itself and the world is ignorance.

Free thinkers (liberals) will try to educate you about your bad choices, but they will not kill you for disagreeing. Conservatives are professionals at defaming, economically destroying or eliminating those who disagree with them.

I have had my bumper stickers torn off or defaced and car scratched because of my free speech comments. Nothing violent or un-American is ever on my vehicle or in my writing!

*"When you violate someone else's automobile because you don't like their bumper sticker, you are unpatriotic, un-American and possibly un-Christian like, as well as, immoral!" 12/22/2019 Dudley Griffin*

*"Try to keep you mouth shut until you know the facts and truth, because you could be spinning people's lives off into the wrong direction due to your ignorance." Putter Dooley*

# CHAPTER 21

## Capitalists, Conservatives, Democrats, Liberals

### Republicans

**Capitalists:** There are differences between capitalists and conservatives. They are separated by moral and economic commitments and desires. Capitalists are an exclusive group; they can be conservative and religious (most often with hypocritical or ulterior motives). They are most often Republicans hoping that a Republican administration will allow them to continue stealing from the public.

Good capitalism is consumer driven; you want something and you go out and buy it, or barter for it and everyone gets what they want. But, there became a whisper of deceit, greed or conceit in about 400,000 BC and it has been growing ever since. It was personal desire.

Producer-driven economy is, "I want to make money, so I will invent or steal an idea, most often not a necessity, and advertise it and sell it and my kids get water skis and their kids' medicine be dammed."

Here I am speaking of social conservatives and capitalist pigs. Unless otherwise stated, when I use the term capitalist I mean a pig, or when I say conservative, I will try to stipulate a social or economic conservative. I am not being profane or disrespectful, I am telling the truth by calling a pig a pig!

Capitalist Republicans and captains of industry are not always social conservatives, but they are usually economic conservatives.

Republicans are not always social conservatives.

Republican presidential and congressional administrations always spend and squander more money than democratic administrations. And Republicans spend it on rich-benefiting projects, not people-benefiting projects. Pork: There is pork for the rich and pork for the poor. Which do you think is moral, and which do you think it is just capitalist stealing?

Republican administrations give money to the rich after taking it from the poor. They are conservatives only when it suits their own value system.

Most wealthy people are really not economic conservatives. Have you ever seen a capitalist who didn't own every expensive toy they could get their hands on? They spend everyone else's blood, sweat and money that they can access. They are economically fiscal with their own money, not yours.

Conservatives and capitalists are not exactly the same person, but for the most part they have interchangeable ideals and goals. It is possible to be a good capitalist and not be conservative; it is possible to be an economic conservative and not be a capitalist pig.

It is not possible to be a capitalist pig without being a social conservative. Conservatives and capitalists like to enslave and degrade people. This is because it makes them feel more important and superior. Why do they want to feel important and superior? Because they are deeply insecure!

You don't need to be a capitalist of any kind to be a social conservative. Stalin was a social conservative. Hitler was a social conservative. They both believed in controlling and imprisoning people who did not agree with them. You can be a capitalist and not be a dictator. You can be a socialist and not be a dictator.

*"I always tell the truth. If I am offending you, then you are doing something wrong."*
Dudley Griffin, 2020

America was not based on freedom for you alone. It was based on freedom for all. It was not based on capitalism. It was based on free enterprise. It was not based on Christianity, but freedom for all religious beliefs.

I know it might be difficult for you greedy, self-absorbed capitalists and conservatives to accept, but America was created on liberal principles of tolerance for all spiritual beliefs! A level economic playing field for all and freedom to tell the truth, not freedom to lie. You damn self-righteous, self-important, selfish capitalists and conservatives are anti-American and dangerous to mankind and the ecology of this earth.

It is commonly understood by educated people that conservatives suffer from "paranoid personality disorder."!

1. They think everyone is out to get them, so they "get" everyone else first.

2. They lie, cheat and steal to get money and power to bolster their fragile egos.

3. They consider anyone who doesn't have their selfish work ethic and greed is lazy and beneath them.

4. They project their own faults onto others by calling other people selfish, greedy and arrogant, only because they can't imagine anybody being any other than they are, or feeling other than they do. You can't be rightfully judgmental unless you, yourself, have felt what the judged have felt.

5. Conservatives think that anyone with a bleeding heart must be weak or pretending for a selfish agenda. That is because most conservative agendas are selfish, and they don't believe anybody could really be selfless.

*Paine wrote:*
*"The more men have to lose, the less willing they are to venture. The rich are in general slaves to fear, and submit to courtly power with the trembling duplicity of a spaniel."*

There are two basic forms of conservatism--economic and social. Economic conservatism can serve a purpose, even though it tends to produce destructive and competitive capitalism. But social conservatism is a major problem in American culture.

Social conservatism is responsible for most of the problems in our society. It is directly or indirectly responsible for creating and sustaining all the poverty, greed, drug, civil rights and intolerance issues in America.

If conservatives would confine their indignation to offenses that really mattered, such as lying, cheating, stealing and crimes against the environment, then their message could be of value to humanity. If conservatives would pay more attention to the Golden Rule and adhere to real, Christian ethics, such as tolerance for other religious faiths, ethnic groups and political views. If they would get with the majority   of people, their message would not cause the civil rights violations and economic strife it now does.

Conservative ideology has forced value systems and moral judgments onto the American public causing our society to think that normal human activities are actually immoral or illegal. And it is almost as if they have made it illegal to be poor or a member of an ethnic minority. Social conservatism is the author of all the prohibitions, intolerance and prejudices that fill our jails and make a large portion of our population guilty by association.

Conservatives suffer from insecurity and superstition which causes them to create religions and nationalities. They do this in order to gain security within a group, but religion and nationality actually tend to separate people, thus creating even more insecurity and superstition in the world. In their minds, conservatives have not left the jungle. They are still fighting the boogeyman and the saber-toothed tiger.

*"Trying to be perfect is not easy, being normal is not hard, being bad is simple. Being diabolic is natural to some people, but it is also a matter of pride with them. Those are usually social conservatives."* Ug

**Conservatives:** They can be Republicans or, in smaller numbers, Democrats. They tend to be people who do not have the broadest view of society and the problems of other ethnicities and economic differences in society. Conservatives would be better off, and it would be better for the world, if they would not get involved with politics, society or religion.

Not all conservatives are Republicans or capitalists. Most Republicans <u>are</u> social conservatives, yet they may not all realize what that means.

There are social conservatives, economic conservatives and religious conservatives, and they do have connections in that most all of them believe in exclusivity, bigotry and protectionism. Social conservatism, capitalism and fundamentalist Christianity (conservatives, capitalists and fundamental Christians), are the causes of all the problems in this country and the world. All the dictatorships are represented in the list of culprits. Most of these afflictions come from a deep, almost primal insecurity within the people who indulge in them. I will say that, because of their ignorance, they think they are doing the right thing, regardless of it being un-popular with the rest of the country and the world. So why do we put up with them?

It is all right to be a bigot, protectionist, fundamental Christian or rabid patriot, unless you persecute others for their own commitments, worship, patriotism or belief in their own causes. Or, God forbid, that you would just persecute them only for not agreeing with your ego.

No wonder God has forsaken us and all our arrogance!

*"Don't forget that the laws of freedom you want for yourself are the same that everyone else wants!"* DG 12/23/19

*"Conservatives are always trying to control what people can do, hear or say. Why would anyone vote for this; that is, if the conservatives continue to let us vote?"* DG 1990s

**Democrats:** People who believe in democracy by the majority of people (not corporations), peace, love and whales. Democrats are mostly liberals, people who believe in the real family values, small town morality, tree-hugging, neighbor-loving, no matter who or what you are. They are not commie pinkos, left-wingers or communists, as Fox "fake news" calls them. These liberals are actually the people who care most about you because they care for people, no matter what their color, religion, mental or physical disadvantages or checkbook.

*"By the way, Democrats are persecuted and put in gulags in 'communist countries' because they don't believe in dictatorship of any kind."* Alexie, Ukraine 2018

*"Democrats can be conservative (most often economically). Conservatives can be Democrats (most often with too much concern for their bottom line)."*
Dudley Griffin

**Liberals:** Don't get me get started on liberals! They are the most apologetic people I have ever met. They love everybody; how gross is that? They let you do what you want to do unless you hurt, violate or obstruct others. Liberals are strange but harmless; pay them no mind; they will not bother you unless you are an asshole!

*"By the way, liberals are put in gulags in communist countries, because they don't believe in dictatorship of any kind."* Alexie, Ukraine 2018

**Republicans:** Let's separate Republican <u>voters</u> from the <u>elected</u> Republicans! Not every Republican voter is a greedy asshole. But most elected Republican representatives are one of those.

First, most elected Republicans come from an upper middle-class district of their city or state! Wait, wait, wait, they still haven't done anything wrong! But when they have money thrown at them, and try to steal elections to get more from the cash cow, then they become assholes.

Republican voters don't need to be tainted by the Republican party perversions. Yet many Republican voters have been raised in families with certain values and limitations, and we all cling to things given to us by birth. And the Republican tradition is to cut off enlightenment toward, and to marginalize, other people and life forms on this planet.

We have to rate others and ourselves on the chart of IQs. it can't be helped. If you are a writer, a singer, an actor, a politician or definitely a businessman, intelligence matters

Intelligence quotient is not something someone can give you like a graduation scroll. It is received by reading, listening and travel. You can't know, actually know, anything new unless you have stepped away from the things you already think you know. And then you can look back and see your error.

Republicans are people who want to be capitalists, yet they still on the surface believe in the flag, patriotism and the American Dream. Somewhere along the way Republicans have lost track of the fact that the people who came here, to America came for freedom, hope and a dream. And most likely their own blood family came for that themselves. Coming to America for all people has meant hope. It's a shame when you get here and those people whose families came for the same reason are willing to deny your hopes and dreams. They say, "I got mine. Go away; you don't belong in my neighborhood!"

I must interject here, if you Republicans and the present tenant in the White House continue to alienate the real thinking people of this country and this world, you will destroy that which even you hold most dear--freedom.

But of course, when a person gets fixated in their mind what they think should be, then even the facts and truth will not keep them from jumping off the cliff or pushing others off.

keep the faith life will
continue in some new form
it may not be yours


Social conservatives do not understand the basic concept of American freedom. If you want freedom for yourself, you must allow everyone else to have the same level of freedom you desire. When you restrict someone else, you are actually limiting your own horizons.

*"Until we are all free, we are none of us free."*
Emma Lazarus,1883

*"No one is free until we are all free."*
Rev. Dr. Martin Luther King, Jr.

*"None of us are free if one of us are chained!"*
Ray Charles, 1993

*"No one on this planet lives in true freedom as long as others are slaves in poverty. We will be the next targets for the same chains."*
JMc

*"Always chose the right decision for the largest number of people. Then, still, you might be wrong, but at least you will be diplomatic."*
Dudley Griffin, 12/ 21/19

# CHAPTER 22

## **Bigotry**

Bigotry in a Country of Different People?

*"There is no room for bigotry in this country,*
*there never has been!"*
The Lone Ranger, in a 1956 TV show.

*"Welcome to The United States of America, the country of big-*
*ots who should know better because they are mostly immigrants from*
*somewhere else themselves!"*
JMc, 12/26/19

Ug, Mug and Thug were walking around on the earth 400,000 years ago. Ug, a female, was a feminist, Mug was a man with a spiritual and creative mind, and Thug was an insecure person who wanted to rule someone, since no one liked him.

Thug saw that Ug and Mug were popular people. Thug sat in the back of the cave and watched Ug and Mug. They were different from him. Ug was a woman, and he "knew what that meant." He thought he had to dominate her to get what he wanted from her. And Mug had curly hair, and loved to carve wooden figures, so he must be different. One day Thug put his log, which he had stolen from Mug, closer to the food and the fire, and told Ug and Mug that they were not quite right and, so they had to eat after him, and feel the warmth after him. Thug was the first bigot on earth.

*"Different" is a bad word to many people! To me it means new,*
*exciting and educational!*
*"Bigotry" to me means ignorance!* DG

As human beings, other people are the most important element of our lives. Bigotry is the mistrust, fear, and/or hatred of other people. And in America, a continent of such ethnic diversity, bigotry is one of the most ignorant, self-defeating and damaging of all national mistakes.

Europe, where most of us came from, is fighting to become a cooperative continent. Many of us progressives, or future-thinking people, believe that this movement to end national sovereignty is the only way that humankind is going to be able to survive.

America is a continent of different people from all over the world; am I right!? Because the different people have come to inhabit this continent only within the last five hundred years, we have not had enough time to assimilate fully and comfortably. If we don't kill each other first, we may create a cooperative society within the next few decades or centuries.

Curiosity and education are what will save humankind, and it is that which has made humans the dominant animal on earth. Now we are our own worst predator, and only wisdom will save us from ourselves!

Republicans are obstructionists. They stop other people, whereas liberal Democrats are questionists. We question other people's choices in order to help them think to help us all find the proper answer. The Democrats tell you when you are wrong; the Republicans hit you over the head until you change or die. Democrats try to find facts and solutions to any disagreement.

The balance of right and wrong is but a viewpoint. If you have the intelligence you will realize that divided mankind will self-destruct, but if we cooperate, we, may I say, may survive.

106

If you are concerned only with your own generation, country and self, then you are contributing to the end of this human life that we have gotten used to. If we continue the way we are going, the future is worse than you can imagine.

If you are so silly as to believe that the apocalypse is going to be to your advantage, please realize that not everybody is going to be able to live in a castle right next to God and Jesus. And how many people do your books and preachers say will ascend into heaven? Start counting; I don't think you are on the list.

Conservatives are one-dimensional thinkers. Self-preservation is their primary concern. They are still on the defensive mentally, as if they were yet in the jungle of primeval times.

Because of this, they rely on organized religion, false patriotism and superstitions to explain their existence. But this actually makes them even more insecure in the world and causes them to be jealous of those who are really free to enjoy and celebrate life outside their groups and control.

Because of jealousy and insecurity, conservatives try to control the world and other people to make themselves more important and self-assured. It is a frustrating situation for everyone else in the world who is just trying to live their own life and let others live theirs.

Conservatives love groups and organizations. It is a way to define their importance and to separate themselves from other people whom they do not understand, are afraid of and look down upon.

Countries and churches, when used the way conservatives do, are actually human limitations and confinements! They separate people and keep them in "their own place." Of course, belonging to a nationality or a religion can give one comfort, but false patriotism and overzealous religion also create most of the cultural turmoil, war and suffering in this world.

This book is not a condemnation of all conservatives or all those who believe in the conservative ideology. But this is definitely a condemnation of all of you who are control freaks. I am using the word conservative in its most negative definition. The true negative conservative is a person who is actively trying to force all the rest of us in the world to think the same as they, believe in the same God and have the same values as they do.

The current assho … sorry, president, is dangerous to this, our, your world, and all, yes all the intelligent people know that. We have to Vote Him Out!

Within this book, for the purposes of literally explaining certain personalities, I have to use commonly known descriptions. I may use conservative, greedy, self-centered, arrogant, ignorant, insecure, insensitive or asshole to describe Republicans.

It may be inappropriate to lump all conservatives together with the capitalist cause, but conservative ideology aids and abets the greed and materialism of capitalism, and so I don't know how else to categorize conservatives. A conservative is a capitalist at heart, whether they have the money to be or not. A conservative may be poor, but they would like to have the power their big brother has, and so they support the capitalist agenda.

There are many members of the silent majority who call themselves conservative. They do so because they have been fooled into thinking conservatism is patriotic and religiously proper. Yet, since conservative ideology is based on intolerance toward "other people," it is definitely neither democratic nor Christ-like.

Most average Americans who call themselves conservative are not really conservative in the strict sense of the word. They think it is the safe and comfortable place to be, but they are not personally prone to intolerance, nor are they committed to the control and domination of other people.

The majority of the silent majority are just folks, and they realize that most of the "other people" in the world are just folks like themselves. What they don't know is that the ultraconservatives are using them to oppress and suppress those "other folks."

Most Americans are tolerant, generous and friendly, but through

their silence they are enabling the conservative establishment to oppress minorities, those of other religions and the poor. Christ would
not approve.

For the purpose of explaining the struggles of mankind, I have
broken humanity down into three main groups. Of course, there are
actually many more groups and subgroups, but by using some imagination it is possible to place everyone generally in one of these three
categories.

The three groups are conservatives, silent majority (middle
class), and liberals. Conservatives can also be called businessmen, and
liberals called intellectuals. Sometimes, to be even more descriptive,
I will call most conservatives accountants and most liberals artists.

All creatures are born into fear and insecurity; it is primal. It is
the mechanism of self-preservation. Humans are no exception.

Self-preservation is the first dimension of thinking; it is the first
rule of life. The fear and insecurity of self-preservation causes all babies of all species to lash out in selfishness, to try to control or dominate their environment in order to preserve their own fragile lives.

Human beings, if all goes well, and depending on how they are
treated and protected, soon achieve a level of security due to our position as the top predator in the world. Almost all other animals must
fight for survival throughout their lives.

All other animals must function in the realm of that one dimension of self-preservation. Humans, if allowed, can expand into more
dimensions of thought and expression, such as, the arts, spirituality
and altruism.

Sadly, many humans are also trapped in the lifelong fear and
insecurity that lesser animals experience. These people function only
within the one dimension of thought and action, which is self-preservation. They are called conservatives.

They are afraid of challenge, the unknown, and ultimately, the
prospect of failure. They are conservative, so they bank on the sure
thing, or they use the minds, bodies and lives of others to enrich themselves.

Conservatives, because of their one-dimensional thinking, are usually very superstitious. They tend to be religious, not spiritual, but prone to controlled and organized religion. They are also enamored with money and possessions, which bring them security in a mind that is insecure!

They feel that orderly, structured economics and life should be the norm for everyone, because their own insecurity dictates it of them. They fear, distrust and often hate people unlike themselves, because those "other peoples" lives may prove their own to be shallow and arrogant.

Conservatives are driven to control things and people. Liberals, on the other hand, live by freedom and want to set the world and its people free.

*Paine wrote in Common Sense:*
*"Immediate necessity makes many things convenient, which if continued would grow into oppressions. Expedience and right are different things."*

People of one dimension, who have not risen above the primal reactions of fear and insecurity, think only in one dimension about life. They do not marvel at the beauty of nature; they only fear it.

Instead of enjoying life, they create religions to control it and superstitions to explain it. They do not celebrate emotions, love and their own six senses, but are ashamed of them and persecute others who do celebrate them.

Conservatives think of intellectuals, artists and freethinkers as a subculture, not quite up to par. Conservatives ignore the fact that all ideas come from these artists and intellectuals, but they are not averse to using these ideas to enrich themselves.

Artists and liberals who do look at the beauty of life and create art and new ideas are thinking in more than the single dimension of self-preservation. Liberal thinkers, who give us all new thoughts and all man-made beauty, think in many dimensions. These intellectuals want to set the world free so we all can feel the sweetness of life and freedom all around us.

God never told you to be conservative. Other conservatives, lonely in their paranoia, have told you to be afraid and insecure and in the box.

Liberals suggest that you smell the roses, think outside the box. That is what most advertising slogans, which originally came from progressives and intellectuals, really mean. "Stop being so anal retentive, stop being so conservative, greedy and bigoted!"

We must rid ourselves of conservative politics. Conservative politicians must be convinced to change their points of view, or they should be voted out of power. Conservatives are the cause of most of the problems in our government.

Conservatives create trouble in two basic ways; first, they make laws and create sins which are impossible to follow, thereby creating a large population of "sinners," "lawbreakers," and "second-class citizens." Conservatives need to create these "lower classes" in order to make themselves feel pure, righteous and more important than someone else.

At one point in the history of man and religion, some very ambitious and devious men realized if they could create a "higher being," a god for people to fear, and then impose laws in this god's name against natural human functions and desires, such as "sex, drugs and rock & roll," then people would feel ashamed and vulnerable when they performed these normal and biological activities. Automatically, everyone was a "sinner." Of course, then these ambitious young men (let's call them conservative capitalists), had something to hold over the heads of the public. (Constantine and the first Popes.)

"My goodness," said these conservatives, "we can extort money and achieve power from this situation!" The "sinners" then became obligated to pay these "priests" money to save their souls and forever faithfully attend their churches.

Laws of the land came from these sins, and the public was also obligated to follow these laws, listening to the conservative sermons and edicts which contained not only spiritual, but political and economic instructions.

And all those who did not want to pay for absolution or listen to the propaganda, or who broke the unjust laws, were outcasts. They became the "other people."

Conservatives create trouble in a second way by ignoring the real problems, refusing to allow systems to be created to protect the public from its own weaknesses or to educate people to fix themselves. Conservatives do this, they say, because all human frailties are sins and embarrassments, and should not be discussed because that will entice people to do them.

No one needs to advertise sex; people will do it whether you discuss it or not. But if society doesn't discuss it rationally and educate about the pitfalls of sex and drugs, it just makes the problem worse.

For the most part, conservative economics has its place, and it can be utilized for the good of mankind, but it often carries with it cultural prejudices. Conservative thinking tends to force certain ethnic groups and cultures into categories of poverty, blue collar or even slave labor.

Conservative economics carries with it preconceived ideas of what some people are worth and what their value is to society. This makes it difficult for these people to advance and improve.

Our society's problems with poverty, unwanted pregnancies, drugs and blue-color crime can be laid at the doorstep of conservative politicians. They like ignorance; it creates problems, and gives them something to bitch about. In reality, conservatives don't actuality want people to improve their lives, because that would end their need for righteous indignation, and it would jeopardize the value of their religious conviction.

After giving the subject of conservatives and liberals many years of thought and study, I have determined that the primary differences between these two opposing groups are "control" and "freedom." Conservatives want everything and everybody around them to be under control, and the liberals want to set everything and everybody free.

Not all conservatives necessarily want to control everything themselves, but they want everything and everyone controlled by some power in which they, themselves believe. Liberals, on the other hand, don't know or really care who is running the world as long as they can be free and as long as the freedom of others is assured.

This is why there is conflict in the world. One group of people wants the world under their thumb, and the other group won't completely lie down, be quiet and let them have it.

Liberals are by nature passive, but they have their limits as to how much oppression they will accept from the conservative slave trader. Liberals don't start the fights, but they are usually accused of doing so because they are the messengers, telling of the troubles in our society, and they are called troublemakers because they don't want to submit to all the unjust rules conservatives have created.

Conservatives have created a whole set of laws against freedom of expression and a whole other set of laws designed to control people from having too much fun. Those are the "Christian ethics" laws, created because, for some reason, many people feel that Christ wanted us to be miserable in this lifetime.

This "Christian" theory is actually based on the insecurity that some people possess and the self-imposed guilt they have somehow connected with religion. These human restrictions have also been supported and nurtured by religious and business leaders who wish to control people.

The moral laws which have been created by conservatives to control our fun are difficult enough to put up with, but the laws they have created to control our economic lives are the ones that eventually cause liberals to speak out with vehemence.

What is interesting about most laws is that basically, on the surface, they appear reasonable and productive. Most laws are originally created to protect the majority of society from harm. They are written to restrict individuals from taking advantage of everyone else. This is a good thing; it is the whole purpose and necessity of government.

The problem is that in our society as it is today, each person, depending on their ethnic, economic, religious or cultural situation, is treated differently by the courts in regard to our laws. In other words, if you are rich, many of our laws do not apply to you. Yet, if you are an African-American or Hispanic or a little outside what is considered the normal lifestyle, you are subjected to the wrath of every law.

The inequity of this is made especially poignant by the fact that corporate crime is responsible for the theft of more money, the destruction of more human life and the creation of more discord than all the drugs and common crime in this country. If you don't believe that, then you have not looked very deeply into the causes of poverty and crime in the United States, nor have you considered all the death and destruction American corporations cause worldwide.

Conservative ideology and the capitalist economics that go along with it are the most destructive forces in this country and the world. This is not a socialist manifesto. I believe in free enterprise, just as most liberals do, but the capitalistic aspect of free enterprise and how it is being manipulated by a few greedy people is what I am warning you about.

Economic conservatives are very aggressive because they think they have a lot to lose. Money and power are a very seductive motivation. What they don't realize is that most liberals don't want to take away their money and power; we just want them to be a little less destructive with it. They are type-A capitalists.

They can have that job. I don't want it. I realize we need type-A personalities to accomplish many things in this world, so I don't want to get rid of them. I just want them to stay in their place and stop mucking with my life and the lives of millions of other good people around the world.

In the Bible it is written that Jesus said, "For what is a man profited, if he shall gain the whole world and lose his own soul?" Matthew 16:26. Economic conservatives have a lot to lose if they continue the way they are going, and liberals are not the ones they have to fear. Conservatives have their own misjudgment to fear more than anything else. Their faith in the stock market and conservative politics is their very worst enemy, and that creates a trickle-down blight on everybody else, including the silent majority and the vocal minority.

There is a group which I call the "vocal minority." 2020, our current president was supported by the vocal minority; they didn't win the real election, but they won his election by political maneuvering. That means we are right and they are wrong!

The vocal minority, mostly ignorant of the political and economic realities, voted for "change" and "difference" that the current president yelled about and tweeted about. What they got was a capitalist, who cares less about them than he does about his hair, the sound of his own voice and his bottom line.

Conservatives and the vocal minority are usually committed to a religious or patriotic crusade. It is their way to justify all the bad things they are doing otherwise. Some are sincere about their religion or patriotism, but it is most often misguided. It will not get them to heaven.

Because conservatives are so aggressive and because they wrap their activities in a flag of God or country, many of the less aggressive people in the middle, the silent majority, are convinced that conservatism is the norm in our country. The silent majority is not to be blamed for this mistake because conservatives own the media, and they are able to make normal life appear to be anything they want.

There is a large mass of people in the middle who do not have the aggressive, controlling nature of conservatives, but they are so passive that they don't have the liberal defense mechanism. This group has been called the silent majority or the "poor and middle class" and it is, in the long run, the most important group of society. It is what society is created for.

The middle class does most of the physical work and fights the wars that the conservatives create. It is also this silent majority who vote within the polling booth or within the marketplace, and they determine what this country is. At times the vocal minority votes with guns, which makes them outside of American morality, lawless and unpatriotic. They do not realize this gives them nowhere to go but downhill.

Just because conservative capitalists are aggressive and they run our industry, military and government, it doesn't mean that they are the center of our culture. Because of their aggression, they appear to be the most productive part of society, but that is deceptive.

Capitalists do not create the concepts that become products or services in our culture. Liberals who are the intellectuals, creative people and artists of our society, are the ones who think up most of the valuable ideas of our world. They are the inventors. And then the ambitious conservative businessperson swipes the idea, employs the middle class to build the product and then sells it back to them.

The conservative capitalists just market the products. They most often don't invent them. But because of their desire for power and money, they are continually finding and developing new products, often stuff we really don't need.

Because the conservatives are the ones who are creating this aggressive business economy, everyone thinks they are the leaders, the smart ones, the people to look up to and copy, when actually the aggressive businessman is the person to look out for, to be leery of.

Until the silent majority recognizes its true enemy and rebels against the aggressive conservative control, this world will continue to have conflict, war and poverty. The poor and middle class needn't work as hard as they do just to survive. The conservative few have forced an economy on us that is working people to death.

The conservative capitalist minority wants more money and power continually, and so they manufacture and sell us more unnecessary products. And we fall for it.

One of the most insidious devices that they have created is the Christian work ethic, the notion that it is un-Christian to be leisurely. The inference is that, if you don't work hard and have lots of material goods, you are not blessed by God, and you are not a good Christian. This is blatant slave labor propaganda.

To proclaim that people who just want to relax and enjoy life are somehow Godless people is manipulating religion to control the work force. It is a common scam that the conservatives and business world have been using on the common man for centuries.

Aside from using this religious philosophy to acquire a large, cheap labor force, conservatives also use it to control the masses, to keep the masses from enjoying their lives too much.

Because conservatives have a hard time allowing themselves to open up, to abandon convention and fully enjoy themselves, they are jealous of those who do. And they are also afraid of the personality that can be spontaneous and free. Conservatives fear the unknown; it brings to life their superstition, it creates insecurity in them and when a person feels insecure, beware. All those around him are going to suffer.

One of the most basic traits of a conservative is hypocrisy. Hypocrisy is the act of ridiculing others for something that you yourself are doing.

Hypocrisy is also a process of lying to yourself. "No, what I did was not a sin, but once you do it, it becomes one!" Denial is the salvation of a small mind. Only a one-dimensional mind can lie to itself.

Liberals are always being ridiculed by conservatives for taking off their clothes, for baring their souls, for admitting their flaws or accepting their human nature. Conservatives are always trying to prove to themselves and everyone else that they are above mistakes, above human nature, incapable of being nude and animalistic.

Recently, in the political comedy of America, we had a conservative talk show host who trashed marijuana smokers while at the same time he illegally used pain killers. And we also saw a conservative gubernatorial candidate who professed family values and groped women on the side. And a conservative governor/movie star who groped, and produced a child by an undocumented woman. Everyone is capable of "sins." Everyone is capable of lying about their sins to save their skin, but only a self-righteous conservative will trash others for being weak as they themselves are.

Condemning others for sins which you yourself are performing is actually a sin worse than the original sin. Professing moral laws, then breaking those laws and denying it is much more sinful and damaging than if one were to just do what felt good and then accept the responsibility for what they did.

For many years liberals have quietly watched conservatives hypocritically ridicule and destroy democratic politicians. We have been quiet because we have felt that it was undignified to play that kind of politics.

Now liberals are getting more concerned about the damage to our Constitution and life-supporting environment caused by conservative politicians. We are beginning to realize that, if we do not fight conservative activities with whatever tools we have, they will destroy our democracy and our world.

We are now fighting back, dignity be damned, because our life and pursuit of happiness depend on it. If you see hypocrisy in action, tell people about it, let it be known. Conservatives must be held accountable for their lies and for the damage they do.

People like "our current president" and his supporters think they are better, more deserving Americans than many families who have been here way longer than their families have.

American Indians, Mexicans, Chinese and Japanese were all here before Christians or Europeans. Black slaves were transported and sold to Virginian colonists in 1619. They were here before your Irish, German and Italian asses ever got here!

*Thomas Paine*
*"When we are planning for posterity, we ought to remember that virtue is not hereditary."*

*Bigotry is usually inherited from your family, religion or country. Bigotry toward other people is most often based on ignorance and false information. It is an uneducated, unfounded and unnecessary hatred founded on some form of fear. Fear of the unknown is created by insecurity!"* JOB

# CHAPTER 23

## Patriotism

Those people who demand and exploit the freedoms of this country whenever it suits their purpose, yet deny others those same freedoms, do not understand or represent true American patriotism. The thing that made our country so unique and powerful in its beginnings was the promise of fairness and equality among its citizens.

Patriotism, like zealous religion, is often a fraternity that an insecure person joins to give himself value.

As an intellectual, I am a pacifist and I abhor violence. This does not mean I am not patriotic, nor is it an issue of cowardice, for if I truly believed that my country were in danger, I would fight and die for it. I am a peacenik because I know that war and death serve nothing that could not be served better with intelligence, diplomacy and common sense.

I want to see humans begin acting more humane, and that is why I have written this book. I have written this because we must halt the direction in which this country is now headed. The exclusionary, over-zealous, patriotic, us-against-them mentality building in this country is heading us into more and more violence here and in the rest of the world.

I am writing this in hopes that we as a nation will come to our senses. The time for a revolution is upon us, and it is my fervent hope and desire that this change can be made through words and not violence. This is a pre-emptive strike against anarchy.

Patriotism from a populous that does not understand what they are supporting allows, and even creates, dictatorship. Second World War German citizens were very patriotic with lots of flags and lots of slogans, just like the United States today.

There are many Americans who think that they are being patriotic when they support the stock market and capitalism and express unquestioned trust in the US military. Patriotism is not meant to be given to the military, to the president or to the businesses of America; it is supposed to show support for the original ideals of America and our Constitution.

Our Founding Fathers would be revolted by what is happening in America today. This country, just as in 1776, is composed of people from the whole world. The minute we exclude anyone from our freedom, we automatically exclude ourselves.

Some people make a very good living keeping our population dumb, silent, afraid and "patriotic." Conservatives in this country use patriotism as a divisive weapon, when it should be a unifying spirit. Patriotism is shabby self-indulgence and a Godless device if it is used only to hate.

Patriotism is a form of love. It is the love of one's country. True and real human love is felt for the soul of a person. So what is the soul of this country? It must be what this country stands for. It must be its Constitution.

To be patriotic is to support the ideals of a country. In America, if we followed the lead of our Founding Fathers, true patriotism would be the mutual agreement of all citizens to support freedom and justice for all.

To be a patriot to hatred, intolerance and war may be patriotism in some countries, but not in America. Patriotism has always been a spiritual ascent here. It has always been in support of the higher ideals of this country and its Constitution.

When Thomas Paine wrote the original *Common Sense*, most of the American colonists still believed in the sovereignty of the King, George III, and in continuing under the governing from England. They were "patriots" to what they were used to, what was comfortable. At the time, they knew of no other way to live.

Paine's writings convinced a continent that their allegiance was misplaced and caused the colonists to seek patriotism in the ideals of freedom. To reject England was a frightening prospect; it didn't make sense on many levels, but it did speak to the cause of freedom and self-determination, which is man's right and his nature.

Human nature is to be free to determine one's own destiny. England did not allow the colonists a choice in their own future. It was not natural for the colonists to continue to be patriotic toward England and the monarchy.

The terrorism directed toward America today was caused by the economic and imperialistic actions and omissions of a small number of conservative Americans. And now the War on Terrorism, which these same people have implemented in our country, is creating dissention within our own mixed culture.

Even though America, upon its concept and inception, is the perfect idea of the Garden of Eden, democratic America is being attacked and undermined by people who are threatened by its concept. Conservative ideology and capitalist ambition feed on ethnic and religious conflict. If the poor and disenfranchised ever started comparing notes, then capitalism and conservatism would soon be rejected.

The War on Terrorism is a diversion, taking people's minds off the real problems of corporate greed and class intolerance. The War on Terrorism in this country, as perpetuated by our own wealthy class, is a form of domestic terrorism against our own Americans. The War on Terrorism and the US Patriot Act are just ways to frighten good Americans into giving up their own freedoms.

*Paine wrote:*
*"Even brutes do not devour their young; nor savages make war upon their families ... This new world hath been the asylum for the persecuted lovers of civil and religious liberty from every Part of*

*Europe. Hither have they fled, not from the tender embraces of the*
*mother, but from the cruelty of the monster!"*

Does this not sound like what we are living through now here in the United States?

Capitalism is not our mother, just as England was not our mother. Freedom is our mother. That is why we came to America, all of us. We must be patriotic to freedom, not to a king, president, army or capitalist businessmen.

People who are patriotic to a flag without knowing what it stands for are fools. Today around the world the flag of the United States does not stand for freedom as it once did. To most people of the world, the star spangled banner stands for greed, corruption, and economic imperialism. If you don't know this, then you have been listening only to the capitalist, conservative news media. And they are very foxy. And they are lying to you.

You are not being patriotic to America if you are supporting the greed, corruption and imperialism of our present conservative, political, capitalist leaders. You are supporting oppression. You are a misguided "patriot."

Many "patriots" have also been taught to believe that Christianity is the only religion of a true American, yet our country is based on freedom <u>of</u> religion. If you understand what that means, you know, it means freedom <u>from</u> religion as well, if that is what you wish.

Christianity is not the only religion. Many people in this country believe in freedom of religion as long as the religion is based on Christ. That is bad thinking.

Many people in this country believe in freedom of religion as long as it's their freedom, but they are not quite sure that "those other people" deserve it. You can demand something for yourself only if you are willing to grant it to everyone else; otherwise, you are being undemocratic, hypocritical and also un-Christian.

The silly thing about many Christians is that they are so selfish about their own brand of Christianity that they don't even feel that the people in the other Protestant or Catholic churchs across the street deserve to be free to worship. That is stupid thinking. You may believe in your own religion, and that is good, but God has many religions.

Some of our Founding Fathers were pantheists, agnostics and Masons. If you care to learn of these faiths, you will find that they are not at all Christian, as fundamentalists know it. If you study Christ himself, you will also learn that Christ was not "Christian" as we know it, because he was not as greedy, bigoted and hypocritical as many Christians are today.

Outspoken, "fundamentalist" Christians are not truly very fundamental in their beliefs when they express prejudice against other religions. Their spiritual, political, economic and patriotic opinions generally come verbatim from some spokesperson, not the Bible. Mostly, these prejudices and propaganda come from a talk show host or church pastor who has an ulterior motive, most often economic.

If patriotism is based on money, then it is misguided. Christ got pissed off only once. He got mad at the bankers in the temple. What would Christ think of the kind of "patriotism" being displayed in America today?

In America, a real patriot is one who supports the ideals of our Constitution, not of our military, and definitely not the ideals of our business class. Patriotism is being proud of the foundation of this country, which is freedom. A patriot is a person who fights, either verbally or physically, to preserve freedom for their family, themselves and (here is the important part) every other American.

The freedoms of religion, speech and commerce are available to anyone who is willing to allow those same freedoms to others. If you do not give them to others, you have no right to them yourself. That is the Catch-22 of freedom. If you deny freedom to others, you lose all credibility within the rights of freedom, and someday someone else will have the right to deny it to you.

124

You are no better than anyone else, even if you are a pure Aryan, Anglo-Saxon, Protestant. You too will still die if someone shoots you, or suffer if someone jails you. Who gave you the right to demand better treatment than any other human? God sure didn't, and you are a poor Christian if you think Christ did.

People, we must realize, with the population growing on earth the way that it is today, we have two choices--learn to live together in tolerance, freedom and peace, or suffer the hell that anarchy and world-wide war will bring. It's up to us here in America to make that choice, or others will make it for us.

At this point in the turning of the world, it comes down to what we do here in the United States. And it comes down to our definition of patriotism.

Should I feel obliged to give my unquestioned allegiance to a president or administration that I feel is, itself, not following the path of true American patriotism? Patriotism is not given to a person, a king, a president, a flag or a piece of land; it is devotion to an ideal.

I do not believe our current president and his deteriorating gang are patriotic to the true ideals of this country. I believe they have confused capitalism with America. They are indeed "patriotic" to the ideals of capitalism and to making lots of money.

In 1776, the colonies rebelled against a government that was supporting business practices detrimental to the majority of the population. Today AIG, Enron, Exxon, Madoff, WorldCom, oil, energy, banking and loan companies and many more corporations in this country are not concerned with the comforts of the majority of Americans; they are patriotic only to the American dollar.

Here in America in 2020, many people think or assume the government itself is the country, and therefore, they blindly give those in power their unquestioned patriotism. The truth is that the people are this country. This country, of all others, has a distinct history that we can trace from its beginnings. It is obvious in viewing our history that those who started America were committed to freedom of choice, diversity, freedom of speech and freedom to be enterprising, and these ideals are what we should be patriotic toward.

Critics of the peace movement say it is unpatriotic. These "patriots" say they are supporting the president and his war on other cultures because it is patriotic. This country is in the grips of a mob mentality, or it might be called a "patriotic" fervor. This "patriotic" mob mentality has the effect of shielding some people from having to distinguish between right and wrong. In the name of patriotism some people feel they don't have to think.

Wars are not won; wars are mistakes that just put off what mankind should really be doing, which is learning to get along with one another.

After 9/11, the "brilliant leaders" of our country did the one thing that is guaranteed to ensure that America would suffer even more terrorist attacks. We went into the Middle East and started killing innocent civilians. Collateral damage in Afghanistan killed thousands of women and children.

Then we pissed off the rest of the world by attacking Iraq and killing a lot more. This is so typical of the cowboy mentality of which America can't seem to rid itself.

If we are going to be part of this world, we need to get with the program--cooperate, assimilate, join. We can still be leaders; in fact, with our diversity of cultures, we should be a good example of unity. But somehow we are not, because the leaders of our culture are still afraid of diversity. They still think this country is for, of and by the Christian white man.

Wealthy white men are still trying to pretend that the white Anglo-Saxon Protestant is the ruler of the world. You know what that will get us? A whole hell of a lot of enemies. It is us-against-them politics, and it is suicide.

There is nothing wrong with being proud of your country. Being patriotic is a warm glow in one's heart, a feeling of being part of an accomplished goal, a belonging to a family. But one must be careful that patriotism is not arrogance. Pride in one's own country based solely on the hatred of another country is not patriotism. It is not a positive; it is negative.  It is not the warm glow of valor; it is a chill, a blemish on the soul of this country.

# CHAPTER 24

## Military and War

*"The Greatest Generation will be the
generation that doesn't go to war!"*
Gloria Steinem

*"We are now dealing with things that
are not written down anywhere."*
JBMc, 2019

*"The history of man is not a blueprint for man-
kind's evolution; it is a list of our mistakes."*
JBMc 9.13.13

If mankind cannot elevate his skills of communication to be able
to end greed and war, then we are doomed. Intellectuals don't start
wars; businessmen do! The middle class does most of the physical
work and fights the wars that the conservatives create. It is important
that the world finds a way to scale down our militaries and rethink
the rationale of war on a socio-economic level. Only about 1% of the
world ever actually profits from wars; the rest of us suffer from it.

Much of the history of the world is written about our wars. Our
history is not as much of a celebration as it is a warning!

War is stupid except to people who profit from it. They are smart;
they make you fight and die for them. A dead man in camo surround-

ed by collateral women and children shows as debit <u>and</u> credit to the capitalists in Washington, DC. So F you!!

Some children are taught that they have to fight for everything they get, including love. That education will not serve the world or its people well. If we teach children the weapons of love and war, but not the diplomacy of life, then we will all fail.

War and many other stupid human mistakes are created by male ego. You buy a house you cannot pay for, you invade Russia, you bet on a horse, and you play Russian roulette.

# CHAPTER 25

## Liberals

I am a vocal, liberal intellectual, bleeding heart, peacenik, and all I want is for everyone to live in peace, dignity and freedom! Does that sound like I am an enemy of humankind?

I personally have had family members, and have known and worked with people who are conservative, hardhearted, war lovers, who don't care about other people's peace, dignity and freedom. Now, who would you choose to be your neighbors, them or me?

Liberal is not a political party; it is the conscience of mankind. If this nation's people continues to ignore the wisdom of our liberal intellectuals, this country will be just like every dictatorship we have fought against.

Liberals don't want money and power; they want peace in the world and peace of mind. Liberals and intellectuals usually have no economic motive for their actions. Because of this they should be paid just to think and solve social problems. If you don't believe this, then give me one rational contradicting argument against it!

Altruism is a foreign subject to some people. Giving without expectations, loving without need, and caring by giving, even when you don't have the money for yourself. A few people really don't like that! And it is because deep inside they are embarrassed.

Conservatives ridicule liberals, but the only invective they can find for us is that we are bleeding hearts. They call us bleeding hearts, but the alternative is to be a heartless conservative. How do you want your grandchildren to remember you, as heartless or warmhearted? If you say heartless, then you are missing the point of humanity. You are confronting the world with your ego, rather than meeting it with your soul.

If you were a shark in the sea, a deer in the headlights, or an ant on the kitchen floor, then that confrontational, kill-or-be-killed conservative attitude would be appropriate. But, as a human being, as the "highest" form of life on the planet, the cowboy, tough-guy mentality is actually self-defeating, destructive to you and to the rest of the planet.

Liberals are humanitarians and humanists. If you do not care about humanity yourself, you will never understand the liberal mind. You will always think that liberals have a selfish agenda, and that is because you, yourself, are selfish. You will, of course, think that these people have the same motives and desires as you do, but these liberals are unique. They care about even you, even though you dislike them.

Liberal causes are everyone's causes--peace, freedom, fairness and tolerance. Liberals want everyone to have the same freedom to live and the same chance to prosper. What is wrong with that?

Liberals fight for everyone. Sometimes they fight to protect people from themselves. The issue of separation of church and state is a good example of that.

Most fundamental religious people want more religion in the government and want fewer restrictions on their propagation of religious dogma. What these people don't realize is that more religion in the government will bring in people of different religions who will want, just as they do, to restrict other religions.

*"Is that too difficult for them to grok? Well, maybe it is. Read folks, read anything and listen to something other than foxy news."*
Grok is in The Hippie Dictionary.
JOB 2020

And more propagation of religious dogma will eventually create religious dictatorships since most religions are not democratic. And which religion, denomination or sect should have control? What if some other group than yours gains control? They will most likely persecute or ban your religion.

Liberals are the people who have fought to keep all people and religions free to worship as they wished. Most liberals don't have a violent commitment to the domination of any one religion, so they lobby to give all religions freedom. But this means all religions must allow all other religions to worship as they wish. This also means that religions must not force their own beliefs on other people. Thus the abortion issue and the banning of the use of any one exclusive religion in schools and government.

The talk show puppets have been lying to you. Liberals are not communists, nor are they socialists. Liberals do, of course, believe in social programs, such as the ones we already have, Medicare and Social Security. We also think it is humanitarian to have other programs, such as socialized medicine, as do the other 13 industrialized nations of the world.

What liberals don't believe in about this country is our rape of the environment, excessive corporate profits, supporting foreign dictators for economic imperialism and capitalist greed that spreads poverty, drugs and crime in this country.

Liberals are not commies, but they do want to help you when you're down. If you get old or lose your money, a liberal wants to help you. Will a capitalist help you? No, he'll be happy to give you a minimum-wage job.

During the Cold War many Americans developed a misunderstanding of liberals. It started with conservative attacks on liberal ideals. In the early 1950s, when people like Senator Joseph McCarthy began preaching about the ills and excesses of Communist Russia and China, they always seemed to associate American liberals and Socialists with those governments.

Eventually, the American silent majority began to believe that liberal thinking was the same as totalitarian communism. It was an innocent mistake, given the propaganda they had been fed, but that misunderstanding has caused a great deal of damage to the economy of America.

In reality, a liberal is a humanitarian, not a totalitarian. The liberal works to help all members of society be comfortable enough not to be forced to become criminals just to eat, and hopes that eventually all citizens will become useful contributors to society.

Liberal ideals also promote an environment in which all human beings will be able to experience happiness in their lifetime. The pursuit of happiness is one of the Constitutional rights that has been overlooked by capitalism.

US citizens who also just happened to be liberals and/or socialists identified with the poor people of America as well as those of Russia, China and all countries. But they did not support the totalitarian governments of Russia and China.

Liberal intellectuals in Russia and China have suffered as much discrimination and have been imprisoned as often as any other segment of those societies. This is because liberals believe foremost in freedom and democracy, which is in conflict with both communist and capitalist totalitarian dictatorships.

It is not treason to be a socialist or liberal and a citizen of the United States. The treason would be to want to overthrow the democratic system of the United States.

No liberals or others I know with strong socialist ideals have any desire to end American democracy. We know that democracy is essential to create the freedoms liberals and intellectuals require to think and to speak as we do.

It is capitalism and communism, the two totalitarian forms of economy and government to which liberals are opposed, because we know that the poor suffer in both of these forms of government and economy.

So liberals naturally support free enterprise and democracy and oppose capitalism and communism because they leave little opportunity for people to be truly free.

Liberals are generally passive, and that amuses conservatives. Conservatives think it is a weakness, but some of the strongest people in the history of the world were pacifists--Gandhi, Christ, Buddha, Dr. Martin Luther King Jr., Joan Baez, Mother Teresa, Baba Ram Das and many more.

Being the reasonable and passive personalities that they are, liberals do not force people to their side. We would rather see the offending conservatives listen to reason and facts and thus change their arrogant ways themselves.

We want freedom, peace and tolerance: the lack of oppression, job slavery, bigotry and prejudice. And we want to accomplish this without killing people to make them comply. Bur if the rich refuse, they will be forcing violence upon themselves. As Bob Marley said, "A hungry man is an angry man." You can't expect a man to watch his family starve and suffer without reaching out to defend them.

In the conflict between conservatives and liberals, the issue comes down to values of truth and self. For a liberal, if truth conflicts with self, truth wins. With conservatives, self often takes precedence over truth.

Liberals think less of money and more about harmony. A liberal intellectual is someone who does not make decisions based on ego or economic gain. He has no personal agenda or economic ulterior motives. A liberal intellectual just wants to reach a place of harmony with his fellow man, God and nature.

To say that a liberal is completely without ego or personal motives is to lie, but the motives are usually less destructive. More than money, a liberal wants a "warm and fuzzy" feeling inside.

Of course, conservatives make fun of warm and fuzzy. They don't understand altruism. They themselves don't usually give without economic motive, so they don't understand the emotional value of unconditional giving. Conservatives think everyone must be selfish like themselves and have an economic or ulterior motive for everything they do.

Liberals think it is "fun" to do something nice. They feel accomplishment from giving without strings attached. They give money without a tax deduction being the prime reason, or without getting their name on a building. Now if that is a bleeding heart, then I'm bleeding.

CHAPTER 26

## Conservative vs. Liberal ... Desire vs. Reason

Artists, writers, musicians and creative people are different from conservatives. Any stifling of the liberal mentality will cause a dearth of art, music, literature and new ideas. Any effort to make artists and intellectuals conform to conservative values always creates a revolution.

We have been in a dark age of political, social and cultural advancement for the last thirty years because conservative control has stifled good thinking in the world.

Liberal ideals are what you will eventually, naturally reach if you think deeply and search for the truth. Liberal truths will automatically come to you if you explore the arts, the philosophies of mankind and the beauties of nature.

If your only main concern is your own survival and success, you will be stagnant and conservative in your thoughts and actions forever. You will miss out on many of the true joys of life--human empathy, altruism, artistic expression and cross-cultural experiences. Does this sound like an advertisement for a hippie kit, an "out of the box", freedom, a carefree and guilt-free life? Well you don't have to go online to order this. It is available free of monthly payments, no surcharge. By the way, there is also no religion or hypocrisy involved. There is no hippie kit to buy to become mellow. It is all in your mind.

If you think of the simple joys of life and accept them as your reward, you will automatically become liberal in your actions toward others. As an open-minded person, you will live a satisfying life in close emotional and spiritual association with mankind of all shapes, colors and personalities. This is no new age versus the capitalist mentality; this is good against evil.

A major difference between conservatives and liberals is that conservatives often alter truth to fit their greed and indulgences, whereas liberals alter their lives to fit the truth. The liberal is the true pragmatist, the true evolutionary human being. Conservatives fight against evolution. They are stagnant human beings. They fight the growth of human understanding and obstruct mankind's ascent toward eventual perfection.

Conservatives, Capitalists and COVID19
March 28, 2020

I am not blaming this disaster on the conservatives and capitalists, as they do us liberals, for every problem in the world, but I think their policies, greed and complacency are responsible for creating the environment for this pandemic. Overpopulation, corporate mistreatment of workers, underfunding for education, underfunding for medical health--are all conservative policies and major factors in this and most problems of the world.

When is the world going to start listening to liberal intellectuals? We have been speaking for your benefit for so long. We have proven over and over and over again that we are only trying to help! Yet even though we have been the messengers of troubles ahead, and have been trying to educate people to pay attention, the silent majority still mistrusts and even hates us.

We are not doing this for money. We are not doing this for fame. We have not made the decision to be unpopular because of great rewards. We are ridiculed for our opinions, and we accept that, because our conscience has made it necessary that we speak out

To accuse liberals of being un-American is the most absurd of lies. Since freedom of speech, of opinions and travel are most basic and essential to the liberal philosophy, it would be ridiculous for a liberal to do anything other than support and nurture the United States of America, where these freedoms are granted to us all.

Yet conservatives can live quite well in a totalitarian regime. In fact, they are usually the ones who administer such forms of government. It is the liberals who are always trying to save our freedoms. How does that equate to being un-American? Liberals have suffered even worse in communist countries. Why would we support politics that persecute us?

The framers and writers of the Declaration of Independence, our Constitution and Bill of Rights were liberal intellectuals. If you balk at that statement, consider: Do you honestly believe that any of the Republicans in Washington today could author such documents as those?

A conservative might use the Declaration of Independence, our Constitution and Bill of Rights as propaganda to get votes, but to write them, he would have to hire a very good liberal intellectual speechwriter.

I am a political liberal because liberal ideals most closely follow the ideals of our Constitution and Bill of Rights, no matter what Rush Limbaugh or Hannity try to tell you. Liberal ideology resides right between and opposed to both communism and capitalism, where most people live.

Liberal intellectuals have created most of the positive, unselfish and imaginative ideas of this world. They are the people who conceived of democracy and free enterprise in the first place, and they should be the only ones allowed to make laws and restrictions affecting a democracy.

138

That last paragraph holds a lot of volatility. I am tempted to say that only democratic minds should be allowed to make laws in a democracy, but that, in and of itself, is undemocratic to say.

The real dilemma of a true liberal, democratic person is how do we keep the conservatives from ruining this world without stooping to their level? We must educate the voting public, and we must do it soon, before the conservatives get rid of the voting process itself.

*"This human world is an intricate scaffolding of 'good intentions.' At each crucial point of this structure a person holds a part of us all together. If any one of us falters and lets go of the dream, our whole castle will fall apart."*
John. 7/12/2006

## Left-Wing

Left-wing is someone or something that is connected with socialist philosophy. The association of the word "left" with socialism refers to the fact that the Left Bank of the River Seine was the socialist part of Paris in the 1920s and '30s. (From The Hippie Dictionary by John McCleary)

The term left has come to mean a communist, or someone who leans to the left of center. Liberals have been called left wing ever since the 1920s, but that is an incorrect designation for today.

Between the 1920s and 1950s many liberals and concerned thinkers foresaw the threat of capitalism to the public, so they reacted by associating with the opposite ideology of socialism or even communism. In many cases these people didn't realize the excesses of communism, and they certainly didn't condone the oppression of a totalitarian dictatorship.

Eventually, throughout the 1960s and 1970s, most liberals realized that both communism and capitalism were threats to freedom and American democracy. Since then, true liberals have established a place of social and economic ideology right in the middle, between capitalism and communism.

Liberals are still called left wing by conservatives, but that is just another one of many propaganda fabrications to discredit the responsible liberal causes. A liberal, above all else, believes in freedom, and that makes it impossible to support a communist totalitarian dictatorship.

If you consider, as most political scientists do, that capitalism and communism are the two ends of the spectrum, then a liberal is actually right in the middle. But we are definitely left of wage slavery, greed, war, environmental destruction, and religious and ethnic intolerance.

Liberals are neither right of communism nor left of capitalism. They are just downright against any "ism" that tries to oppress and control people's lives. Even yours, Mr. Capitalist!

NO, liberals are not left wing, we are centrists.

# CHAPTER 27

## Totalitarian Dictatorships, Left or Right

For the majority of the people, it matters little which dictatorship is above them. They get screwed with both and both ways.

All people who live in a dictatorship fall into the same categories and are treated in the same way. Powerful people become greedy, normal people are worked to death, intellectuals are persecuted, and the weak and tired are jailed and discarded.

Totalitarian means, in essence, that the populace is under total control by the leaders or "government" of the country. It is a control thing--government by a small committee or by one person. And there is usually a strong military presence, keeping the people under control.

Both fascist (right) or communist (left) are basically conservative forms of government. A totalitarian dictatorship is a controlling government, and control is the most prominent aspect of the conservative philosophy.

Controlling the media, the money, religion and thoughts of its population is a major concern of conservative politicians. Dictatorships also insist and rely on controlling the media, money, religion and thoughts of their population.

Both left or right totalitarian dictatorships are bad for the people and, of course, are incompatible with democracy. Conservative political ideology is also incompatible with democracy; that is, unless it is held in check by a strong liberal opposition. Without the middle ground, the liberal, we would soon be under the thumb of a dictatorship. Left or right, it matters little; they will both take away your freedom.

# CHAPTER 28

## Intellectuals

*"Because something is happening here, but you don't know what it is. Do you, Mister Jones?"*
Bob Dylan

*"I have a lack of patience with mistakes, mine or anyone's, and a hatred for larceny and stupidity, even mine."*
JOB, 2020

We refuse to apologize for being intelligent. Just because we speak out, just because we think we have answers does not mean we are arrogant snobs. To be intelligent is the inner goal of all human beings. It is what sets us apart from all other creatures.

Our Founding Fathers were intellectuals. Franklin, Jefferson, John Adams, Madison, Monroe and Thomas Paine were all accused by small minds of being big-headed. These men if living today, would all be called left wing, liberal, intellectuals by today's conservative, fundamentalist Christians. And yet those conservative, fundamentalist Christians could not do what they are doing or say what they are saying if it weren't for our liberal, intellectual Founding Fathers.

*"Intelligent people know what they don't know, dumb people don't know that they don't know!"*

When are conservatives going to wake up to the fact that it is the liberal ideals that give them the freedoms to be the greedy bastards that they are?

Intellectuals are not your enemy; they are looking out for you. We are the ones who have fought for your freedom of religion.., for all religions! We have fought and are fighting still for your freedom of speech, sex, reproduction and politics.

Seventy years ago, Joseph McCarthy and Richard Nixon, two discredited conservative politicians who were arguably arrogant and opinioned, started accusing intellectuals of being opinioned and arrogant, and ever since, the silent majority has mistrusted intelligence. That has been a very bad thing for this country and the world.

Intellectuals are the potential salvation of the world. We are the people who thought up all of the systems used in government and business, and we should be given more control over how they are used. Right now, they are being abused badly.

Intellectuals (artists and writers) are the people who create all the important (thought-provoking, creative and enlightening) socially relevant books, movies, music and art. We are the people who keep the world from being boring.

Conservatives are the potential destruction of the world. They are the people who took over all the systems used in government and business and made them competitive and destructive.

Conservative lawyers and accountants are the people who have taken over the production and selling of books, movies, music and art. With distorted emotions and exaggerated themes, they are the people who are making the world intolerant and frightening.

The intellectuals, artists and creative people are the ones who have intellectually created everything. In prehistoric times the first person to leave the cave to build a house was an artist or intellectual, and everyone thought he was crazy.

Conservatives always think creative people are crazy. The first person to get up off the ground and build a chair to sit on was definitely a crazy creative person.

The person who invented the wheel was probably kicked out of his or her tribe. The Wright Brothers were considered nuts by everyone around them, and so were Alexander Graham Bell and Steve Wozniak!

If it weren't for intellectuals and artists, we would still be living in caves. And there wouldn't even be any paintings on the walls.

The problem is that once the capitalist types and accountants realized that a buck could be made from that house, chair, wheel or computer, they jumped in, took over and exploited it. The intellectual who created the idea is often left behind.

Capitalist types are pushier, Type A personalities, unashamed of taking advantage of other people. So, slowly but surely, they have filtered up into most of the positions of power in politics and business. Artists and intellectuals who came up with the concepts of business and politics are forgotten.

Accountants and conservatives in this society and in history have always been the established, stagnant, culture, which does not move until someone else gives it a push. Accountants always think that new ideas are crazy until they figure out they can make money on them. Then they often steal the idea from the creator and become rich. Here in 2020, several TV shows show how this is done. *The Profit* is one of them and xxx and xxxx!

John D. Rockefeller was a fine example of many, and maybe most, capitalists. He didn't invent oil, steel, or railroads; he just took (in some cases stole) the ideas and made millions. He was, by training, an accountant.

The definition of intellectual is a person who deals with circumstances by using abstract thought rather than merely relying on basic visceral, animal emotions or reactions. That abstract thought is what separates humankind from all other animals. If you get wet, you build a roof. If war fails, you become friends.

144

If you are not intellectual, then you are in essence the same as all other creatures. Depending on your value system, that means you are no better than other animals.

Abstract thought eventually leads to questions, such as the meaning of life. It leads to inspiration with nature and spiritual awakening. This avenue eventually creates a selflessness, a feeling of acceptance as a member of society rather than as the center of the world. It is the evolution of mankind to a place of stewardship of the world instead of dominance or suppression of the world. It is as close to God as we can get.

Conservatives and capitalists feel threatened by intellectuals, and rightfully so, because intellectuals have a tendency to expose the treachery and excesses of capitalism. Because of this, capitalists and conservatives have mounted a campaign of persecution and misinformation to discredit intellectuals.

With disdain, intellectuals are often called liberals, a label of which we are actually proud. Conservatives also call us commies and left-wingers, both of which are untrue.

Contrary to the beliefs of most of the silent majority, intellectuals are not communists. They believe very strongly in the freedoms that are not accepted in communist or fascist countries.

An intellectual, by nature, is someone who seeks the truth, and we require freedom of thought and action to do this. We are not compatible with dictatorships.

Intellectuals are feared, hated and persecuted in communist as well as fascist countries, because they also expose the treachery and excesses of communism. More intellectuals were sent to gulags in the USSR than almost any other segment of the population.

In the USA, powerful people with economic attachments to capitalism are afraid of what intellectuals will tell the silent majority about capitalism, so they have discredited Intellectuals. The silent majority now thinks that Intellectuals are their sworn enemy. This could not be further from the truth. The only hope for mankind is more and deeper intellectual thought.

There are basically two types of thinkers in the world: accountants (also known as conservatives) and intellectuals (also known as liberals). Accountants adopt and manipulate established facts and laws, while Intellectuals are the ones who discover and create those facts and laws.

Left and right brains. Accountants use mostly the left side of their brain. Intellectuals use mostly their right brain. Artists, writers, architects and deep thinkers are intellectuals. Most lawyers, most politicians, most business leaders, middle management and accountants are bean counters and conservative by nature.

Intellectuals write all the socially uplifting books, plays and movies. They develop all of our culture's valuable ideas. They create all the "intellectual" concepts.

So why does the silent majority hate and fear them? Why? Because they have been told to by a conservative capitalist press and right-wing politicians who fear the intellectuals' information, which will jeopardize the capitalist economic stranglehold on the general public.

John D. Rockefeller was an accountant by profession. He did not create anything, but he stole inventions and ideas from others to make millions. Sure, many capitalists become philanthropists, but with their money it is an easy drop out of their bucket.

We have let capitalists exploit us like this for far too long. They are destroying this world with their greed, and they are enslaving and impoverishing the majority of the rest of the population while doing so.

Silent majority ... whom should you trust--an intellectual whose career is finding the truth, or a capitalist whose career is finding money?

When I use the word intellectual and call them the thinking people, I know some folks will believe I'm being arrogant or inferring superiority. But trust me, I'm not. One of the lessons learned by being intellectual is that everyone of every level of intelligence has an equal value in this world.

Aside from psychopaths, all kinds of intelligence and all levels of interest are necessary to create this society. The absence of the businessman, the farmer, the mathematician or the musician will diminish this world

Intellectuals are important because they think deeply about the meaning of life, and they usually do so with unselfish motives. They believe in the possibility of Utopia, a world where everyone is satisfied, where all needs are fulfilled and peace and freedom prevail. And they know that place cannot exist if selfishness is allowed to dominate.

Intellectuals are the messengers of trouble in our world. They tend to think on numerous levels of a problem. They think of solutions regardless of personal gain, because they most often have no personal financial expectations from the outcome one way or the other.

Through multi-tasking in their minds, intellectuals are capable of seeing all the sides of an issue. They walk in the shoes of others. Because they have no ulterior motive, they are willing to find options that are completely democratic.

Often, people think intellectuals have personal motives. Those who accuse intellectuals of having selfish intent are usually, as Freud said, projecting their own greed or motives onto the intellectual.

It is possible for a person to be completely altruistic. Humans are capable of being truly selfless, and that trait is usually found in the person of an intellectual.

Strangely enough, the other segment of our population that is capable of this completely egoless, giving and nurturing personality is the large silently majority. The middle, lower middle and poor classes of America, the family farmers, laborers, carpenters, factory workers, small business owners, office workers, waitresses and truck drivers of this country are, for the most part, fair and pure in their relationships with others.

This large middle class and poor class have much more in common with the intellectuals, the liberals, and even the hippie radicals, than they think. The liberal intellectual wants to set people free. It just makes good sense to him. It makes a better world for all of us to live in. It's more fun when your neighbor is happy and not trying to steal the food from your garden.

The problem is that the established military industrial complex feels threatened by the intellectual messenger because his message undermines their control of the silent majority. The intellectual tells it like it is, and that reveals the greed and corruption of the capitalist. If the middle class and silent majority ever learned these truths, the ruling class would suffer their most feared loss, the loss of profits; not income, but profits. Ninety-nine percent of the world population works of an income, one percent mikes a profit, sometimes from working but most often from lying cheating and stealing from the ninety-nine percent.

Intellectuals are always bad for big conglomerate business. They are the messengers, and the powerful people always want to kill the messengers because they keep their power by suppressing information about their fallibility and corruption.

The power politicians and industrial leaders silence the messengers most often by discrediting them. That is why they are always saying that intellectuals and liberals are radicals, revolutionaries and unpatriotic. But, you know, communists say the same thing about intellectuals.

All dictatorships and totalitarian governments, both communist and fascist, treat intellectuals the same way. They persecute them, call them second-class citizens, freaks of society, radicals, hippies and bohemians.

The industrial establishment is using its own private PR representatives, the network news media, to trash the intellectual message and liberal ideals. They have been doing so since the 1960s.

Mostly, all that liberals want to do is help America maintain the basic ideals of our Constitution and democratic process. That is our motive. If that is personal gain, then we are guilty.

The conservative establishment and their conservative media

have so frightened the middle class and silent majority that these people think that intellectuals are threatening their way of life. This is capitalist B.S. The people taking things away from the American public are the conservative politicians and capitalist CEOs.

Intellectuals don't start wars, businessmen do! Intellectuals don't raise prices and lower wages, businessmen do! Knowing all of this, why do so many people in this country distrust intellectuals and support capitalists?

Intellectuals and liberals have somehow gotten the reputation of being arrogant snobs. The working class and silent majority have a misunderstanding of what arrogance and snobbery really are.

Someone who spends a lot of time thinking and worrying about the situation of the world and warns you about the problems is not acting superior to you ... they CARE about you!

Someone who traps you in a bad, low-paying job, enslaves and impoverishes you, then lies about all the good things they are doing for you, and laughs about it on their yacht ... that is an arrogant snob!

Many middle-class Americans think that conservatives are their kind of people because they push the right buttons of family values, patriotism and religion. But do you really think those capitalists who have a gazillion more dollars than you do are going to join you for a beer at your local tavern or bowl a few games with you? No! And they sure can't sympathize with your problems as a middle-class bread winner or homemaker. It's the liberals who are closer to you in lifestyle, interests and frustrations.

It is amazing how the silent majority will celebrate a man for being smart enough to make a lot of money and ridicule another man for being a liberal intellectual. "Smarts" come in many forms, but shouldn't we judge a person's intelligence on what it produces for the world rather than what it brings to his own bank account?

Knowledge and truth are the highest endeavors of mankind. Only through an unselfish search for truth will we create a world of peace, freedom, generosity and tolerance. This may all sound like a lot of New Age mysticism to you, but if you can find a flaw in this philosophy, please write a book about it.

The nature and purpose of deep thought is to find the truth. An intellectual is always trying to find the truth, not just truth for himself, but the final truth, truth for everyone.

In this process an intellectual learns, and is actually forced to consider, all levels of a decision. A deep thinker is always concerned about how an action will affect all those around them and how it will affect future generations as well. Searching for the truth is an action against selfishness.

Capitalists and accountants have a hard time understanding this kind of thinking. They feel every decision must have a personal motive. But intellectuals are built differently. They get satisfaction from seeing the world and people's lives run smoothly and peacefully. That is their reward.

Of course, it is unrealistic to believe intellectuals will be completely impartial. Intellectuals are going to be partisan toward people, and capitalists are going to be partisan toward wealthy people. Which of these is better for the whole population of America?

Accountants have their value. Accountants can run the infrastructure of the world, but they should never be allowed to make the rules as to how it is run. Capitalist-type people have their value. They are often good at efficiency. But we have to control them, or they will steal everything for themselves.

Soon, our democracy and our freedom will be completely gone if we continue to let the accountants and capitalists run this country. Our natural resources, air and water will also disappear. And we will infect the rest of the world as well. It is already well on its way to happening

The stupid thing about this process is that the accountants and capitalists are not even aware of what they are doing. They think they are doing the right thing. They are convinced that they are ensuring

150

democracy by spreading capitalism. But, as we have discussed, democracy and capitalism are not the same thing.

We need more intellectuals, educators, people with humanities and liberal arts degrees, making the rules in this country. Stop voting for lawyers and accountants.

Lobby for candidates who have a real concern for the average people. Dump those politicians who are interested only in big business and big money.

> *"Those who know, know. Those who don't know,*
> *don't know they don't know!"*
> DG, 1970s

The Republican party has lost its connection to the ideals of the Founding Fathers and the Constitution that they created. The Republican party is the party of the tyrants we left the old country to get away from.

I propose that we kick the Republican party, not its members, but the party itself, out of this country just as we kicked the Crown out in 1776.

I believe it is necessary to have a two-party system to maintain a democracy. We need two strong, common sense, political parties, so I suggest we choose the Democratic party and the Green Party to function as our political entities. After all, our environment and its health will soon be our most important problem.

Competition is necessary at some times, and good fun once in a while, but it will destroy more than it produces if we let it become our moving force or only reason to live.

## CHAPTER 29

## One-Dimensional Thinking

One-dimensional people are folks who have not gotten past the paranoia of primal fear and competition with all other creatures. One-dimensional people act and react as if they were still in the jungle with saber-toothed tigers about to pounce upon them. They are in competition with everything and and everyone.

*"Greed is man's only predator!"*
John 11/1/2005

Man became the most dangerous predator to all other creatures some five million years ago. Now the only predator man has is ourselves. We can make this world hell, or we can make it paradise for all of us. We must stop competing amongst ourselves!

The germ that is killing mankind is insecurity. Insecurity is brought on by recognizing yourself as an individual, but not liking what you see in yourself.

Knowledge of self has bred insecurity in some people (one-dimensional people). Insecurity, in turn, creates selfishness, jealousy and greed.

The "Law of the Jungle" does not apply anymore. By now we should be way past that. We should be adhering to the "Law of Cooperation." Mankind has advanced so much intellectually that we should be using common since now. We have made all the mistakes over and over several times. Aren't we intelligent enough to learn from our past?

The first thing is to stop listening to the one-dimensional people, the greedy people, the capitalists. They will do well no matter what hell they make this world, but the rest of us will continue to suffer until we tell them to stop feeding upon us. And, believe me, we have the power. All we have to do is stand up for ourselves.

Start listening to the multi-dimensional people, the intellectuals, who know that the only way for us to survive and be free to pursue our happiness is to cooperate with each other, not to compete with each other. Help your neighbor, and you will help yourself.

# CHAPTER 30

## Multi-Dimensional Thinking

1. The first dimension of human thinking is of self, as all creatures at birth.
2. The second dimension of human thinking is recognition of others as beings.
3. You may then reach the third dimension of compassion for others.
4. The fourth dimension is commitment to doing things for others, without recognition or payment.
5. The fifth dimension, only achievable by saints and gods, is giving your life to help others.

The human brain is capable of thinking in many dimensions. Some people use that ability and some don't. We are originally born, as all animals are, with one dimension, one thought--the visceral urge for survival. As we humans grow, depending on the environment we are in, our minds can expand to other dimensions, such as art, philosophy and altruism.

A family with art, conversation and books in the home will more likely breed children and adults with curiosity, and therefore more dimensions, to their thinking. The one thing that raises us above other creatures is our curiosity, which, in turn, stimulates our multiple dimensions of thinking. If we do not utilize these dimensions, we are not reaching our potential as humans. We are not really human.

Many people, because of the circumstances of their birth, are not able to take full advantage of their minds. They may think only in the basic one dimension or, at best, only several dimensions throughout their lives.

The more dimensions in which a person thinks, the closer they get to perfection. This is, of course, why some religious leaders discourage education, because it breeds rebellion from the prejudices and restrictions of organized religion. It is the same reason conservative political and business leaders suppress mental exploration and open, uncontrolled education.

As a person moves into higher dimensions of thought, he becomes less selfish and more tolerant of others, because he sees all the ramifications of his own action upon others. With each new revelation about your surroundings, you have a better understanding of how important cooperation of man-to-man and man-to-earth is. You are thinking in more dimensions. You are getting closer to harmony within life.

And what is the trigger that leads mankind into the process of thinking in more and higher dimensions? I believe it is literature, art and music.

Man has the potential for magic moments of creation. When a person creates a new thought or idea, it is ecstasy. I feel sorry for those who never feel what a musician, artist or poet feels. Feeling that creation triggers new dimensions in the mind. To create is like "god"; we must all express the "god" inside us!

Sports and sports competition, on the other hand, focus mostly on the one dimension of self, winning and selfishness. And, oddly enough, as art and music are dropped from the curriculum of most schools, sports are vigorously funded.

Art and music give the mind non-judgmental, noncompetitive, yes, even nonsensical avenues of thought. This has a tendency, actually a spiritual power, to cause someone to reach for new dimensions of communication. It enables the mind to consider the thoughts and circumstances of others.

The key to multi-dimensional thinking is being able to step into someone else's shoes, being aware that others have the same feelings as you do, knowing that they hurt and bleed like you. Have some awareness and concern for the consequences of your actions. This is the road to perfection.

Every human child, every antelope, salamander, dragonfly and worm is born with one-dimensional thought--self-preservation. If they don't, they won't survive.

But we are humans, and especially in America; we don't have the predators hanging over our heads as we once did, and as all other creatures do. So why do the capitalist businessmen and conservatives still think only with this one dimension of their brain? Why must they always function within the aggressive, kill-or-be-killed mentality?

One of the things that happens when you learn to intellectualize is that you begin to question everything. And shortly, one of the areas you start to question is your own thinking and your own motives. There is a short step from this to the point of realizing that selfishness and greed are among the most destructive, most contrary thought processes.

Some people believe that thinking of others and being unselfish is being weak. They feel that it is contrary to the natural mechanism of self-preservation. But this again is one-dimensional thinking.

Selfishness is actually suicide for our society right now. At the rate of greed and selfishness in this world today, coupled with the population growth, we don't have much more time before anarchy and world-wide conflict are our reality.

We must think in terms of cooperation as our solution or we are doomed. If we do not think of everyone else in this world as our brothers and sisters, they will soon become our enemies.

# CHAPTER 31

## Silent Majority and Middle Class

The silent majority, this largest portion of the American public, is generally by nature nonpolitical, quiet, hard-working, generous, tolerant, and often religious. But God help them, for they are also often ignorant of who their enemies are.

The silent majority are people who tend to trust authority figures, such as presidents, congressmen and clergy who push the right buttons of family values, such as chastity, temperance, thrift and patriotism. But these figures of authority don't always have your best interests at heart.

While presidents, congressmen and clergy are telling you to be patriotic, virginal and thrifty, they are sometimes out there spending your own money on the sins they warned you against. It pays to know what your role models are really like.

Some people feel it is too much trouble to learn all the many things that are out there, and for many subjects, that is true. I am ignorant about brain surgery, and it does not affect me in the least.

There is nothing to be ashamed of in being ignorant. It means that for some reason you have not been given the facts or have not come in contact with the truth.

It is not always your fault when you are ignorant, but it is your fault if you remain so. I agree it is wrong to be intelligent and arrogant about it, but it is worse to be ignorant and arrogant about that.

There are some areas in life where ignorance is dangerous. One should never drive a car without knowing what red, green and yellow lights mean. Likewise, ignorance about those who govern you, those who have the power of peace and freedom over you, is very detrimental.

To be politically informed is difficult; it takes some work. One must find sources other than network news. All the established media news and views are paid for by corporations, and they have an agenda, an economic agenda!.

To hear new views on the same old subjects, one must read alternative magazines, listen to public radio and seek out reputable news web sites. One must listen between the lines and one must definitely not listen only to voice like Limbaugh, O'Reilly and Hannity. Just look to see who pays their salaries.

To be a true citizen of a democracy and maintain your freedom, you must be informed. If you do not stay informed and question the policies of your politicians, they will become arrogant and steal away your freedoms. That is just the way of power.

To be an educated citizen of a democracy, ask questions. Listen to both liberal and conservative commentators, and don't believe everything you hear until you have heard enough to make your own decision. You are only a free person when you make your own decisions.

Right now, conservatives have the ear of the silent majority, and because of that conservatives get passive support from this group. I know if the silent majority began listening to the facts, they would find reasons to question conservative propaganda.

Arrogant patriotism or jingoism is usually held by people who have no ability to see the world from other people's shoes. Conservative propaganda tells the silent majority that the rest of the world looks to America as the benevolent father, the savior of the world. In truth, most of the rest of the world thinks of us as greedy, meddling, arrogant and ignorant to the facts of life in the rest of the world.

It is frightening to be ignorant and uninformed, unaware of the majestic things that are going on in the world around you. It is natural to be frightened and a little bit defensive toward the unknown. In primal man's history anything that was new automatically posed a threat to life.

Conservative propaganda feeds on this mechanism and keeps the population in a state of ignorance, feeding it only enough information to keep people afraid, defensive and blindly patriotic. This is not reasonable human behavior in today's world.

Because of ignorance, many Americans today are reverting back to the primal urges to run from or attack anything new and different. Both of these reactions are bad for world politics and for the future of our freedom.

Humans are the most powerful family of animals, not because we ran from or attacked the unknown. We are strong because we think about the unknown and determine whether it really is a danger necessary to defeat physically or if it is something to befriend. If conservatives had done all the thinking for the world, we would still be eating horses and would never have gotten up on them to ride.

If something is unknown or frightening, the real human reaction is to go inside our brain and figure out how to avoid a confrontation. Maybe to join forces, or defuse its danger, and then only as a last resort to go into battle to defeat it. How else did such a small, fragile creature as man survive and conquer all of the rest of nature? The wise man knows that in battle, everyone suffers.

We must learn who and what our real enemies are. Intellectuals do not enslave us economically and lead us to wars. Businessmen control our lives with money and send our young men to war for more money.

It is the man in the three-piece suit who forecloses on you or cheats you on interest. The man marching in the streets against the oil industry is not picking your pocket. It is the oil industry that is picking your pocket.

In this jungle we live in today, it is the greedy minority who are our enemies. Our worst enemies are not terrorists from other countries. Our real enemies are the economic terrorists in our own country who

159

are responsible for creating the hatred that created foreign terrorists.

The silent majority is composed of good people who have been misled into thinking that capitalism is the American way of life and that capitalists will protect them from all evil. If you look closely and realistically at your life, balance all the pain and gain of your economic and physical world, I am sure you will see that most, if not all, of your troubles can be traced to the banks, auto industry, insurance company, stock market, U.S. military, congress and phone solicitors.

When was the last time a liberal, intellectual, ecologist, peacenik stole a dollar from you?

Just because you are in the majority doesn't make you God! Just because you are in the minority does not mean you are the devil!

There are those who will say America has flourished under capitalism and that this form of economy has created our happiness and it will continue to do so. Sure, up to a point in our history capitalism made America the strongest country in the world. But, unless you have been under a rock, you must be able to see that the greed of capitalism has reached a place of such avarice that it is now dividing, suppressing and destroying many people in this country and world.

As for the naysayers of change, as Thomas Paine said, "We may as well assert, that because a child has thrived upon milk, that it is never to have meat; or that the first twenty years of our lives is to become a precedent for the next twenty."

What is wrong with us? We have seen it again and again when a conservative administration takes over Washington from a liberal administration. The majority of the poor and middle class are doing all right and the government has a surplus. There's a chicken in every pot, and then things start to change.

The poor and middle class start to suffer, the government has a deficit and the rich get a tax break "to stimulate the economy." When are we going to wise up?

What happens in times of financial comfort is that the large middle class and silent majority start thinking in terms of being rich.

They start having capitalist illusions, and then, when the next election comes along, they say, "I'll vote for a conservative. He is always working to push money to the top, so when I get to the top I will have more money."

Not good thinking. In the process of pushing the money to the top 10% of the population, all the other people, the 90% of the population, get the short end. Are we really that stupid?

If you don't already have a $150,000 a year discretionary income, or $300,000 (available) in the bank, that is to say you don't have to lift a finger to make it, and you can spend it on whatever you want, then you have no damn business voting for a conservative. In fact, you're cutting your own throat if you do.

That is what the two-party system has come to. If you are upper middle class, middle class, or poor, you have no chance with a conservative administration. With the Democrats, you at least have a fighting chance. They're not perfect. They often try to straddle the line, but at least the liberal history is there.

If you have to get up every morning and work to survive, to pay the rent and feed the mouths, you are foolish voting for anyone other than a liberal. People must learn the nasty little difference between capitalism and free enterprise. Capitalism benefits only 10% of the public; free enterprise benefits everyone.

# CHAPTER 32

# Lies, Misrepresentations and Misunderstandings by Conservatives

Conservative spokespeople are continually voicing inappropriate portraits of liberals and making inaccurate statements about liberal ideals.

*Apocalypse: Self-Fulfilling Prophecy*

Right now, the leadership of this country calls itself "faith based." But, no religion I have ever studied would dare to be as greed-based, prejudice-based and dictator-based as this present administration.

What is it about people who "find religion" that makes them so intolerant of others? Not just intolerant, but demanding, obstructive and destructive. Why do they want to force everyone else to be as blind as they are?

I am opinionated, but I don't kill people because they don't believe what I believe. I'm intolerant of fundamentalists, yet I don't want to pass laws that say they can't believe what they want to believe or worship the way they want. But that is what fundamentalists do to everyone else. And then they have the gall to say that "God" made them do it.

Self-important, shortsighted busybodies want to be inside of everybody else's bedroom, and want to control everyone's reproductive process. And now they are almost purposefully destroying the environment of this world because they think the world is going to come to an end anyway. God and Jesus are rolling in their graves if they ever did exist, and if so, they now are dead.

I believe "God" does exist, yet I do not see him as fundamentalists do. God to me is not the creator of my triumphs or mistakes as most religious people feel. God is life, and the good things of life. And Jesus if he did actually exist is love, tolerance and peace. He is not greed, war and intolerance as the present leaders of our country believe.

The forsaking of Mother Nature right now by capitalist "born-again Christians" could well be the breaking of the seventh seal. They are doing "the Devil's work."

In Jewish/Christian writings, just as in all spiritual texts, you can read anything into them that you want to believe. That is the purpose of religious writing, to stimulate belief in and dependence upon a particular doctrine. But, believe me, any real God of any real value would never warn his people of the imminent end of the world and then expect them to hasten it by their greed and violence.

Why would a Christian who is supposedly going to ascend into heaven, want money and power here on earth anyway? I suspect those who look forward to the end of the world and who are profiting from bringing it about are actually the anti-Christ, and they don't know it. They are self-fulfilling the work of the Devil.

Nowhere in the New Testament does it really say that Christians will be awarded earthly riches as an indication of their faithfulness to God. Biblical riches are peace of mind.

Those of us who really love God and his creations are doing God's work to save them. Environmentalists, teachers, social workers, artists, intellectuals, healers, doctors who care, these are Christ's workers, for that is what Christ is said to have done when he was on earth.

You don't really believe television evangelists are doing God's work, do you? They are the people Christ kicked out of the temple.

Look, whatever gives someone comfort is OK by me, as long

as they don't try to force their brand of comfort onto me and other people. If they do, then they are not just God-fearing folks; they are terrorists.

For thousands of years we have given Christ. Buddha, Oden, Ra, Mother Nature, royalty, capitalism and Silicon Valley a chance to make our lives comfortable and worthwhile! They have all failed us many times. I suggest this is the time for us to come together as human beings, or should we wait for another savior? How has that served us in the past? No, it is time for us to come together! Mother Nature seems to be our best, perhaps only, supporter, but we have to save her now, even before we can save ourselves.

February, 19, 2020: Today our current president promised farmers in Bakersfield, California that he would bring them lots of water. How does he plan to do that? Coming from a president who fights all ecological, pubic health and global warming issues and is against birth control, how is he going to make it rain so we can grow crops to feed our ballooning population and also give people household water? The farmers are already getting most of the water and households have to conserve water. Our anti-environmental president is promising to give the public more water, and the conservative farmers are voting for him. How stupid is that?

February, 20, 2020: Today I read that the conservatives of Idaho want to annex the conservative parts of Oregon and California, because they are feeling alienated being surrounded by liberals.

What do the liberals do to them? Force them not to worship what they want, no, force them not to have children, no, force them to stop charging over 10% interest, or force them to stop getting 100% profit, no!

No, liberals, using common sense, are asking them to be good human beings and protect our planet. Liberals don't beat up conservatives for wanting to make a living. We don't even beat them up for wanting to squander. We ask them!

Liberals <u>ask</u> conservatives to conserve! We <u>ask</u> them not to squander our earths resources. And if someone's actions are contrary to democratic and moral laws we may have to enact and uphold rational laws to help all of society.

Why do conservatives feel alienated? Are they uncomfortable because we liberals ask them to clean up their act to help save the earth?

# CHAPTER 33

# Birth Control and Saving the Planet

*To "Ms. or Miss" Wright and*
*All Other Conservative Feminists*

No liberal, "socialist," intellectual is asking you or any of your shiny-faced friends to use birth control or have an abortion. "We" are lobbying for all the women of the world (including in the Third World and of all religions) to have the freedom to use these options. This is to help save the world from over-population and to give women what we think are their human rights.

Birth control and real sex education, not abstinence, are the proper solution. By the way, anyone with a drop of brains and any knowledge of mankind's history knows abstinence is a hoax.

The real issue here is saving humankind by getting it to stop having so many children! One child per two people would slow the death of all of us, and then we would have to start working on not consuming all the food, nails and bolts and lubricants of the world. Natural resources are necessary for life on earth. That would be water, hydrogen, sun, soil and oxygen.

The mechanism of self-preservation is not fear; it is lust for life. Man is the only insecure animal. Our mind, and its recognition of itself, is our "carnal knowledge," and therefore our gravest flaw.

Most anti-abortion organizations are run by men, and under the surface most men blame women for any of these procreation issues. Yet unless you are totally ignorant of the situation, you will know that it takes two bodies to perform the act of procreation. And men are usually, maybe about 97% of the time, the aggressors. So I think women should make all the rules about birth control or abortion.

Miss Wright, a conservative feminist is fighting on the wrong side.

Sense I have not heard from or about her for a few years, I don't know if she is still fighting that battle; if not, pardon my commentary about you yourself.., but I am still adamant that women should make the decisions about what is done to or with their bodies.

CHAPTER 34

# Good People

Good People by nature are often naive. There is nothing wrong with this kind of naïveté. It is an openness, a trusting nature, a child-like confidence, and it is basic faith in mankind, generosity and tolerance. The opposite is skepticism, superstition and insecurity, and that is the basis for greed and intolerance.

In our society, where we are free from the worries of predators who would eat our bodies, a little naïveté is refreshing and safe. It would be completely safe to be open and trusting if it weren't for a few misguided human predators who are out there.

Conservatives would have you believe it is human nature to be selfish. "Greed is good."

Liberals think differently. We know that only a small number of people are really selfish. All we need are a few well-placed laws and the proper amount of social conscience to control these greedy folks.

What makes humans different from all other animals is our capacity to rise above the struggle just to survive and to feel tolerance and compassion for other humans and animals. The silent majority is basically a tolerant and compassionate group of good people who are being used for their muscle and their money to make the capitalist class wealthy and powerful.

There are so many good people in this country and this world who are minding their own business, just surviving, keeping their families alive and together. These people are not hurting anyone, not lying, cheating or stealing from others. They are working hard to survive and be responsible citizens. Why are they the ones who always come in second?

The silent majority doesn't really benefit from the greedy conservative world as it is today. And I know they don't approve of the cutthroat, competitive atmosphere in which they are forced to live today.

The silent majority would really rather see the world become a friendlier and easier place in which to live, but they don't know how to change things. I am sure they support conservative politics only because they are confused about who the good guys are, and they don't think that their one small voice matters anyway. It does matter, and it must be heard.

The good people have been told for so long that it is unpatriotic to speak out. They have been brainwashed into thinking that the demonstrators who speak out for peace, the environment and less capitalist materialism are commies and traitors.

It is not the people who speak out against government excesses who are traitors to democracy; it is those who are silent who threaten our freedom. People who speak out are, by the act of speaking, supporting democracy and freedom. Those who are quiet are the ones who are allowing our freedoms to be taken away.

Good people, by your silence you are supporting those who are causing your pain. The radicals and demonstrators who are telling you about the problems of our society are not the cause of the mess. They are just the messengers of its existence.

Good people, speak out against those who are causing the poverty, intolerance and war. Don't let the bad guys win. You can tell the difference between a good man and a bad man. I know you can!

Capitalist pigs, liars, cheaters, drug pushers and deceivers of old people, your time has come to an end. The silent majority is not going to stand for it any more. The good people have a voice, and they are going to speak out!

Vote selfish conservatives out of office. Elect liberals who believe in true democracy.

*O, God, man is searching for and waiting for heaven.*
*Why is he looking for less than what he already has right here*
*on earth?*
JOB, 8/18/03

# CHAPTER 35

## Do-As-I-Sayers

People who meddle in the lives of others for moral or religious reasons are "Do-As-I-Sayers." To the best of my reckoning, they are basically insecure people.

These folks rely on superstitions and unsubstantiated moral laws to guide their own lives and to affect their treatment of others. They use semi-moral authority to push others around and to make themselves self-important. They are often hypocritical. Ask them where they were last night and if you can see their bank statements.

# CHAPTER 36

## Live-And-Let-Livers

We don't care what you do as long as you don't inflict it on other people.

# CHAPTER 37

## Cooperation or Catastrophe

*"I believe in adopting the American Union, rebuilding the EU, and helping to create other Continental Unions that will some day come together to form the World Union, because that is what we need to do to survive peacefully."*
Ug 400,000 BC

On this earth until now, selfishness has been accepted. It has been considered a normal part of life. In a world with unlimited resources and just a few people, greed, although destructive, can actually be tolerated.

Those who are selfish and greedy have told us only the strong are meant to survive and succeed. They have convinced us it is the way of nature. But I am here to tell you such conflict and struggle is not meant to be the way of man, the way God intended mankind to live.

Selfishness and greed have been an annoyance for some time, and the majority who are not greedy and selfish have suffered in silence until now. It is not possible for us to ignore the wrongness of selfishness and greed anymore.

I am convinced that mankind was meant to rise to a place of prominence on this earth and then to become its wise leader. Everything I see in the joy and creativity of man and his capacity for generosity, tolerance and love indicates to me his capability to become a responsible steward for this world.

I can see no other reason for a just God to place such an able creature as man upon such a vulnerable earth. No righteous creator would conceive a world of such beauty and then introduce one last animal with the intent and ability to dominate and destroy this beautiful planet.

I am convinced that the "carnal knowledge" we are told that the snake in the Garden of Eden gave to us was actually "knowledge of self" and a desire to satisfy self in a material way. Carnal knowledge is not sex. Sex is natural. Sexual gratification is sought and experienced by all other creatures, whereas material gratification is man's domain only.

I believe selfishness is man's only flaw, and right now it is dominating mankind and ruining the world.

Whereas Christ vented his anger at the bankers, he lived with prostitutes. Selfishness and greed are the only human traits that guarantee we will not reach perfection. We cannot be in harmony with our world if our unnatural desires cause us to mistreat and exploit other creatures and the earth itself.

A shark kills to eat, a bird only borrows the tree for a time, a snake and a bee will bite if tread upon. Only man kills for game or pleasure, possesses trees and earth, and forbids other creatures from crawling upon his domain.

As the earth becomes smaller with our population growth and as fewer people own more land which they choose to keep from others, the emotional state of our population will become increasingly anxious and competitive. Greed and selfishness will progress to those who have nothing, and the hungry man will rise up to take food for his child to eat.

In coming years, tolerance, cooperation and understanding of the troubles of others will become as important as concerns for your own welfare. This will come about because your neighbors' conflicts will become yours. Crowded streets will result in negative behavior. Hunger and poverty will become a fight for self-preservation.

Some people will say this is a reason to build taller fences, but other, wiser ones will tell us that open gates, generosity and friendship are the only ways to solve this impending difficulty. Greed and selfishness are the causes of our world conflict today. To neutralize these is the only peaceful solution to the problems of life on this planet.

This has become obvious now even to business people, who have seen that if we don't have welcomed migrant workers, our economy will suffer and then even capitalists could lose their preferred way of life

# CHAPTER 38

## Cowboy Mentality

First, to establish my right to speak on this subject, I will tell you that my father's family came to America on the second boat of Pilgrims, The Fortune, arriving at Plymouth Plantation on November 11, 1621. My mother's family was already living in North America hunting dear and buffalo. She was born in an unfinished home being built by my grandfather in the Panhandle outside Lubbock, Texas. Her family crossed America to the West in covered wagons, and I am 1/64 Native American. I cut my first steer, branded my first calf, and killed my first deer by age 11.

I have an aunt and uncle who worked cattle all their lives. I have uncles who were rodeo riders. I punched cattle myself before I was big enough to reach the gas pedal of the ranch Jeep in which I later learned to drive at age 12.

The pioneer/cowboy spirit in America is on one hand the most basically heroic, and on the other hand the most fundamentally destructive, human persona. At times in the creation of this country, we had need to be arrogant, strong and violent. But today that violence and arrogance are counterproductive to a peaceful, rational world.

Our fixation with guns has created a nation that kills more of its own children than any other country. People say they are protecting themselves and family, but that is ignorance, and maybe an out-and-out lie.

Numbers show us that for every one criminal who is subdued by a household gun, there are literally hundreds of family members who are killed in gun accidents at home, not to mention all the thousands of friends and family members who are killed in fits of passion by those guns.

The facts show that you are actually putting your family at risk by owning a gun. This alone would cause a rational person to destroy his weapons. But then, we are not dealing with rational thought, are we? Let's face it, we are dealing with the male macho ego.

Don't use "the right to bear arms" excuse for your reasoning. Don't dishonor the fathers of our country by saying that they meant citizens should own half a dozen assault weapons, MAC-10s and 9-millimeter semi-automatics.

Don't dishonor the writers of the Second Amendment by thinking they intended it to justify the indiscriminate sale of deadly weapons to just about anyone who could pull a trigger.

Our fixation with guns is not our only indulgence in the antiquated pioneer spirit. Many Americans have an underlying attitude that everyone else, anywhere else, is only there just for America's benefit.

We are now the prominent, if not only, major imperialistic country in the world. We are not actively trying to physically capture new land for ourselves, but we are invading other countries politically and economically for their natural resources.

A dream I once had as a young, naive boy sums up the attitude of many Americans. In that dream I was walking down the street, and I was able to look ahead to the next block before I got there.

In the next block all the people were standing frozen in time, waiting for me to walk by so that they could come alive and do their thing. They were not really people, but just automatons waiting on a movie set for me to venture by so they could make it look like life was going on even without me.

I thought I was the center of the earth. I thought everyone else existed just to please and fulfill me. Many Americans think America is the center of the earth, and everyone else is there just waiting for us to come by and use them.

That is the same way Greece, Rome and England felt in their days of power, and they have all faded as we will someday. The only way America can succeed and survive graciously is to consider treating the people in the rest of the world with the dignity they deserve.

Our pioneer spirit has caused us to do some despicable things to people, things that we condemn others for doing. We destroyed numerous valuable cultures on the American continent in our quest and greed for land and freedom. In the end, we are losing our own freedom because of the way we pursue that freedom.

The cowboy mentality, guts and guns, has also forsaken us in this modern world because it sets us apart as an unthinking, unfeeling society, which is at odds with the rest of the modern industrial world. It is time now that the United States of America grow up to the values of the 21th century. It is time to hang up our six-shooters.

It is time for us to take charge as the respectable and reasonable society we profess to be. It is time for us to make amends for past civil rights mistakes in our own country and only then we can truly become the fathers of democracy, freedom and justice in the rest of the world.

In 1776, the diverse cultures of the American colonies came together almost as one to create the United States of America. At that moment we did not look at our differences, but at what made us the same human beings in need of freedom and justice for all.

Throughout the years since that "moment of greatness," we have slowly digressed into being separate people again, thinking only of our own personal hopes, fears and wants. We are now a country of individuals with individual dislikes, enemies and prejudices. We have forgotten about the spirit of cooperation which first made this country strong.

Even in 1776 we were a diverse culture consisting of English, Irish, French, Dutch, German, Russian, Spanish, African and Native Americans. We were Catholic, Protestant, Dutch Reform, Jewish, Muslim, Agnostic, Atheist and Pantheist. Our differences didn't make us weak; they made us stronger.

If we are to progress as a nation and have a positive effect on creating peace in the world, we are going to have to relegate our pioneer/cowboy spirit to history. True, it got us where we are today, but many times with infamy, and it is today a detriment in many ways to our future.

If we continue to believe that we are right just because we are American, and everyone else must listen to us, we may someday soon find ourselves alone, talking to ourselves.

*"The opposite of prejudice is, to post-judge, postjudice meaning to judge people based on personal experience and after seeing their behavior yourself."*
Postjudice, a new word, coined by John McCleary in the late 1970s, and printed in his book: The Hippie Dictionary, in 2002.

*"Think about others and yourself as being in the same category."*
Mug, 400,000 BC

# CHAPTER 39

# Religion

This chapter is not halfway through this book because it is only halfway important; it is one of the most crucial subjects in our lives.

I am a fool to even venture into religion, but I can't help it. Someone has to try to put it in its perspective. I am here to say that if we don't put religion into its place of personal preference and speak only of it and act only on our convictions within our own homes and churches, then humankind is doomed.

Religion is personal to each person, everyone else has their own idea of religion, God, heaven and hell.

It is like trying to describe a color to someone. Green is a palm tree to some a pine to others. Pain is an ach to you, a knife to some else, and itch to others. Love is a worm feeling to some, a dizie spell to others, and a

I have had as much experience with religion as most people in this country. Read the new testament twice, and much of the Old Testament. I sang in the choirs of Pentecostal Churches, and was married in that church. Most of my maternal family was Pentecostal or Seventh Day Adventist. I think I spoke in tongues once. Yet, I have seen the most egregious bigotry and hatred in my life expressed in the Christian church. I have also known some of the most wonderful people in church just as I have in bars, hippie communes, art co-ops, rock and roll bands and anti-war demonstrations.

On the one hand, mankind is capable of great beauty and grace, but on the other, we are the most destructive creature on earth. If your religion is not directed toward enhancing the harmony of this world, then God has nothing to do with it.

You are not smarter than God, so don't try to put his motives into your words!

"In God We Trust" does not mean in Buddha we trust, or in Christ, Muhammad or Confucius! It means in God. God is bigger than all our petty divisions and squabbles!

Religion is man's desire for unity, but organized religion is divisive. Unity means with all creatures and forms--the fish, the rose, the other man, the mountains and trees. Above all, be respectful. Respect them and respect yourself.

If you want to be a good, spiritual person, respect what God and Mother Nature have done, not what they have done just for you, but for all creatures.

> *"We should be beating crucifixes into plowshares and editing the Old Testament into a romance novel and the New Testament into a work of fiction."*
> Dudley Griffin 10.4.05

# CHAPTER 40

# Religion in Politics

In the beginning of man, the reason for religion was to put everything in harmony. The golden rule is the answer back from all gods. Harmony is what all leaders should wish for. A politician who does not follow the golden rule is not a spiritual man, and therefor not in harmony or sympathy with the slave or beggar, and is therefore is not a good leader.

Most fundamentalist Christians don't really know what they believe in. They are convinced that they are right, yet they don't really know why, since their beliefs are based on a faith that someone created for purposes other than spiritual--for power and money. There they are again--the roots of all evil, as the Bible says, money and power.

Christians do know what they don't believe in. They don't believe in abortion, gay marriage, or freedom of sex, drugs and rock & roll. They are "do-as-I-sayers."

Since their intellectual level is shallow, based only on self-fulfillment and selfishness, they do not care about the negative effects their beliefs have on other people. They think they know what they oppose, but they don't realize the repercussions.

Most fundamentalist Christians don't believe in freedom for other people, but they want freedom for themselves to do what they want to do. This is Christian hypocrisy. What fundamentalists don't realize is that they rely heavily on the liberal ideals of freedom.

What fundamentalist Christians don't realize is that the "separation of church and state" was created to protect religion from itself. So if a Catholic regime takes over the government, they can't outlaw the Baptists, or if a Pentecostal government takes over, we won't all have to talk in tongues before every ball game. Get it? Separation of church and state protects freedom of religion, every religion, including yours.

Fundamentalist Christians are not only arrogant, but also naive. Naïve arrogance, that oxymoron, best describes the state of religion in the world today. To believe that you are the only one who knows the truth, and yet the truth you stand on cannot be proven, does that make any sense to you? And for a faith to determine the existence of humanity while being squeamish about sex, that is humanitarian heresy.

Fundamentalist Christians insist that they are right and that everyone else is not only wrong but also must comply with what they believe in. And they don't just leave it at that, but they force laws on others to make them change. They will even kill someone to save them.

I am a liberal intellectual, and they call me arrogant. I say I am right, but I would never force anyone to follow my way of thinking or kill them because they are wrong. The only time I would endorse a law prohibiting someone else is if their actions were obstructing the freedom of others.

If you don't believe God belongs to everyone, then you are putting limits on God. You must think that He is just like you, with prejudices and favorites.

In the beginning of every religion, God is benevolent; he does not judge, nor does he condemn. But, likewise, he does not have favorites. He loves the shark and he loves the butterfly. But then the mind of man comes along and needs justification for its insecurity and greed, so we attribute laws to God, and we craft them to support our own agenda. No, folks, God does not love Jews better than Christians or Muslims or Buddhists or, well, you get the picture!?

If there is a God, the only sin he would condemn would be greed. The only God worth worshiping would be he who wipes away our insecurity. To be like the rockfish, unafraid the moment before being eaten by the shark. To be like the deer, unmoved before being flattened by the Ford. That is true life. Christ and cash, God and greed, religion & $, those are abhorrent to me and most true spiritual people.

> *"The worst Christians are those who mistake their own greed*
> *for God's gifts."*
> JMc, 12/17/19

# CHAPTER 41

## Freedom

Freedom is the inner drive for individuality, which is one of the most basic human traits. It is not a gift given by others, but a right that comes with being human.

Homo sapiens alone possess a true self-awareness, and that is what makes us such productive animals. To take away a person's freedom is to deny them their basic human instincts of curiosity and exploration, which in turn produce our most valuable trait, that of creativity.

In 1776 we found our voice through intellectuals and writers patriotic to freedom, such as Thomas Jefferson, Samuel Adams and Thomas Paine, and we found the strength to oppose our economic and cultural oppressors. We revolted, and all the world agrees we had the right to do so. The people of the world appreciate our profound wisdom in doing so, because we gave them permission to fight for their own freedom. Now it appears that we must do it again.

To paraphrase Thomas Jefferson, "Anyone who thinks they can be ignorant and free, never was and never will be free." We must have the freedom to be different and keep the right to be equal.

You cannot have freedom without democracy, or democracy without freedom. Freedom is one of those concepts that cannot be possessed to the exclusion of others. Only the democratic act of giving freedom creates freedom.

## CHAPTER 42

## Commerce and Free Enterprise

*"There are two kinds of politicians, ones who care about the people and ones who care about the money. Who do you want to vote for?"*
Abraham Lincoln probably wrote or said something like this at one time!

The path of commerce has taken a dubious course. It used to be, "You give me that, and I'll give you this in exchange."

Then it became, "But I want more for mine because I think it's better than yours, and I just deserve more than you do anyway."

Today, it has become, "I am now making all the rules! From here on in, you sell only as I say you can, and you are prohibited from competing with me equally."

Free enterprise began as the ideal concept of equal exchange of goods, services and money for other goods and services. Everyone was meant to get what they wanted out of the deal and go home happy.

After all, commerce and business were originally just the negotiations for commodities necessary to sustain life. The problem is that at some point, luxuries and extravagant toys became commodities, and greed, ego and larceny entered the business world.

Today, business is more like a crime scene than a gentlemanly exchange of necessities. And what is worse is that we now have the greedy people making all the rules of business engagement.

Modern commerce, the "exchange of money for goods," is a necessity in our world today. It is necessary because of our expanded population, migration to big cities and ownership of most of the land by the government or by a wealthy few.

Because our society is getting away from an agrarian and rural life, we can no longer grow our own food or make all our own stuff. As we moved further from the production for our own needs and wants, a manufacturing, distribution and merchant class emerged.

This commercial class of people is important to our society's existence. But this group of people, call them capitalists, has become so powerful and arrogant as to think they are actually the most important people in this society.

For some reason, capitalists keep forgetting that they need the workers to make the products to sell back to those same workers. It somehow slips their minds that, if they don't keep the majority populous happy and well paid, this working-class will no longer be able to buy the stuff they manufacture.

Capitalists also forget that they, for the most part, have very little to do with the things they sell. That's right, capitalists are paper pushers, or actually, they make the decision as to what paper is pushed where!

Does the capitalist invent the things he sells? No, an artist or intellectual invents or creates the things he sells!

Does the capitalist make the things he sells? No, workers make the things capitalists sell.

Well, maybe the capitalist markets what he sells. No, a creative person writes the advertising!

Then the capitalist just sells these things. Well, no, actually a salesman sells them to people.

Does he deliver it? No, truck drivers and salespeople do that!

So an artist or intellectual invents something, workers build it, artists market it, salespeople sell it and other workers deliver it.

What does a capitalist it do?

He makes money on the blood, sweat and tears of all these other people.

Good ideas and invention of things are most often thought up by creative people who don't always have the possibility, ability, desire or ambition to make money by developing those ideas. Without the capitalist and his money-driving development, then the ideas often never come to fruition. That is the money-type person's value, but they should never be celebrated as the creator of something just for giving money to make it happen.

Money is the reward that stimulates technological advancements. Intellectuals and artists realize this and appreciate the role of capitalists. But capitalists have to realize the role of others in the whole process.

All we want is a little more respect. They need us to develop the ideas that they sell, they need us to build them, and they need us to buy them afterwards.

We, the majority of the population, need the wealthy manufacturers for convenience, but that doesn't mean we couldn't live without them. And, for the most part, our lives would be quite a bit more enjoyable, simpler and easier without them.

The rich need us more than we need them. The wealthy would not be wealthy without us, and besides, many of us would not be poor if it weren't for them.

After all, one of the reasons for the migration of the subsistence farmer into the city was large corporations and land owners who made it hard to exist in the agrarian life anymore. Add to that the advertising seduction to own more junk and indulge in the temptations of the city life.

We need commerce, but not on the scale at which it exists today. And it need not, and should not, be at the level of greed and corruption it has reached in recent years.

Free enterprise is the form of commerce we should strive for, not capitalism. Capitalism, as I have already brought to your attention, is only 150 years old in this country. Free enterprise, the level playing field for all, is what this country is based on.

Freedom of commerce for all, not control of commerce by a few. Capitalism as it is employed today in this country is a backward step in the evolution of man. The door toward mankind's freedom from economic and religious tyranny opened in this country with the Declaration of Independence in 1776. Slowly, the greedy tyrants have been allowed to take control again, and they are closing that door.

Capitalism can be a part of the free-enterprise system, but fists must be taught, and sometimes even forced, to maintain a certain level of morality. Capitalism as it is wielded today is just like the feudal system we left the Old World to escape. Have I said this before? Well, believe it!

When you study the history of the middle class's slow decline back into economic enslavement, you find that those who benefit most from it are the same people who created it, and the same people who are continually telling us it is the American way of life. The capitalists.

Liberals, the only group of people who continually complain about this tragedy, are the ones who are continually accused of causing it. Yet for the most part, liberals are not affected positively or negatively by this economic decline. We may have to tighten our belts, recycle or change our occupations, but we adapt easily. Many in the silent majority are unable to adapt as well.

Liberals, who have objectivity and a clear perspective on the situation, have a pragmatic view. They adapt to solve problems. Change has always been the strongest of mankind's attributes. Society should be listening to the suggestions of our liberal intellectual community.

Silent majority, stand up for your rights. Speak out, with your vote and with your pocketbook!

Capitalist, look deep into yourself. Can you find a soul willing to step into the shoes of a poor man? Can you see the spirituality in generosity?

Through this small book I am trying to awaken the capitalist to the pain he creates and warn the silent majority of the slavery they are in. I am trying to avert a tragedy in our society and in the world.

If things don't change, if capitalists don't become more reasonable and if the silent majority doesn't start getting a better break in life, there will be a conflagration, a conflict between the haves and the have-nots. I am trying to keep that from happening. I'm only the messenger.

My worst fear is that those in power right now actually want to see a revolution, want a war of economic and ideological opposites, an Armageddon. Many of the "leaders" now in our "government" profess fundamental religious beliefs. It is possible that, with their misguided theology, they actually look forward to a world war of ideologies?

They think, of course, that they will survive to lead afterward. What they don't understand is that they are on the wrong side. They don't realize money and those who use it as a weapon are the real anti-Christ.

The only time in our written knowledge Christ ever got mad was at the money-changers.

This country is meant to be a free-enterprise society, with enough socialism and welfare, used correctly, to protect our people and our country from the ravages of poverty and starvation.

I believe in a free enterprise/socialized form of economy. Free enterprise creates a comfortable life for those who can and will work for it. Social programs are the benevolent conscience of a moral society to protect those who either physically or mentally cannot support themselves.

# CHAPTER 43

## Socialism and Welfare

*"A cold heart is a dead heart!"*
Source: An old native saying from your culture and my culture,
and all cultures, actually!

Karl Marx did not invent socialism; it has existed for millions of years in tribal and simple village cultures. Capitalism, although named only within the last 150 years, has its roots in the monarchy, aristocracy and feudal systems of Europe and many Asian cultures.

It is godlike to give support to the young, poor, aged and uneducated, so that they might survive and eventually reach a place where they can be of value to themselves and society. Social programs are the conscience of a society where humans care about other humans.

What is wrong with good will? What is wrong with taking care of your fellow man? The Bible tells us to support the poor, children, widows and the aged. It is not a crime to want to help others in need; it is a crime if we don't.

Whether you know it or not, our country was created on many socialistic concepts. Widows and orphans of the War of Independence were provided for. Free libraries, fire protection, police departments and education were social ideals which were created and instituted in the early United States of America.

The idea that welfare is a subversive concept or a communist plot has been forced upon us by capitalist businessmen who are so greedy they can't stand to see anyone else get something for nothing.

If you look at the giveaways in this country, you will see that, per capita, rich people get more government handouts than the poor do, by far.

The whole conservative philosophy against public welfare programs goes even deeper than just greed; it is a superiority complex.

The wealthy, of course, feel it is their right to get paid by the government not to plant crops, or to pretend to experiment or plan to develop something. They think it is their right because they are more important than poor people, who aren't devious or hypocritical enough to fabricate these things.

The conservative business community also has the twisted belief that, if the poor are not kept poor and uncomfortable, they may not clamber for underpaid jobs in bad working conditions. And they may, for once, be correct.

Also, the concept that financial assistance is something to be ashamed of is an idea that has been taught us by conservative "thinkers." It is the "Christian work ethic," the notion that it is un-Christianlike to be in a position to have to take "charity."

The inference is that, if you are poor, you are not blessed by God, so you are not a good Christian. This is particularly hypocritical since the reason many people are poor is because of the impossible competitive atmosphere created by capitalism and conservatives in this country.

Not everyone is going to be able to compete, even in a reasonable free-enterprise system, let alone a greedy capitalist environment. Get used to it; there are going to be people who fall through the cracks.

So what should society do? Should we wait for the poor and disenfranchised to steal something or become disillusioned drug addicts, so we can put them in jail? No! A respectable society supports its people, educates them if they want, and helps them achieve a better life; but above all, a civilized nation does not let people suffer.

The demonizing of welfare and those who must rely on it is a particularly cruel mechanism of the conservative establishment. It is destructive on several levels.

First, everyone must realize social systems are a necessity in any civilized culture. If you know the history of small villages and towns, you know that folks do and must take care of their own.

It is not good for a village or town to let a person financially suffer to the point where they become more than just a burden, but a danger to society as well. This also applies to larger social groups. As Bob Marley wrote, "A hungry man is an angry man."

The "burden" to help a person or family is less trouble than to have to deal with the consequences of their criminal acts because of their poverty or despair. It is not really a burden; it is an obligation to the community and to individuals to help them.

Most importantly, everyone needs to change their attitude toward the folks who have to use welfare benefits. These benefits are necessary to support and protect those who are having troubles in this difficult world.

If a stigma is placed on welfare, then the community is reluctant to support it, which, as I have said, is bad for the community in the long run. If the recipients of welfare recognize the stigma or experience the animosity of the community, they feel disenfranchised and will lash out.

The main reason for the drug culture in this country is the disillusionment that poverty creates and the negative attitude toward welfare created by conservative ideology. Conservative attitudes have forced a whole segment of our population into poverty because of prejudices or unfair wage and labor practices, and then these disenfranchised people, through no fault of their own, fulfill the conservatives' expectations.

In this and most every other case, prejudice is a self-fulfilling prophecy. If society alienates a person because of expectations of their failure, they are most likely going to fail because of the negative treatment they receive.

Many Americans have developed a misunderstanding of socialism and welfare. It started with conservative attacks on the liberal ideals of helping the poor, the disadvantaged and the elderly.

Eventually, the American silent majority began to believe that socialism, welfare and even just liberal thinking were the same as totalitarian communism. It was an innocent mistake, given the propaganda they had been fed, but that misunderstanding has caused a great deal of damage to the economy of America.

In reality, a socialist is a humanitarian, not a totalitarian. Socialist ideals are aimed at helping those who can't help themselves. It makes no difference why they can't help themselves. It could be for social, mental, educational or physical reasons.

Americans who believe in social programs identify with the poor people of America, as well as those of Russia, China and all countries. We do not support the totalitarian governments of Russia, China or America.

The Great Depression and President Franklin D. Roosevelt created many social programs in America, and Presidents John Kennedy and Lyndon Johnson created more. These programs were designed to help the poor and disenfranchised citizens get out from under debilitating poverty, achieve an education, be able to contribute to society and eventually experience some part of the American dream.

Welfare and free enterprise need not be incompatible in American society. A proper mixture of both would help to balance our economy more equally among the majority population. But there is an element of our wealthy population that considers welfare or anything that resembles socialism to be a threat to their agenda.

These people don't oppose welfare on the grounds that it is bad for people or for society. They oppose it because it may cut into their own economic profits.

Did you know that at one time, John Wayne and some of his friends were the biggest recipients of welfare checks for not planting cotton? And at the same time he verbally ridiculed welfare mothers for getting small checks to feed their children.

Since the 1970s, all of these programs have been slowly dismantled or made ineffective because of conservative disapproval. The stigma of an assumed connection to left-wing ideology has worked against these important social and educational programs. Because of this, the economy of this country is fast becoming polarized into the two vastly separate groups of the very rich and the very poor.

The reason the social systems in this country are inefficient, fraught with abuse and corruption is that every four to eight years the Republicans take over the administration of these departments. With each change in Washington, DC, or state capitols swinging to the conservative side of the aisle, businessmen who do not want social systems are put in charge of them.

They know it wouldn't look good on their record if they outright dismantled programs to feed poor children, so they cut funding or make them so inefficient that they are slowly becoming unworkable.

This country cannot afford to have conservative minds make policies about government agencies that affect the poor, health care or education. They continually gut them or privatize them to make lots of money, and then abandon them to chaos.

> *"The basic difference*
> *between the conservative and liberal mind*
> *is freedom."*
> Dudley Griffin

Conservatives pass laws to force people to comply with and adhere to conservative ideologies. Many of these are against the cultural norms and economically impossible to follow. Liberals ask only that people be allowed the freedom to make their own choices and that they have a free media to supply them with the options.

There is a big difference between suggesting to someone that they follow your moral, religious or political ideals and forcing them to do so. Killing someone because they don't agree with you is a conservative M.O.; it is not a liberal option.

Many social systems were created at the beginning of our democracy. Benjamin Franklin devised the free (socialized) library system and free fire department system. What's wrong with socialism? Every village or small town in the world runs on a socialistic morality. Are we going to let greed destroy mankind and the world with us?

Socialism is a democratic economic system. Free enterprise is a democratic economic system. Capitalism is a dictatorial economic system! A free-enterprise and socialism economy allows the freedom to be enterprising for those who can compete in the system, and provides a safety net for those who cannot. It is the moral and actually, if you read your Bible, the Christian way. Presently, we just marginalize, imprison or institutionalize people who can't compete in dog-eat-dog capitalism.

I believe in a rational economic food chain. As with the food chain of the animal and natural kingdoms, human economic sustenance should start from the bottom. All nutrition in the animal kingdom travels up from the smallest creatures through the chain until it eventually reaches the top predators. This makes for a happier society, everyone receiving the food that they need. It's natural, it's democratic, it's socialistic, and it is the opposite of trickle-down.

Socialism, free enterprise and democracy mean: we can achieve, with our own help, the ability to support ourselves, all of us.

Socialism, free enterprise and democracy could solve all the problems of the world if the capitalists, fascists and religious fanatics would keep their violent, bigoted, greedy thoughts to themselves.

Socialism, free enterprise and democracy could solve all the problems of the world if the capitalists, fascists and religious fanatics could stop being insecure!

Socialism, free enterprise and democracy could solve all the problems of the world if people would realize they could, themselves, be the poor, the disadvantaged, the minority, the other religion, and/or the loser.

We are not talking about communism. Socialism is benevolent communism, just as free enterprise is benevolent capitalism.

# CHAPTER 44

## New Deal Again

The Roosevelt New Deal was a system whereby the U.S. government put money into the building and repair of the national infrastructure, roads and bridges, etc. Art, education and small businesses were also subsidized.

What this did was give money to the working class and improve their standard of living. And then, of course, they would spend that money to improve the economy. All of what they made in salaries went back into the economy.

Of course, big businesses, those who build roads and bridges, complained because they wanted to make a profit by gouging the government for the contract and paying employees a small percentage wage.

Eventually, big business won out. We haven't seen anything like the New Deal since the 1930s. What we need is a new, New Deal.

We have to get money into the hands of the poor and middle class majority. Not just for their comfort and not just because it is the moral thing to do, but because it would solve many, if not all of the economic and social problems of our country.

For no other reason than it makes good sense, we should find ways to employ the poor, and if they are unemployable or even if there are no jobs, we should give them a living wage anyway. That will move the economy. It will eventually get back into the pockets of the wealthy; you know it will, but it should start as income and welfare to the people at the bottom.

There are those who will say it is unreasonable to give money to those who do not work for it, but the problems created in society by poverty are even more unreasonable. Some people feel that it is un-Christian-like not to work for a living, but it is even more un-Christian to sit back and see people suffer and not give them a living wage.

Our government often gives money to businessmen and farmers for not working. Who deserves it more, someone who already has plenty or someone with nothing?

If you think there are no funds available to give to the poor, then you have been listening to capitalists and big businessmen. Get a bunch of university professors together, and they will give you an economic plan that will supply the poor with what they need, and the rich won't even suffer in the process.

The greed of capitalists is what has created poverty, and yet they don't even realize they would still be rich even if they allowed the poor to have enough to be comfortable. Somehow, the power over other people has become more important than the money itself. Call it the "Ego of Power."

If you give a tax break to the rich, only part of the money will go back into the system. They tend to hoard and protect their profits; you know they do! But if you give money in the form of wages and welfare to the poor and middle class, it will all go right back into the economy, and the rich will eventually see it, but only after it has improved the quality of life for the majority.

If you think about it, a "trickle up" system is better for all people and for the country. The best way to get this money to the poor and middle class is to pump money into public works, infrastructure repair, education and then, as a last resort, welfare.

The strange thing about government money, even with oversight, is that it seems to get squandered. Graft and corruption seem to happen, and large amounts of the money disappear. But if you think about it, the money doesn't really belong to the government in the first place. It is tax money from the people and for the people. If it gets something constructive done and goes back into the system through the hands of the poor and middle class, then at least it has accomplished something. Usually, these huge amounts of tax money mysteriously end up in the hands of large contractors and corporations, and then only a percentage of it gets back into the system.

If we could find ways to get this tax money to smaller contractors, artisans and individuals to repair our infrastructure, it would improve the quality of life and then filter back up to the rich anyway. Even money into the arts and grass-roots entertainment, theater and dance troupes would enhance our lives and then move right back into the economy.

Capitalists will have to tighten up their offshore belts for a little while, until the economy gets healthy again. The money will start to flow back to them again, and by then it will have created new hope and security for the poor and middle-class masses.

Give a dollar to a rich person, and half of it goes into foreign goods, tax shelters or entitlements. Give a dollar to a poor or middle-class person, and it will go right back into the economy and circulate over again. What makes more sense to our society and our economy?

# CHAPTER 45

## Abandoning This Planet and
## Colonizing Some Other Place in Space

So you think it is time to abandon this planet and colonize some other place in space!? Well, it is expensive and time-consuming and, frankly, it is too late for that to save mankind. Plus, if done, only the "best people," the most wealthy, right religion, who-you-know people would be sent.

We should and could clean-up our act right here and not have to go through that farce. It was started by Wernher von Braun. You know, the Nazi V2 creator.

JFK did not advocate it or the use of space as a weapons platform. He asked the Russians to cooperate and benefit from the moon landing. But almost every other Republican/conservative U.S. president or administration since has supported it. It creates jobs, but depletes the resources, and yet looks good on your resume.

Even today, if we concentrated upon life on Earth, we could save most of this planet. But, birth control, eliminating corporate planned obsolesce, and producing a world-wide subsistence welfare and health program would expedite fulfilling "God's" hope for all creatures and this world.

CHAPTER 46

# Greed
# &
# Money

Greed is not good. It is destructive; it even destroys the greedy!

What the greedy man seeks is his undoing and the undoing of his victims. We must learn to live in cooperation on this earth, or we will all die in competition with each other. With the constant growth of the world's population and the shrinking of natural resources, some day greed will have to be outlawed, or we will live in anarchy and die in competition.

There are people out there who are still promoting wealth and not promoting sustainability. Corporations give you hope for fame and fortune, yet they are just stealing from you. Peace and happiness is not connected to money except in a greedy capitalist society.

*"War, bigotry, religion, greed, these are thing we should dispense with, for the sake of humankind."*
JOB, 1990

Money is the root of all evil, as the Bible says. Why do we continue to ignore that fact? It is the one thing that will keep us from the Garden of Eden for sure.

It is a wedge between people. It makes some people arrogant and others envious. It is the cause and the means by which one person enslaves another.

If you are a Christian or a spiritual person of any religion, indignation toward greed and the pursuit of money should be your most ardent crusade. And what about the people who use it to enslave others? They should be the enemies of all moral men.

Money is an interesting commodity. Since we stopped making money from precious metals, what we now call money is just a promise. It is a promise that somewhere on down the line we will be given something else of value for what we sold or for the service or work we did.

Buying and selling with money is just like barter or exchange of goods, but without the middle man. Although money is handy to carry around and allows time in between selling your cow and buying bales of hay, it also has some very negative qualities.

Money seems to have more dimensions than the goods it buys. It seems to promote greed; it is easier to steal than a bale of hay, and somehow it creates grandeur in one's mind more than the cow it used to represent.

People get really uptight and possessive about money, yet it is only paper. Money itself is not really that important in life, except, of course, if you don't have enough of it to be physically comfortable or to keep you from stealing from others.

Money can only buy you love that others can also buy! Money can only buy you happiness that can also be taken away by an act of man or the whim of nature. Real love and happiness don't require money.

A large portion of the population in this country is under the false impression they are free human beings living in a free country. Yet many, if not most, of the citizens of this country are technically enslaved by the economic system that exists here today.

Anytime anyone else has control over your means of livelihood, food or money, then you don't have full control of your own life. You are at the mercy of others.

The reason times are getting tougher for most people is that the rich are siphoning off more money all the time. They are also finding new ways for the poor and middle class to spend money, creating more unnecessary products.

And the masses are making it easy for the rich by being greedy themselves. We are spending money on things we don't need.

Somehow, the normal, average, working people have let this happen. They are so impressed by money and power that they will support those who have it, thinking that they must be right because they have the money and power.

Strangely, in political discourse when someone asks whether America is doing well, people automatically think about the economy of big business. They forget to think about the economy of the average person. In case you haven't noticed, it is getting worse all the time.

The economic situation of the majority of the people in America is in critical decline, and on top of that our freedom to be able to stop it are being eroded. Conservative politicians and capitalist businessmen have forgotten about the people they are supposed to be protecting and the workers with whom they are in partnership.

Corporations are gobbling up smaller companies, controlling all manufacturing and services, but not doing a better job of manufacturing or serving.

The term "follow the money" which became popular through the Watergate break-in and conspiracy, is an important concept today. It goes both ways; where is the money coming from and where is the money going?

Who is benefiting from a particular situation? Always follow the money. Never trust someone who has money to gain in the proceedings.

If we do not question people about their ethics and their motives, it is our own fault if we become their slaves. To a greedy person the best society is an ignorant one.

It will not be long before the business community lobbies to abandon money altogether and to use credits instead. This will be a very dangerous and crucial decision for us to make. We must watch out for the wolves in sheep's clothing.

Money is too often used as a weapon by the rich. Keeping other people poor has always been the way the wealthy control the world. If we want a democratic and humanitarian society, we must create a world free from economic worries.

Are you familiar with the way money is handled on *Star Trek*? Gene Roddenberry created a society without economic conflict, and perhaps that is our future if we are to survive.

Conservatives and capitalists would benefit the world by watching the whole catalogue of *Star Trek* TV shows and refraining from watching *Star Wars* movies. All humanity would benefit if the socially aggressive and intensely militaristic people of this would would choose more humanitarian media entertainment.

# CHAPTER 47

# **Work**

In primal and tribal societies people worked only to feed, clothe, house and protect themselves. Then they created art and played with family and friends the rest of the time. They had active social and family lives because they worked only for the essentials. Today we work and slave for a lot of stuff we don't need, and our family, social and spiritual lives suffer.

In our society today, whenever the news media talk about how the economy is doing, what they are discussing are the profits of large corporations and whether capitalist America is getting its fair share. They equate a healthy economy to how big business is doing, how much gross national product is being produced and sold.

Sure, they mention unemployment, but only as a concern for how it will affect productivity and consumer buying power. A better measurement of how well this country is doing, and how poorly would be to discuss the amount of credit and mortgage indebtedness the middle and lower classes have.

The fortunes of big business do fluctuate, but for the largest corporations and their CEOs, it has been mostly up, steadily up. Yet for the majority of the people in this country, it has been down, mostly down.

The majority of the public has no concept of inflation or deflation. For us, it is mostly recession. If you compare how much work we do, how much pay we get, and how much deeper in debt we are each day, it is obvious most people are not benefiting from our society's riches.

Gross National Product is a deceptive measurement of a society's worth. Are all of these things we produce contributing to a better life? Are we happier because we have all this stuff?

Some of you may remember when a four-day work week was being discussed during the 1950s. Boy, that sure did scare the pants off all the capitalists in this country! So what did they do? They invented planned obsolescence, started creating a lot of silly, unnecessary trinkets and figured out the possibilities of advertising. That got us back to work.

If we would readjust our manufacturing and economic systems properly, we could reach a place where everyone had work available and a living wage, and we wouldn't be using up all of our natural resources. The first step is to concentrate on manufacturing essential products to improve our infrastructure and stop producing so many luxury items and impulse-buying commodities, which fall apart or are rejected within a few months.

The real first step in fixing our economy is to stop listening to conservative capitalists' ideas and get some liberal intellectuals to work on creating true solutions that will benefit the majority of the population. Capitalists have a tendency to forget what a democracy is.

# CHAPTER 48

## Stuff

More stuff to buy means more money for the corporations, and less free time to spend with our families. Stuff that breaks after a few months or years means we need more money to replace it, which means more hours of work, less time developing our culture and more money for the corporate CEOs.

It used to be that an artisan made a product or tool of the best material he could so that it would last long, do a good job, bring him respect and future business. Now a company makes flashy things to look good, but from cheap materials, so they last only a short time, requiring that you buy another one sooner. And, of course, you have to work for the money to buy them.

Planned obsolescence will someday be a crime punishable by incarceration, when we no longer have water to drink and air to breathe. Why don't we get smart as humans are supposed to be and start passing laws against wasting our natural resources now?

We have to stop making so much stuff! We must tone down our economy and cut back on advertising. Some people will be outraged at these ideas, but are they willing to face the alternative?

Disregarding the impact on our environment, the gross, unthinking materialism of this society is not mentally healthy. Placing all your hopes and dreams on things, rather than feelings and emotions, will leave you mentally and possibly morally bankrupt.

Some of you might think that what I say here is just New Age, counterculture hokum, but it is mainstream reality. Our environment is dying because of the manufacture of worthless stuff, and our minds are atrophying because of a lack of creative thinking.

When the white man came to America, the Native Americans were amused by his attitude toward stuff and land. White men built houses surrounded by fences to protect their stuff.

Native Americans thought this was strange since the fence kept the white men inside their small pieces of land with their little collections of stuff. Yet the Native Americans were outside where they had the use of everything God provided and were free to use the whole world as they knew it.

Native Americans owned almost nothing, were held down by nothing and possessed by no possessions. And then the white men stole the land from the Native Americans, who didn't even own it, and built a bigger fence to keep themselves inside.

The real sad ending to this story is that the Indian culture was proud and free until the white culture showed them what they were missing. Then the Native American people became miserable. Stuff and the accumulation of it can take away a person's pride and freedom.

# CHAPTER 49

## Technology

Our lives and world are being affected both positively and negatively by technology. Technology is a wonderful thing when used properly, but humans are always able to make a double-edged sword of everything we touch.

The problem is that we let the wrong people make the decisions about how our technology is used. We have left these decisions in the hands of businessmen. Businessmen are, of course, going to make decisions based on economics and profit first, and then, maybe, if they have any morality at all, they will consider the real needs of mankind.

Intellectuals should be in charge of the use of technology. Unlike businessmen who think on one dimension, intellectuals contemplate all aspects of a subject and all possibilities of a product, whether it be economic, social or moral.

In a perfect world all technology would be used for the enhancement and betterment of human life on the earth. It would not be utilized solely to make money or used as a weapon to kill other people.

Originally, all creations (including art) were conceived to improve our lifestyle. For centuries, new ideas, new tools, new weapons, new toys, even new luxuries, improved our lives in some way.

There has always been the incentive to invent weapons to protect ourselves and help provide food. But recently much of mankind's weapons technology is as dangerous to the inventor as it is to the intended victim.

In early ages, sometimes unnecessary or frivolous inventions emerged for the amusement and comfort of mankind. But recently these "luxuries" have proven to be counter-productive and have actually become a threat to our intellect and our lives.

The problem is that now much of what we produce consists of new, frivolous toys and unnecessary luxuries. These commodities are not essential or even important to our existence or even our happiness. We have become so jaded and bored with life that many people feel a new DVD player and bigger screen are essential to their survival.

The real negative aspect of these new toys is that they are suppressing our creativity and hindering our communications with other people. We have replaced art, literature, theater and philosophic discovery with shallow entertainment. Electric games and picture phones are taking up all our time and dulling our intellect.

And, of course, these new luxury items and electronic diversions are also eating up natural resources, polluting our air and water and destroying the future of the whole human race! Materialism, planned obsolescence and advertising are burning up our world and dulling our senses.

Why do we continue to produce these trinkets? Because capitalists are running the world right now, and they are always in need of more luxuries to sell to make more profits.

Of course, we could stop buying these trinkets they sell on TV!? If we were intelligent enough to realize what this junk is really doing to our lives and environment, we would "just say no to TV toys!"

If liberals were running the world, you could have a lot more fun for less money. The world wouldn't be crumbling, and wars wouldn't be waging. You are following the wrong God--money, profit, materialism and technology are going to be America's downfall. The problem is, we will take the rest of the world and all the people in it with us.

CHAPTER 50

# Media

*"We have to have education and true information to have people intelligent enough to rule themselves. Otherwise dictators will rule over them."*
DG 4/20/20

Are they changing minds or controlling minds? All media, conservative or liberal, is good as long as it dispenses facts and opinions, until it crosses the line when it indulges in outright lies, or actively suppresses the voice of its opposition.

I can't prove that lying is un-American, but I'm damn sure that controlling the flow of information is subversive, even treasonous. Remember Nazi Germany and the USSR!? Any place that has only one source of information is a totalitarian dictatorship. America is supposed to be a democracy!

Even if you do not agree with what another person says, you are not a patriotic American unless you allow them to say it, and are willing to defend their right to do so. Anyone who does not want other opinions to be heard must have something to hide, and therefore their own morality and validity is in question.

Deceit has no place in a democracy. If you deceive someone to get them to vote for your agenda, then you are living by the rules of dictatorship.

Liberals know that all voices are important. Even if they are lies they give dimension to the truth. If we hear only one side of a subject, we have no perspective to find the truth.

It may seem like a contradiction to hate someone's ideals, and yet support their right to live them and voice them. Yet this is what democracy and freedom of speech is all about. This is what it means to be a good American. It may not be easy, but it is the high road. What you must do is make a better argument for your truth than they have for their lies. Hopefully, they will change because of what you say and others will follow.

Someone who is telling the truth has nothing to hide from the words, opinions or even lies of others. I believe that humans have a built-in mechanism that eventually finds the truth, a bullshit filter if you will. But in order for it to work, people must be given all the facts, fairly and equally. That is why some people try to monopolize the media.

Conservatives complain about the "liberal media," and liberals complain about "conservative media." First, to understand and explain these circumstances, a distinction must be made between news media and entertainment media.

The "entertainment media" consists primarily of movies, sports, TV shows, music, literature and, to some extent, fine arts. The "news media" is daily information and is voiced traditionally through radio, TV, newspaper and news magazine sources.

There is, of course, cross-over media. Books, songs and movies can contain "news." News is also separated into political information or just facts of interest, such as the report of a traffic accident. When liberals or conservatives comment on news bias, they are obviously referring to political, economic or social content.

To understand the conflict and confusion most people have about conservative and liberal media slant, you must understand first that there are two opposite disciplines at work necessary to produce and distribute the media. In both news media and entertainment media, there are the administrative people and the creative people.

It is a generalization, but one supported by many facts, observations and experiences, that most creative people are more intellectual and thus more liberal.

Administrative or business people are, of course, most often more business-oriented and conservative.

Conservative administrators run the front office of the media and entertainment industries. Creative people, such as writers, artists and deep thinkers, are essential to media production; they write the movies, stories and commentary.

Many people in the working press are liberals. After all, most writers are intellectuals and most intellectuals are liberal. But the people who own the news media and run it are conservatives.

Almost all media is owned by large corporations, which are, of course, conservative. This means that the writers may be liberal, but the management is most certainly conservative.

What happens is that the liberal writer has to be careful not to get too good at his craft. He must be cautious about what he says and not be too persuasive, or else his career could mysteriously disappear.

Conservative businessmen and legislators have discovered that education and information are their worst enemies. They cannot lie to a public that has access to the truth. So the conservative capitalists have slowly but surely, over the last 100 years, taken over the news and entertainment media.

Because the mass media, TV networks, most newspapers and radio have fallen under the control of a few people who have a selfish interest in capitalism, our democracy is slipping fast. No government, however benevolent, is going to remain democratic if it is not questioned and held accountable for its decisions.

Our forefathers established a form of checks and balances using the presidency, the Congress and the Supreme Court to control a potential run-away administration. The fourth element of that overseeing mechanism was the news media, protected by the First Amendment.

In the last 200 years, most notably in the last forty years, those checks and balances and freedoms have been eroded. But what is most damaging to our democracy and freedom has been the last 20-year trend toward larger media conglomerates. As long as a few rich people own most of the mainstream media, there is no real freedom of speech; at least there is no proportionate distribution of facts.

Our Founding Fathers tried to ensure that we would have information about both sides of every situation available to us so we could make informed decisions about our own destiny. That system has been weakened by conservative laws.

Many people watch only TV for all of their news and outside information. Most people have access only to mainstream large corporate media. They are not seeing both sides of the political story. Most Europeans know more about what is going on in our country than our own population does.

Me thinks the conservatives protest too much about the "liberal press." A slanted liberal press is a fallacy; it is actually a lie. Liberal press is mostly a fact and fact-finding function. Conservatives who run things don't honestly believe the media has a liberal slant. They have inside knowledge that the mainstream media is definitely conservative. They just accuse the media of having a liberal slant in order to convince the silent majority that it does.

Conservatives own the mainstream media. How could it possibly be a liberal voice? The conservative media is not a monopoly yet, but it is an overpowering majority of the voice heard in this country.

But the mainstream doesn't totally own the airwaves yet, and they have no control over the Internet. So, conservatives, if you think the media is liberal now, just wait till the public realizes the lies you have been telling. And watch as more good people in the media get fed up and find their own voices.

Voting to expand the number of media sources that one person or corporation can possess in one market is an un-American act and could possibly create a dictatorship in this country. Urge your Congressperson to be a good American and protect our diversity of information.

The conservative media majority voice is only part of the program to control minds. The process of dumbing down the public is the other part of the move toward a capitalist dictatorship.

The process of dumbing down has been created for two different reasons. The first, as I have said numerous times, is because the conservatives know that an ignorant person is easier to control. The second and in some ways the most insidious reason is to save money.

An important thing to know about the entertainment and media industries is that creativity and experimentation cost them money. If the audience is sophisticated and creative, the entertainment industry must come up with new themes and unique ways to engage them. "Smart" people won't put up with the "same old shit" all the time.

For every success in attracting an audience, the entertainment industry has hundreds of costly failures. For this reason the media is always trying to simplify the tastes of the populous.

The dumbing down of America serves two purposes: It saves money, and it makes people docile--easier to sell junk to. But in the meantime, the most destructive side effect is that it is killing sensitivity and creativity, thus suppressing the development and expansion of our culture.

People who don't read have no idea what they are missing. Reading adds so many more dimensions to the mind, its potential for exploration and its available levels of joy.

Whereas most TV and movies entertain rather than inspire the mind; books give people much more creative stimulus. The majority of mass media lowers the expectations of people.

Lowering the expectations is the same as lowering a person's creative expression. Conservative businesspeople like low expectations from their customers; they thrive on a lack of education or imagination in their customers. Creative or intelligent people are not so gullible; they are harder to deceive or sell a pig-in-a-poke (bogus goods).

# CHAPTER 51

## Monopoly Is Not a Game

Monopoly Is not a game today; it is a <u>real</u> economic <u>reality</u>! And it is a destructive social and economic problem.

*"Only the rich play it like a game. The poor feel like the ball that is being hit, the bullseye shot at, or the racket being abused!"*
Dudley Griffin, 1/2/20

Capitalism is the creator of monopoly, not the game, but the real larcenous practice of controlling prices and salaries, which happens when one company controls the whole market in any one place.

Capitalists do not believe in free enterprise. They believe in monopoly, where they and only they have the power and right to be prosperous. And capitalists have been slowly eroding all the checks and balances that our Founding Fathers created to make prosperity possible for everyone.

The irony of the popularity of the game of Monopoly, which seems to promote greed and insensitive combative competition, is that the first person to invent the concept of that game about capitalism was actually opposed to the business practices of monopolies and the existence of capitalism and its anti-democracy activities.

Her name was Lizzie Magie, a liberal, and she invented the game that became Monopoly in and around 1903. Her creation was intended as a way to expose the negative aspects of land monopolies. She had it patented as The Landlord's Game and created two sets of rules; one, the anti-monopoly game, where all where rewarded when wealth was achieved, and second, a monopolist set of rules where the objective was to crush opponents.

In the 1930s a man named Charles Darrow swiped the idea and begin marketing it in the more competitive form of "corporate crush." He was an unemployed heating "engineer" and most likely a conservative, but he went on to being a millionaire from his theft.

To give America back the American Dream, America must reinstitute monopoly laws. Monopoly gives corporations the temptation to steal from the public when they own a whole industry

# CHAPTER 52

# Competition

The opportunity for individuals to prove their abilities and worth is a natural activity in the world of self-preservation, sports and business. Someone has to win, and someone has to lose. But in a modern, civilized and democratic society, competition must be fair, or it is immoral and it is a lie.

Fair, equal competition is the economic ideal upon which this country was founded. Free enterprise, a level playing field for everyone. To achieve that playing field is one of the main reasons the colonists left their old countries.

We started this country to escape feudalism, and what do we now end up with? The greedy people have changed our free-enterprise system into capitalism, which is exactly the same as feudalism and wage slavery.

Capitalism is not based on fair and equal competition. It is based on winning, and it is based on finding any advantage possible, illegal or immoral. And now these business practices have permeated every aspect of our lives. It is now considered the American way of life to cheat in order to get what you want. This is not American democracy; this is greed, folks!

Is this what our great country has come to? The unnatural drive to win at all costs has taken over all morality.

Almost all advertising is lies. The business class has stacked the deck against the working class. Our new motto should be "In Greed We Trust."

Greed has its roots in insecurity, and insecurity has its beginning in the American extreme emphases on winning in all competition. The importance we have now placed on winning has made insecurity an American epidemic. And these negative personality traits of greed, insecurity and competition all seem to feed on one another in a vicious cycle that is destroying a nation and its people.

Insecurity, the opposite of self-confidence, is one or our society's most damaging human traits. It is the root cause of the excessive, competitive nature of many men. It spawns greed, blind, competitive commercialism and arrogance.

The ruling class, the businessmen and military leaders are good at creating insecurity. They make a living from it.

To combat insecurity, people become competitive. Greed, materialism and self-importance are the most obvious results of competition, the most natural way to combat insecurity. Greed and materialism consume people, destroy the humanity in mankind and are now eating up the earth's resources.

This vicious cycle must be ended. Today, with the population as it is, competition and greed are the most destructive forces in the world.

Remember, before you shoot me, I'm only the messenger. I didn't create violent competition; the czars of big business did. And also, I didn't make the laws of kindness, peace and love; Christ, Buddha, and other spiritual leaders did. I'm only telling you about them and how they fit in you life.

Competitive spectator sports, especially the violent ones, such as boxing, football and stock car racing, are mechanisms designed by businessmen to give the working class someplace to release the hatred they have for their life of work and strife, the hatred they would otherwise have for the businessmen who enslave them.

Oh, and by selling tickets to these "blood sports," big business also gets a chance to take back some of that money they paid you in your shit job. This is psych 1A, and any educator or intellectual can tell you this. Do you remember the coliseum with gladiators against Christians? The same thing!

Big business has you right where they want you. They use your body to make their products and then sell you stuff to make you forget about your troubles. Alcohol and spectator excitement keep people's minds off their problems.

And the spectacle of violence and deceit is part of the excitement and power. Somehow in this country we have come to the conclusion that to be a real man you must be unsportsmanlike, vicious, larcenous and sneaky.

Some people feel that as long as you win, it doesn't matter how you do it--lie cheat or steal. And you know who does this more than anyone?! Cowboys and capitalists!

How did we get to this low point in man's history? What is possessing us? Why do we forgive rich people for doing things we know to be wrong?

The problem is that if humans get lazy or too comfortable, they become vulnerable and forget the common sense that protects them. When this happens, other, more ambitious and devious people usually materialize and try to take advantage of the sleeping population.

Success in business and industry is supposed to be determined by excellence. The successful businessman is supposed to be the one with the best product or service. Everyone knows that is not the case today. Most business success today is reached by screwing someone else. Businesspeople call it competition, but most moral people call it criminal.

Competition is productive and rewarding if it is conducted by gentlemen. Since we are not in the jungle anymore and since imminent death is not the penalty for coming in second, it is immoral to lie, cheat and steal in business dealings, thereby destroying families for a little more money.

Businesses today achieve their economic dominance by destroying competition, reducing the quality of their product and service and lying about their product or service. You know this is true. You know that most advertising is lies, and unless you are living under a rock, you know about planned obsolescence.

Call it business if you want to, but most economic endeavors conducted by men, in this day and age are more about runaway egos, insecurity and jealousy. It is mostly an effort to get past someone else and up the competitive ladder.

> *"I've tried to adapt to this capitalist way, but I cannot. Maybe I am a man of the past. No, maybe I am a man of the future?!"*
> John, 8/18/2003

# CHAPTER 53

## Psychological Obsolescence

### Image is Everything

There is a corporate/industrial underworld. They do things clandestinely because they know the public would not approve. Price-fixing, planned obsolescence and tax evasion are three of their many crimes. The media sometimes reports it, yet too many people only hear corporate media or when they hear of these crimes they cannot believe that people we have such respect for could act in these ways. Fear would be a more appropriate emotion for the American public to have than disbelief.

It is appalling that now the industrial underworld has created a new form of obsolescence. In the last 75 years or so, the advertising industry has grown and changed from a product information resource to a source of fiction. It creates dubious facts, attributes and desires, fabricates people, places and situations to sway the masses.

Present-day advertising creates attitudes about products rather than telling you the attributes of a product. Advertising tells you if something is cool to own, not whether it is worth owning.

And now advertising make things obsolete by making them undesirable. This is just as odious as making them fall apart. It also makes it easier for manufacturers to create poor quality goods, because the product is thrown away before it wears out.

Today, advertising is sometimes our most entertaining media, and that is a sad commentary on the state of business and industry in general. If it is only annoying or entertaining, advertising has become a psychological medium. You can't believe anything advertising tells you, so what do you do, enjoy the actors, pictures and CG?  I suggest that you read *Consumer Reports*.

Corporations are not being civil or humanitarian any more. Even though our courts have given them human status, they have chosen to become inhuman.

# CHAPTER 54

## Creativity, Art, Literature and Music as a Peaceful Alternative to Insecurity, Competition, Greed and War

*"Some people like dictators, because they*
*cannot make their own decisions."*
JOB 4/20/20

One of the most insidious aspects of the conservative mind is that it can cause a person to forsake the future, not his own future, but the future of others and of mankind as a race.

Sure, a predominant conservative activity is the amassing of a monetary legacy for his children and family. But through observation of the species, I have come to the conclusion that this exhibition, as with much of their philanthropy, comes from ego gratification rather than actual spiritual love.

Capitalists are economically expedient, concerned mostly with the bottom line, today's profits. This is brought on by having a one-dimensional mind interested primarily in personal self-preservation. Without having dimensions of thinking that can explore beauty, life force and the concept of future, conservatives put the education and survival of our children and their own children at risk.

Greed is a blindness to the future of mankind. The oddity of conservative mentality is that it is concerned with controlling other individuals, yet not concerned with the specifics of what to do with them once they are controlled.

In an effort to control education, conservatives are actually suppressing education. They are particularly disturbed by raw creativity, and they do everything within their power to obstruct it. They must realize instinctively that it is a threat to their control.

Although creativity is the source of all things and ideas produced in this world, it also stimulates rebellion and experimentation. This scares conservatives to death. What they don't realize, or maybe they do understand and guard against, is that this rebellion and experimentation are the core of true human nature, human value and human advancement. This creativity is all directed toward becoming perfect, which the conservatives realize means; no lying, cheating and stealing and that means they are out of a job.

Without pure creativity and open mental exploration, mankind becomes stagnant and susceptible to totalitarian control. Ignorance is essential to a dictator's success. Conservatives love ignorance, unless it comes from Bus Ed.

In the effort to ensure that the world's economy flows to and through themselves, conservatives contrive to keep people under control as a work force and a buying public. They do this primarily by organizing and suppressing education.

Conservatives have need of a workforce, but they usually have little concern or plan for what these cash cows are going to do other than just supply them with work and money. Liberals and intellectuals are becoming disturbed by the way in which conservatives are dumbing down a large portion of society and then leaving them to fend for themselves.

Capitalists and conservatives don't like free and affordable education for everyone. You can't lie to a person who already knows the truth. Because of this, funding to schools is always cut by conservatives and because of that, higher education is again becoming more exclusive to the rich.

Curriculums are also "legitimized" by conservatives, and therefore education is becoming more controlled, creativity is being suppressed and the curiosity of children is dying. All of our systems are being systematically destroyed as more and more of the money is sifting up to the wealthy, and they, of course, are paying less of their fair share of taxes.

Yes, unrestricted education breeds rebellion against the conservative norm, but it also breeds creativity, ideas and invention. Like "Big Brother," if conservatives have their way, no one will question, no one will feel or think or create. It will make it easier for them to control us and sell us stuff, but in the end the world will be one big, gray cement box.

Free education has created much of what you see around you. It is the American way, and it is our strength. Education, free and unrestricted, if left alone, will also eventually solve all of our social problems, but we need freedom to think.

We have to evolve to survive. The key to the evolution of man is adaptation. And how can we adapt if we cannot think or learn?!

Conservatives complain that colleges and universities are "hotbeds" of liberal activity. That's like saying boardrooms of large corporations are hotbeds of conservatism. Well yes, people do congregate where they're most comfortable.

Conservatives are, in essence, accusing "someone" of "somehow" purposely staffing schools of higher learning with liberal professors in order to subvert the youth of America against their capitalist propaganda. Again, that's like saying that boardrooms of large corporations have been rigged to promote capitalist goals of greed and corruption.

Come on, guys, it is the nature of these two places that attracts the participants. To start with, there is big money in corporate boardrooms, and of course capitalists are going to gravitate there. Education is found in universities, and so intellectuals go there. Sadly, there is much less monetary reward in teaching.

There are obvious reasons that liberals predominate in colleges and universities. The pursuit and teaching of higher education involves intellectual activity, which is basically the search for truth. Liberals hold truth in the highest regard.

Conservatives are often uncomfortable with "free thinking" universities that seek "the truth," because they are usually only looking for "a truth" that supports their economic, religious or political agenda.

Intellectual exploration, particularly in liberal arts, humanities, sociology or history, will eventually lead to a liberal view of life and society. Liberals usually gravitate to higher education because of their need for intellectual stimulation.

Conservatives gravitate toward business because of their desire to control stuff, and there's more money in big business than in education.

The one true and dangerous threat to democracy, to America, and to mankind as a whole is ignorance. Mankind's intelligence and ability to solve problems has been the one element which has lifted us above all the other predators on the earth. Our pragmatic "ability to solve problems" has allowed us to survive and prosper in an environment which has made extinct many other creatures that are bigger and stronger than we are.

Education, information and knowledge make men free! Why else would every dictator and totalitarian leader try to control or suppress these resources? Automatically, if a person wants to control education or the news media, then you know they must have something to hide.

I don't actually think conservatives have consciously undermined education and social services in an effort to orchestrate the decline of our society, but many of their cost-cutting and anti-social programs have accomplished just that.

We must make rational decisions about funding with an eye to the future of our country and world. Funding for preschool and after-school programs is more productive than money for police. Financial support for school art and music programs is a more positive solution than building jails.

Why are our schools suffering so much; why is our penal system so well-funded? Control--it is easier to have a lot of criminals than to have a lot of educated people. Educated people ask questions, they demand accountability, they will not be suppressed.

An ignorant society allows oppression by the wealthy class, which creates poverty, which, in turn, creates drug use and petty crime. The wealthy class knows how to handle crime. It's control. Build more prisons. Maybe if they keep it up, they won't have to build any more schools. All the people will be in prisons.

A government that does not involve itself in the prevention of problems is not a responsible government. A society that uses only punishment to solve its problems is not doing its job properly.

Conservatives are on a mission to dumb down the American public. They know not what they do. It is not only anti-American; it is against the natural laws of self-preservation.

Teach your children to be creative, literary, musical and curious; that is, if you want them to have peaceful alternatives to insecurity, competition, greed and war.

Teach yourself creativity, literature and music if you want to have peaceful alternatives to competition, greed and war.

CHAPTER 55

## Ecology and Environment

Why would a person climb a tree and jeopardize his or her life to save that tree, if not for a higher purpose? Environmentalists don't make money; they are just trying to save this world. They do it for your children and theirs and other generations to come.

Motives .... Why would the ecology movement lie to you about the dangers of pollution and materialism? Are they making money by doing so?

Why would capitalist Industry lie to you about their effect on the environment? Are they making money by doing so?

Environmentalists have only the <u>saving of the world</u> to gain by what they do. Capitalists have a lot of money to save by continuing to pollute the world. Which of these two groups have the purest motive?

If capitalist Industry had any concern for the future of mankind and any morality, they would say, "We have a problem here. Let's fix it!" Pollution is created by businessmen in the process of making money, and now to keep that money flowing, they are lying to you. They are protecting pollution.

So the silent majority has been told they should hate tree-huggers. Is that girl up in the tree destroying the future of mankind? That tree-hugger is trying to get our society to be more economically responsible today so that tomorrow we don't suffer the physical consequences of pollution.

When ecology demonstrators disrupt a working man's livelihood by halting corporate greed, they are doing so to protect that working man's future. If we could get capitalists to be more conscientious toward the environment, future jobs and future lives could be saved.

The silent majority must learn who their real friends are. They must objectively view the motives of the capitalists versus the motives of the demonstrators and tree-huggers.

The demonstrators on the streets are speaking out in your behalf. Stop listening to the lies of the conservative talk show puppets who get their money from capitalists and their scripts from corporate annual reports.

This is your world too. Fight for it, or die when it dies!

# CHAPTER 56

## Foreign Policy

We have no foreign policy in this country right now. Our "foreign policy," if you want to call it that, consists mainly of overthrowing governments who will not cooperate economically with our corporations and replacing them with dictators who will.

Our government presently has only a capitalist agenda with imperialist designs, following a battle plan of pushing weaker countries around in the world. Our world vision is to rape its resources for corporate profits and exploit cheap and child labor in other countries, while creating poverty, drug addiction and crime in our own country.

In the name of spreading democracy (mostly capitalism), our armies and money have killed millions of "rebels" who just thought they were being patriots to their own country. We certainly don't have much to be proud of in the way of foreign policy.

We are a country considered to be a democracy that supports dictatorships for a price. We most often support these dictators against their own majority population. No wonder much of the world hates us!

Much of the world has a negative attitude toward our vision of "saving the world" and the rest is afraid that we will come to their country to "save" them too.

I can't tell whether the capitalists really think they are doing the right thing or if they are just making too much money to care. What saddens me most is the silent majority in our country who honestly believe that our government is the savior and conscience of the world.

They can't understand why people in other countries burn our flag and shoot at our soldiers.

A real foreign policy would be to censor all dictatorships as we do Cuba. And then consider some way to help them become more democratic, not more capitalistic, but more free-enterprising and democratic.

Another strange twist to this "foreign policy" of ours is that we give taxpayers' money to dictators to allow our corporations to make money in their country. It is another example of large corporations getting even more economic help from the overtaxed workforce of America. If we could see any real advantage to the working poor in this country, it might be acceptable. The working poor are getting poorer every day.

The silent majority is exposed only to the mainstream media, and they hear only the capitalist propaganda. Their ignorance and prejudices are not their fault in that respect, but if they continue to believe the conservative lies, America will have no friends left in this world.

The middle class, the silent majority, the working classes, the poor and the liberal intellectuals of this country must band together to protect the United State from its own leaders whose agenda is only profits. We must vote out all politicians who are patriotic to capitalism and not to the Constitution of the United States.

# CHAPTER 57

## To Lying Politicians and Talk Show Hosts

When you lie, you are automatically admitting you are wrong. It means that you don't believe telling the truth will get you the desired result, which is the trust, respect or control over those to whom you are talking. That means you know you are wrong and are unworthy of their trust and support. You want someone's support and trust, so you lie to them. Sounds twisted, doesn't it?

Of course, the general public may not know you are lying. They may be your followers, and therefore, they trust you to tell the truth. After all, you have been telling them all along that you are telling the truth.

The public may not know you're lying and that your cause is wrong, but you know you're lying. How does that make you feel? Or are you able to justify lying because of the money and power it brings you? Are you comfortable with the fact that your cause is bogus and you are a liar?

Of course, there are some people who genuinely don't know that they are wrong or don't know the difference between right and wrong, or they may just be immoral and don't care. Which of these are you? Why not make it simple for your salvation. Just to start by saying the truth that you know to be the truth, with two or three reliable and "truthful" sources, not Fox "news," of course!

You must also be aware that all the intellectuals know you are a liar, and your cause is a scam on the American public. Yes, all the intelligent people know you are bogus, and they will tell history that you are a liar, and your cause is a greedy scam. Can you live with that, or is the money too good to allow you a conscience?

You can change. You can stop lying. You can reverse your direction and become a hero to the world. You can help to save the world by stopping your lies about how good capitalism is for the people. Stop telling the people that capitalism is not killing the world.

The freedom to lie was not granted to us with the freedom of speech. Freedom of speech is a sacred thing; if you lie using it, then you are condemned.

Freedom of speech works only if the truth is spoken. If a person lies, he is not exercising his right to free speech. He is just plain breaking the rules of free speech.

The moment lies and deception are used, freedom of speech becomes useless, we are back to communication anarchy and our culture suffers. The silent majority has been brainwashed for so long by "smooth-talking" scam artists that they don't know who their real friends are.

The bottom line is there are a number of people in this country who are lying to you. The only way you can be sure someone is not making a fool of you is to know both sides of the argument.

Liars are lazy. Its so much easier to lie than to tell the truth. Liars don't concern themselves with studying the facts because they are most often just saying unsubstantiated stuff that came from someone else anyway.

Liars can't prove what they say, so they don't often let themselves be questioned. They never expect to have to prove what they say, so it doesn't take much preparation.

Political liars know that the silent majority won't question their lies if the lie fits into what they already believe or hope or want. Lying to support a person's fears is also a slam dunk!

Professional liars know that once they say it, it becomes truth in the minds of their followers. Even if they had to retract something, it wouldn't matter. It would have already registered and would stay in the minds of those who wanted to believe it.

The reason liberals have been so much less effective in convincing the silent majority of the corruption of the conservatives is that telling the truth is so much more difficult and precise than lying.

The main reason liberal ideology is so difficult to explain or defend is that it is based on the truth, and it relies on telling the truth. It is harder to speak the truth because it requires knowing and following the facts.

Someone who is telling the truth wants suspicious people to ask questions. We are not afraid of questions. That is part of the teaching process. But in order to have that confidence to accept questions, you have to know the facts.

Liberals, who, I might add, are most often likely to tell the truth while trying to save the world are not as flamboyant and quick with words as conservatives, who, I might add, are more likely to lie to save their bank accounts.

Conservative talk show hosts are a unique kind of liar. They get paid very well to lie, and they do so with a great amount of panache and arrogance. These guys blithely spit out unsubstantiated words. ofIt's their show, and no one is there to question what they say. If they interview someone, they can always delete whatever they don't want their audience to hear.

I'm convinced that down deep inside, everyone really knows what is good and what is bad, what is true and what is false. We sometimes choose to look the other way for our own benefit or economic expedience. In this day and age, that is a dangerous way to live. Accepting lies could be the death of us all.

I once had a bumper sticker torn from my car. Who ever did it scratched my car's paint in the process. I wonder what they would think if someone did that to their automobile ego?

It was not a libelous sticker, nor did it advocate any murder or illegal activity, unlike one sticker seen often during Bill Clintons administration that said, "Where is Oswald when we need him?"

With one ignorant move someone stole my free speech from me, and they probably thought that they were being a patriotic American. But no, they were being as anti-American as they could be.

Their stupidity was playing right into the hands of all the totalitarian dictators this world has ever seen. Whether they knew it or not, they were as guilty of allowing the killing of Jews and imprisoning of Christians as Nazi Germany and Stalinist's Russia.

# CHAPTER 58

# Terrorism

Some people will say the terrorist attack of 9/11/2001 was the most infamous event in the history of America, but in the long run, how it was handled by our government could become the biggest disaster in the life of this nation.

The terrorist attack mostly just damaged our ego. But the war on terrorism itself, instituted by the U.S. government administration at that time, has damaged much more because it has opened the door for the conservative oppressors within our government and industry to violate even more of the freedoms that were given to us under our Constitution and Bill of Rights.

The war on terrorism has been more damaging to this country than the terrorism itself. The USA Patriot Act has wiped out hundreds of years of freedom, and the atmosphere of paranoia has changed the personality of this sweet nation into a country of suspicious and intolerant people.

The regime in power at the time of 9/11 was in need of something to divert attention from the economic disaster of the stock market and the treachery of the capitalist CEOs of Enron and Worldcom. The Trade Center attack could not have come at a better moment for the President and his friends.

Paranoia has two dangerous effects; it causes uninformed and hysterical people to cease rational thinking altogether, and it provides a tool with which unscrupulous people are able to herd those other people anywhere they want them to go. That is exactly what happened on 9/11.

You cannot fight terrorism by exiling yourself within an armed camp. By definition, the terrorists have then won the war, for they have terrorized you within your fortress and cut you off from the freedom to experience the beauty and wonders of this world.

Terrorists will always find the one flaw in your defense. No matter how paranoid and isolated you make yourself, you will always have some flaw in your defense. The only way you can beat terrorists is by giving them no reason to terrorize you.

Our government has made exactly the wrong choices to defeat terrorism. The cowboy and super-ego mentality of our current regime is not intellectual enough to realize it is not cowardly to admit that our enemies may have a good reason for hating us.

We have created the terrorists ourselves by our actions in the Middle East and we are making more terrorists with each bomb we drop and each woman and child we kill.

I have for many years spoken out against America's military and economic involvement in the Middle East and our capitalist and oil imperialism throughout the Arab world. That imperialism is what caused the 9/11 attacks on the World Trade Center and the Pentagon. That terrorism justified, in some people's minds, the adoption of the USA Patriot Act into law.

And now that Patriot Act can be used against me for speaking out against America's military and economic involvement in the Middle East and our capitalist and oil Imperialism, which caused the terrorism. The people who are most responsible for causing the atmosphere that created the terrorist attacks are now in a position to silence those of us who want to change that atmosphere and stop terrorism.

An even more profound terrorist attack on this country was the one Enron and Worldcom inflicted on the American people. And how the Enron and Worldcom terrorism was ignored by Washington will eventually have an even more damaging affect on this country than 9/11 did.

# CHAPTER 59

## Evolution Now or Revolution Later

### Where Did We Go Wrong?
### and How Can We Fix It?

This is serious. It is no time to ignore the messengers. No one wants to see our country dissolve into another Civil War as in the 1860s, but we are getting close.

There are people in the USA today who are seriously mistreated by the system, and there are liberal intellectuals in this country who know it is not healthy for a nation to fester as we are now. We feel the pain of this country's people.

As Thomas Paine said, it is inevitable that change will come some day one way or the other. Eventually, people will become so fed up they will revolt against the tyranny. If it is done now while we still have the semblance of democracy, it can be done peacefully with a consensus of the majority.

But if the powers that be today are able to steal any more of our freedoms and achieve any higher level of arrogance and totalitarian self-importance, there will be in our future another violent revolution, death and anarchy that will far exceed our War of Independence and Civil War. And no one, not even the conservative dictators, will profit from that.

We must start relying on the wisdom of our intellectual minds. Only benevolent, tolerant, cooperative and generous thinking will save us now.

I awaken in the morning and look at the front page of the paper, and I am reminded again how badly mankind has failed. Of all the intelligence, creativity and beauty humankind possesses, we are still wallowing in war, poverty and need-based crime.

Need-based crime? A hungry man is an angry man (Bob Marley) and also a possible criminal in order to support his family and their needs.

If I were to list all the problems of the world and assess the cause for each crime and inhumanity, it would all come down to the actions of a small number of people and a few simple reasons. Military, political, religious businessmen who are greedy and want to control the spiritual and financial lives of everyone else.

Are we going to let them continue to do this to us? It is our world too, and there are a whole hell of a lot more of us than them! I am an intellectual, and I want to set you free. I do not want to force you free, I want you to find your own freedom.

# CHAPTER 60

## Laws That Create Law-Breaking

*"If you want things fixed, ask an intellectual. You may not like the way he looks or smells, but self-pride and ego won't get in the way of his ideas. If you want this democracy to work, rely on intellectuals. You may not like the way they dress, but greed will not disrupt their decisions."*
Dudley Griffin

Poverty and despair cause anti-social behavior, and poverty and despair are often caused by societies marginalizing or forgetting people.

The conservative attitude of controlling people and the laws based on conservative thinking are forcing many people to break laws. If you don't trust people, you automatically make them untrustworthy by your attitude toward them. You force them to rebel against your rules. It is basic human nature, understood by the liberal mind, but overlooked or ignored by conservatives.

The do-as-I-sayers are people who do not trust people to do the right thing, and therefore, they want to force everybody to do as they say, even though, if you look into their own lives, they are hypocritical and are doing things contrary to what they say others should do.

Judge people by their actions, not their words.

The live-and-let-livers are the good people who are just trying to conduct peaceful, productive lives with a reasonable amount of prosperity and happiness. They, the live-and-let-livers, don't care what you do except when it hurts others. Your body is your body, and your mind is your mind. We sometimes warn you of the problems your actions cause for yourself and for others, but we will not advocate stopping you unless others suffer. Every person is physically in the center of their world, with everything going on and radiating out us. But most people don't try to have everyone around them praise, honor and defer to them because of that.

"They," the do-as-I-sayers, don't care what their actions inflict on other people. Most people think that they are the center of the earth; only the arrogant people make a big deal out of it.

Bigoted economy does not work for anyone except the wealthy. Immigrant workers stimulate small and medium-size business. The 2019 Nobel Prize winners have proven this. Social welfare does not harm the economy. Only the wealthy 1% capitalists believe otherwise and fight to end welfare support.

The corporations don't like small businesses taking "their" profit from them. And they also don't like having a society of people who will work for slave salaries, on which the corporates have no control. Business people don't like having a society of workers who will take a below-living standard wage who are not buying the high-priced crap that they are making. These are mostly our undocumented immigrants. We have to compromise on our ethnic prejudice and celebrate the hard work and sacrifices these people endure just to survive.

Benjamin Franklin said that compromises may not make great heroes but make great democracies.

"We" have to force a revolution of attitude in this country and the world. I believe strongly in the basic laws, ideals and systems of this country as do most good-hearted and respectable people.

I also believe most people of this country are respectable and good-hearted. But there is a core of leaders and businessmen in this country whose only allegiance is to power and money. "We," the live-and-let-livers, are the good people who are just trying to conduct peaceful, productive lives with a reasonable amount of prosperity and happiness. "They," the do-as-I-sayers, are conservative-minded, power-seeking, religious bigots and capitalists.

"We" have to stop letting them push us around. "We" have to first recognize who "they" are, and then start boycotting them, stop voting for them and stop buying "their stuff."

"Their stuff" is what is imprisoning us. Conservatives crave control of others, and the material goods "materialism" that they have infected upon us is how they control us. The advertising industry has convinced us that we must have all these things, and we have given them our souls to possess them.

The middle-class majority are the potential heroes of democracy and human freedom. A large, informed public is the solution to the hatred, war and intolerance in this world.

The "public," the "masses," possess the common sense necessary to create a utopia, a Garden of Eden here on earth. Our Founding Fathers knew this! That is why they tried to give the power to the people.

The creators of our democratic self-government knew that "the people" could and would, in the long run, compromise for the sake of the well-being of all. They knew that "the common sense" resided in the common people, not the rich and powerful.

In case you haven't noticed, things are getting worse for more people all the time. More debt, more stress, more medical expenses, less time with the family.

If you are happy with your life and financial circumstances, that's wonderful, but look around you. Is your happiness based only on the "stuff" you possess? Is all of it paid for? Meaning, have you paid off the debt that you are in to possess this stuff?

Society has placed its trust in the wrong people. We have come to believe that, if a person is a successful businessman or a lawyer, then he must be qualified to lead a government and create its laws.

Yes, but what kind of government does a businessman or lawyer want? The application of law in this country has come down to the issue of which of the lawyers is the best liar. The business world is much the same, and there is definitely no democracy in a corporation. Business is a totalitarian activity.

So the people who are now making the rules in this free speech, democratic country are well versed in lying and are experienced dictators. Fine, that makes a lot of sense.

Freedom of speech works only if the truth is spoken. If a person lies, he is not exercising his right to free speech; he is just plain breaking the rules of free speech. Power will corrupt anyone, but even more so someone who already has a taste for money. People seem to lie easily when money is the issue.

We have trusted people who are not trustworthy. They have their own economic agenda. We have been told by these businessmen and lawyers that this is a capitalist nation when actually capitalism is incompatible with democracy.

The silent majority has been led to believe that businessmen and lawyers are their friends, and anyone who thinks about that for a moment will realize it ain't so. Capitalists are your friends as long as you pay your bills and keep quiet. The silent majority has just become lazy. They are not paying attention to what is going on around them.

Common sense tells us not to employ the wolf to care for the sheep! Yet, in the U.S. government we do this all the time. No matter how many times the wolf disappoints us, we continue to give him the keys. Where money is involved, it is far too much temptation to a capitalist to give him the keys to this country and its economic prospects.

The people who make decisions about our economics should be intellectuals and educators. Their motives are much more benevolent than those of a businessman, and they understand far better the concept of economic and political democracy.

A businessman can be counted on to construct loopholes for himself and his friends. Intellectuals can be counted on to find loopholes for humanity.

A true democratic government must be devoted to the majority's interests, or it becomes a dictatorship run by a few people devoted to the interests of a few. We are very close to that right now.

We must separate business and state. We cannot have a democracy with corporate CEOs running the government.

Some people, especially those who are afraid of government controls of their business dealings, are against democratically run government. They say they are against big government because it is wasteful and impersonal. But they are actually opposed to a large administrative government because it scrutinizes their economic activities.

It is true that a big government can be wasteful and impersonal, but the real reason conservatives dislike a large government is because it exposes and curtails their own unscrupulous business dealings. If they can have their kind of government, they will support it. You see, conservative administrations actually create larger governments during their times, but it is a government that only agrees with their shenanigans.

We must stop putting our faith in people who have a personal economic agenda. Money is the root of all evil, and it has been the reason for every totalitarian government that has ever existed. A person's economic motives should be scrutinized before he is allowed to represent a democracy.

The silent majority thinks all the marching in the streets against oil and power companies and in support of the environment is some crazy hippie love-in, but this is serious. It is a life-and-death struggle against selfish and greedy people.

Liberals have actually been too quiet, too subdued, for too long. We are not confrontational by nature. It takes issues of real life-and-death importance for us to act.

But we have a lot of good ideas and solutions. That is what liberal intellectuals have to offer to the world. The world should be listening to these people. Not businessmen and lawyers.

*Paine*

"If there is any true cause of fear respecting independence it is because no plan is yet laid down. Men do not see their way out; wherefore, as an opening into that business I offer the following hints; at the same time modestly affirming, that I have no other opinion of them myself, than that they may be the means of giving rise to something better. Could the straggling thoughts of individuals be collected, they would frequently form materials for wise and able men to improve to useful matter."

Mankind's most vivid force is the ability to fix things. Included in that, of course, is knowing when something needs fixing. Because of man's knowledge of self in relation to other life, he is able to feel love, hate, comfort and pain. If man is displeased or pained by something, he can change it. All other animals just submit to their fates. Man is the only one who can fix it and alter the future.

To fix the mess we are in, we need to stop listening to people who receive an economic reward for creating the mess in the first place.

Reducing or dismantling the production of luxury items and frivolous commodities might seem like a drastic and even painful prospect. But it cannot be nearly as painful as starving to death, dying from lack of water or asphyxiating from lack of air.

These are in the future of your children's children if we do not change our attitude toward our air and water quality. If we do not better control the manufacturing of stuff in this world, we will not have the natural resources to live at all in forty years, let alone build the *newest robotic camera cell phone* model.

The most difficult concept for some people to accept, and yet the most important element in the creation of the United States of America, is a smooth and workable combination of freedom, coupled with rational laws within democracy. Both reasonable freedom and common sense social restrictions are necessary for the kind of uplifting and productive democracy our Founding Fathers envisioned.

It is more complex than just compromise. The problem is that some people want too much freedom for just themselves and more control of everyone else but themselves.

Those of you who proclaim you are a Jeffersonian or a Hamiltonian, or a Federalist or States' Righter are missing the point. These people, our Founding Fathers, were for the most part beyond names and egos. They were creating something new, self-government, an icon for humanity, a blueprint for the ages.

All countries, just as people, are born individuals, selfish and self-important, but if they learn in their progression as they age, they come to understand that they are only a part of humanity of the whole world. If a country and its people do not realize this, then they have not evolved as humans or as a country.

Mankind needs restrictions. Nature is chaos, and that is the way it is meant to be, but mankind has such a frightening potential for destruction that we need restrictions. Sovereignty of cities, states and even governments in this world is becoming counterproductive.

Each person, town, state or government has individual needs, but in the long run when they conflict with the big picture, the world, they must take second place. That is why we fought the Civil War, to keep the whole together so that it would not fragment this continent into conflicting values and desires.

We have a strong and just foundation for our country and our world--free enterprise, democracy, our Bill of Rights and good will toward all men. But the house that has been built on that rock has flaws. We do not need to tear down what we have. We do need to repair and to strengthen it.

I propose that voters start voting for people who actually live the same way they do, candidates who have the same economic concerns as their own.

Elect people with humanities and liberal arts degrees, not law and business degrees. Elect people who are interested in sociology, people and living, not business, money and conflict resolution.

Communism, the opposite economic ideology of capitalism, has been largely rejected in the world; it is time to do away with the other oppressive form of economics on this planet. Common sense would say that we should aim for an economic system right in the middle between these two offending opposites. It is time to create a form of free-enterprise/socialism that gives everyone the opportunity to benefit from their own hard work and yet protects our society from the problems that poverty creates.

If we had an astute and intelligent government, one that truly believed in our Constitution, freedom and democracy, it would work to curtail capitalist greed and promote truth in advertising and business. If we had a truly benevolent government, it would introduce a form of socialism into many essential occupations and infrastructures.

A responsible government would pump money into road and public works repairs, education, and the arts, and subsidize the poor. This would put money back into our economy and serve to create productive and useful human beings at the same time.

Is this too complex for our society to comprehend? Intellectuals see it. Although many Americans will oppose and be frightened by such drastic changes, this is the evolution of mankind.

If the economic situation of this country continues as it is going right now, we will soon have a small 10% of the population with all the money and the rest of us 90 % struggling to stay alive. That is exactly what the Founding Fathers of the United States were trying to avoid when they wrote the Declaration of Independence, the Constitution and our Bill of Rights.

Our Founding Fathers envisioned a country where the businessmen and working class worked in unison to create a good life and a peaceful society. They knew that, as long as there was economic tyranny and extreme poverty, there would be unrest, revolution and anarchy.

We left the Old World to get away from the feudal system, and now it has followed us here to America in the form of capitalism. We do not have another continent to go to in order to escape from the oppression of capitalism. We must stop it here.

Capitalism is greed and selfishness. For years we have counted on it as a way of life. For years we have considered it to be the way things are supposed to be. But now, to save our lives, we must turn completely 180 degrees and start treating others as we would have others treat us.

Looking at the timeline of our population and environment, it is obvious to a thinking man that we, the humans of the world, don't have much more time to experiment with the wisdom given us during the last 300 years. If we don't act now, all is lost.

If we are to save this world, mankind and any semblance of human dignity, we must embrace peace, love, tolerance and generosity.

It is going to be difficult at first to reject some of the human traits witch we have long believed basic to our humanness, yet it will become easy once we see the rightness and the results.

Just because some traits seem to be basic human nature doesn't mean that they are correct moral behavior. We humans are, above all, evolving creatures. The fact that something seemed to be proper behavior yesterday, does not mean that we must cling to it today. And most rationally, we must question certain actions since all evidence of common sense proves that they are destructive to humankind.

There have been monumental changes in the history of mankind triggered by a simple thought. There have been massive emotional transformations in the thinking of mankind precipitated by one simple act.

A 180 degree turn would make this world paradise. We are capable of it. We must do it!

This is one of those times in history when we need a movement, event or moment that changes not only the physical, but the actual psychological, history of mankind. If not, humankind does not have much more history to write.

The average person today is bombarded by television which we feel we must watch, and then the ever-expanding computer world for which we spend hours in learning curves and then the iPhone cyber babble called social media that actually separates us by space and time; so no wonder we are not accomplishing anything for all of us as humanity!

# CHAPTER 61

## Lawyers, CEOs and Industrial Chiefs

Democratic governments should not be run by lawyers. Such governments, which pretend to favor the masses, should also not be run by businesspeople who profit from the laws of government. Democratic governments must be run by educators, historians, scientists and liberal arts professors. Or at least these kinds of people should make all decisions that affect the well-being and future of the masses of people who are the world. For that is what democratic government was meant to be, by the people for the people. Maybe we should come up with a new term for democratic governing.

Nowadays most lawyers and doctors do not choose those professions out of conviction or passion. They choose them for wealth or status. Those who do choose these professions for altruistic or spiritual calling are soon disillusioned. It doesn't have to be that way. Greed has gotten in the way of two formerly lofty and respected professions.

# CHAPTER 62

## Children, Education and our Future

### The dumbing down of the public

The media, corporations and many in government representatives today are involved in dumbing down the public, and that starts, of course, with children.

Corporations don't like to guess about what the people want to buy because that costs them more money therefore, they don't like educated, free-thinking and curious people. They dumb down through advertising.

Governmental administrations sometimes don't want to have too many questions asked about what they are doing, and so they like passive people. So they dumb down.

Our Founding Fathers sought free education for the public so that the people could advance, move on, become good citizens! Now, with the commercialization of all higher education, our education system is dumbing down.

And, parents, what you teach your children will most possibly come back to haunt you or bless you. Choose well what you teach. What you do today to divert, pacify or quiet your child could push them into ignorance or rebellion, from which you and the world will later suffer.

Also parents: chose to be parents. Don't just let it happen. Use birth control if you are not ready to have children, whom you will have to love, nurture and teach to be good citizens of this planet.

**And**

**To "Ms. or Miss, or Maybe Now Mrs." Wright and All Other Pro-Overpulationists**

*"I'm only trying to save the world from overpopulation."*
JOB

No Godless liberal is going to force you to use birth control or to have an abortion. Only conservatives force laws on people. Liberals are fighting for a woman's rights and freedoms in the US Constitution. We are not asking to change the Constitution as you are.

We are only asking you to use common sense and save the planet and mankind by choosing to control your procreation.

If life on earth reaches the critical point of self-destruction because of too many babies, then authorities will have to ask you to stop fucking, and then if you don't, we will all have to vote for alternatives. Then if the majority chooses mandatory birth control, the authorities will make you follow the rule of law. I know better; no one is going to stop people from having sex, but every egg does not have to hatch.

No, silly girl, there is no mention of abortion in our Constitution, but it is explicit in our Constitution that a woman has the right to have one if she wants it. And, by the way, there is no mention of fetuses in the Bible.

The liberal community and Planned Parenthood have never considered abortion a proper solution to population control or family planning. Birth control and real sex education, not abstinence, are the proper solutions. By the way, anyone with a drop of brains and any knowledge of mankind's history knows abstinence is a hoax.

If you conservatives didn't fight realistic sex education and birth control (in the world,) we would have a handle on population and unwanted pregnancy. Your naive rhetoric about sex education creating promiscuity is yet another self-deceiving pronouncement. Sex does not need advertising! Young people will find it no matter what "grown-ups" do. It is God's gift of creation. Only rational understanding of the pitfalls will slow it down.

Conservatives think only in one dimension. They are concerned solely with their own survival, and be damned with the problems of others who are poor, trapped in oppressive societies, or ignorant (usually because of conservative meddling).

Liberals think about the problems of other people and other generations. Note the term you have given us: bleeding hearts! But what is the opposite of bleeding hearts? Heartless! And that is what conservatives are.

I doubt you will read this, and if you do, your mind will not be able to handle it. So I will tell you with the wisdom of spiritual knowledge far older than Christianity, you and those like you are so out of touch with the realities of life that you have become the anti-Christ which you fear so much.

Peace, the Golden Rule, and may you change before your soul is lost.

*PS, 12/27/19: "The situation of overpopulation has become a life-or-death situation for the human race. Don't you think it is time for Christians to get real and accept birth control and abortion under common sense laws of nature? That is, unless you are committed to the apocalypse for the sake of your "faith," and to hell (sorry) with everyone else on earth! Apocalyptic thinking is a self-fulfilling attitude. If you look forward to something, you will work toward it or let it happen."*
John Bassett McCleary.

# CHAPTER 63

## Reflections on Slavery and an Apology

### To the Descendants of Slaves

Slavery was incompatible with the principles of the American Revolution. We know that now, but at the time it was an issue that could have ended the dreams of a nation if we did not compromise.

Ignoring the hypocrisy of slavery in our Declaration of Independence and Constitution was the only big mistake in the creation of the United States of America. It is an oversight that has haunted us ever since and continues to damage our national personality to this day.

Historians will tell you with unquestioned certainty that, without the compromise we made on slavery, this nation would not exist in the form we have today, good or bad. Those same historians will tell you that our compromise on slavery has also threatened this union, as we know it, from the very beginning several times throughout our history.

Ridiculing ourselves for past mistakes and second-guessing past decisions is a not productive use of our time. We know that the outline given us by our forefathers is the moral high ground, even though we have thus far been unable to complete the dream.

The only way to justify our ideals of freedom is to move on and make sure the end result of our experiment is a realization of the original intent, which was "liberty (freedom) and justice for all."

The one cultural trait, the one devastating human flaw, that caused us to compromise on slavery 232 years ago, is the same social failing that still haunts us and continues to create all the pain and suffering in our world today. Greed and selfishness caused humans to become intolerant of other humans, thus creating slavery and inhumanity upon our own mankind.

Prejudice causes more prejudice; segregation creates more justification for segregation and prejudice. In every case, prejudice is a self-fulfilling prophecy. If you disenfranchise a person due to expectations of their failure, they will, of course, fail because of your negative treatment of them. Slaves are a product of slavery; ignorance is a product of ignorance.

# CHAPTER 64

## Reflections on Manifest Destiny
## and an Apology to Its Victims

Most Americans of immigrant heritage are sorry we stole this country from the Native Americans and Mexican-Americans. And that's a start, but we're not willing to give it all back.

I, for one, don't think giving Native Americans the right to run gambling casinos is an appropriate compensation for our theft. From what I see, it plays right into the hands of the capitalist movement which was responsible for stealing the country in the first place. Gambling is just another way to enslave people and separate them from their property.

I think an appropriate way to apologize to Native Americans and Mexican-Americans and to give back some of what was taken, is to welcome them into the American dream. I feel that equal citizenship, equal rights and equal freedom, given sincerely without question, are the best compensation we can give.

## CHAPTER 65

# "Bleeding Hearts,"
# and "Warm and Fuzzy"

This is the only humorous and sarcastic chapter in this book. If anyone of you honestly believe that bleeding hearts and warm and fuzzy are subversive activities and a communist plot, then you are truly twisted.

# CHAPTER 66

## This Is Not What GOD Intended for Man!

This is not what God had in mind when he created mankind. If you think that this society would be acceptable to any real god, then you do not know what deity is!

CHAPTER 67

# The 1960s Revolution

*"Let's all get together, become hippies, figure it out and fix it!"*

The hippie movement is the most important cultural development of the last 100 years. The only mistakes of that movement were its clothing statements, its youth, rebellion and thus a tendency to offend the middle class.

This book is a liberal manifesto. And though I may be critical of the government of the United States, I would be just as critical of the French, New Zealand, or North Korean governments if I were living in those countries and they were being as violent and undemocratic.

I have both chosen this country and been chosen by it. I was born here. This country chose me. I also spent much of the Reagan and Nixon years trying to find another country to love and to live in. In the end, I returned home to the United States because of my passion for this country and its potential.

The phrase "Love it or Leave It" is strange since the reason we hippies are demonstrating about the excesses of this country is because we do love this country, and particularly the concept upon which it was created.

This country is in more peril today than it has been since the Civil War. And, as with the Civil War, the threat is not from outside the country, but from within.

In fact, the threat is from the highest levels of our own government. We are being lied to, cheated and stolen from by the military, industrial, capitalist, and conservative powers in this country. Our freedoms are being eroded at an alarming rate. More damage has been done to the American Constitution and our freedoms by Republican administrations than by any invading army or foreign government.

Anyone who does not know this to be true is not paying attention or is not interested in knowing the truth. The fact that the majority of the American people are unaware of the threat to democracy and their own freedom is appalling. We must get the information out there in spite of the conspiracy by the conservative networks and media.

Talk, write, email, phone, carry placards, demonstrate.

We must have an intellectual revolution. It must be peaceful, but forceful. It must be a change brought about by the power of the pen and the mind. No violence must be used. That would only play into their hands. In fact, they are doing everything within their power to create violence so they can suppress it and make themselves even more powerful.

We have seen what they did with 9/11. The oil companies brought about 9/11 by their imperialism in the Middle East and then used it to elicit sympathy from the great, ignorant masses to start this war, to get more oil and to become more powerful.

These misguided men, drunk on power and privilege, must be shown the strength of the pen, of truth and of common sense. We must use our minds, the one faculty that raises mankind above all other animals and brings him closest to God. All we have to do is tell the truth, loudly and clearly, and we can save this world from the men who wish only to exploit it.

The year is 2020: the USA is being run (I will not say governed) by a pack of corporate CEOs and conservative capitalists who have no idea what it is like to be a normal working person. Corporate businessmen should never be allowed to administer a democracy since the businesses they are accustomed to are normally run as dictatorships.

The world is getting crowded. The more people in this small container, the more important cooperation is. If we don't cooperate, we will die in a conflagration of anarchy.

Everyone has the same problems we do. We are all suffering from the same pressures. It is how we deal with these pressures that makes the difference. If you want to live in a perfect world, you must treat others perfectly.

Everyone is different, yet everyone is the same! If you can grok that, you will have solved the problems of this world.

Be aware, this is a spiritual revolution, not of any one god, but of all life itself. Get out and see how beautiful this world is. Look into your creative side. Enjoy the life of living. Kill your TV.

Thomas Paine was one of the first voices of reason in the American experience. I, for one, will not let his vision die.

Liberals are going to have to get tough in the only way they know how. We must speak the truth long and hard. This book is the opening volley of words in an effort by the intellectuals and liberals of this country to take America back to its roots of freedom and democracy.

In this book I have accused conservatives and capitalists of lies, theft, abuse of power and hypocrisy, and I stand behind those accusations. But I also know that these people cannot help themselves. They are driven to that kind of activity by their basic nature.

Due to a different set of values, capitalists feel little or no compassion for others or remorse for their actions. Their one-dimensional thinking causes them to be selfish. For this, I feel sorry for them, yet it will not deter me from confronting them with their transgressions.

As a liberal intellectual, it is my nature to be fair and compassionate toward capitalists and conservatives, but I must still expose and hold a light to their hypocrisy and their crimes. My deepest hope is that they will see the error of their ways and eventually change into cognizant and productive human beings.

Respectable human cultures usually have a "social contract." This sacred contract, though mostly unwritten, usually states that all members of society have a place and a value, and they must be supported and kept healthy in order for society to continue functioning.

The United States and its capitalist leadership have forgotten about the importance of such a social contract. This lapse in understanding of and compassion for human needs has created a confrontational atmosphere that will destroy America and the dream upon which it was founded.

Workers must be given more respect by corporations. Families must not be looked upon as just consuming units. People should not be just numbers.

The arrogance of corporate CEOs is dismantling the creation of our Founding Fathers. Money has taken precedence over life itself.

Most government decisions in this country today are made for economic expedience by capitalist dictators, not of the people, for the people or by the people.

We, you and I, rich and poor, Democrat and Republican, cannot let this happen. We must stop allowing businessmen to make decisions determining the life and death of people. If you consider the difference between people and businessmen and understand the evil of greed, you will agree that it would be much better if people had the power of life and death over businessmen, rather than the other way around.

Very good movies, very good songs and very good books often combine pathos and humor to tell a story. I am sorry to say that, yes, this book contains very little humor to entertain you on your pathway to the message it offers. It mostly has facts, anger and hope, sadly because in our society and government today, there is very little to laugh about.

America has lost its soul in the pursuit of wealth. The arts, culture, true beauty and deep thought and contemplation have been replaced by reality TV and uplift bras. There will not be much to laugh about until we find our souls again.

The darkest hour is just before dawn, and this is indeed one of the darkest times in this country's history. Our government is run by criminals who are masquerading as Christians. Christ would never condone what these people are doing. The American public must rise up inside the voting booth and create a brighter day for tomorrow!

I am going to leave you now, but I will not leave you alone. If you want to quiet my words, you might kill the messenger, but you will never suppress these ideals, for there are many others like me.

I am John Bassett McCleary and I approve of this message. I am an American patriot, and I am mad as hell, and I'm not going to take it any longer! 3/26/03

Power to the people, and may all of the many gods bless America and the whole world.

> *"Reagan, Nixon, Bush, Bush and Trump, you should be ashamed of yourselves! Everything you did was to benefit the wealthy and to enslave the rest of the population!"*
> Ug 400,000 BC

CHAPTER 68

# Open Letter to Millennials

## Day One

I don't worry about what you are doing to your own life; I care, but I don't worry! I just don't want you to fail, and by doing so diminish the world as we know it, flawed as it is. My generation, the LOVE generation, at least made an effort to save the world and improve it, and in doing so we put off 1984. What are you going to do?

I am still concerned about stupid things other people do because, if they continue to keep doing these things, they will have effect on themselves, you and me!

I can bet you that most of the people running this government today never watched *M.A.S.H, Star Trek*, or *Wall Street*; they definitely have not read the good parts of the Bible!

You can't intelligently vote, question authority, or voice dissent unless you have facts, and by facts I mean the true facts. And facts indicate high I.Q., the Ignorance Quotient

Nothing is more powerful than an idea! You Millennials will say that a sil-chip is more powerful, but without the idea first, the chips would not exist. Now with all these chips producing new ideas, some people are altering tomorrow. There are good tomorrows and bad tomorrows. We must, MUST, find a way to control bad ideas or talk people out of bad ideas. The media, all the media, must be taught to be moral or we, I mean all of us, will suffer and may not survive. Every human being who believes in the Golden Rule should, <u>must,</u> vote out those who do to others what they wouldn't want done to themselves.

The real twist to this is that anything you do in this small world you are actually doing to yourself, and definitely to your family and children! A gated community cannot protect you from your own stupidity and greed!

I am very impressed by the ingenuity of man, but if the ingenuity of man is killing man, I want to take another look.

If you think you are a geek and you think nobody likes you for who your really are, then you may be a geek. There is nothing wrong with that, but thinking nobody likes you is going to make sure no one will want to like you. Be positive about who you are, and don't let peer pressure bring you down. Someday you may be an individual, and only individuals do really new things.

I wish we could receive wisdom from our mother's milk, but in lieu of that, we must find someone who is calm and gives a voice to everyone else, then listen to them.

He who is in possession of the truth must first question that it is the truth and then be quiet until he know it is true.

## Open Letter to Millennials
### Day Two

People who read make better political, economic and personal choices. No, this is not a liberal wet dream; there is something about a word coming through the eyes and being translated into a word that creates a visual picture of that word which expands a person's intelligence and curiosity. It makes common sense that, if you know all the facts, you will make the best decisions. As well, if you listen to only one source of media or political discussion and don't read or listen to other possibilities, you will maintain your ignorance, and soon you will be recognized as a fool.

The male ego is not only the most dangerous weapon on the earth, but it is also the only self-perpetuating weapon.

So here are a few questions, suggestions and comments for people who don't want to answer questions, take suggestions or hear comments:

How do you give tough love to a masochist? How do you tell the truth to an egotist? How do you reprimand an insecure person?

Of what value to anyone is bigotry? Does it make you happy, does it make them happy, does it make the world a better place?

Don't stop me now!

People, stop doing crazy things! It does not produce the best image of your efforts or passion. You may be correct in your crusade, but you will cheapen your message by killing other people, or running around naked with a cross around your neck, or with your misspelled tweets, or your assault weapons.

Countercultures are both a refuge from the status quo and the offspring of the corruption and stagnation of the status quo.

Love conquers all that wants to be conquered.

Most people want love, peace and friendship, but then, why haven't we made it happen? It's easy to do--just stop being self-centered, greedy and bigoted.

Vanity is very dangerous to the creative process. It may make you money to begin with, but the bigger your ego, the longer your prison term.

All the wonderful ideas that creative people come up with to advance the comfort and knowledge of mankind are usually eventually usurped by the accountants and capitalists, who then use these "health and labor-saving" devices to siphon off the income of the working man.

Find a hobby that is outside the computer-driven world of social media and gaming. Several reasons: one, you may, no you will, get bored someday when your mind expands. The other, you will get fat, lazy and destroy your health and live a short life because of body abuse. Your genes, your exercise and your food, drugs and drink will determine your quality and length of life.

Nobody, except maybe Mick Jagger, always gets what they want in this life, and I'm sure he would have something to say about that.

May your god bless you and not curse others!

## Open Letter to Millennials
## Day Three

There are some things I can learn from you, such as how to re-program my cell phone every six months to compensate for industry changes. So is this what you want to accomplish in your life, to learn new programs and hardware over and over and over again?

I am pretty sure I will not be able to change the habits and minds of the "Greatest Generation" or even most of the people of my own age, but maybe I can awaken you Millennials up to new/old concepts of social and political rationality.

Two of the most dangerous activities humans do in their lives are driving a car and smoking tobacco cigarettes. If you really want to reduce your life expectancy, add texting or talking on the cell phone to create the troika of death.

The world is suffering from demented egos, demented competition and demented capitalism. If everything is going well, your ego will do you well, but when it comes down to real life, you better start using common sense. If you get your ego involved in any activity of your life, it will diminish your objectivity, your common sense, and your compassion. No human is the center of the earth. We are all on the earth together, and we are affected by one another. Let's try to be helpful, courteous and kind, and maybe then we can all have a good life.

If I place money or material things before friends or family, then I am one really screwed-up person.

Catfishing, oh, that's one I love! Catfishers, you are breaking most of the social and moral laws, and what's worse, the laws of your own self-respect. Don't pretend to be what you are not, because then you become nothing. Don't lie to other people about who you are, because then you are lying to yourself, and those are two of the worst sins a human being can commit.

Anyone who lies is both immoral and a criminal. "Thou shalt not bear false witness," from the Ten Commandments. If you lie you are forsaking your own convictions and your own validity. It is a horrible reflection on your person. Why would anyone want to become a pariah to society and to themselves?

We have to find a way to deal with human conflict using something other than violence. After all, we are potentially the best communicators among all the creatures of the world.

Don't transfer your own hang-ups or prejudices to the actions of others; they may actually be perfect human beings, and there are many of them out here. Real life is not a reality TV show!

If you don't know the meaning of any word in this letter, please look it up. There is a correct word for every situation. Precise communications are most responsible for humankind's greatness.

## Open Letter to Millennials
### Day Four

<u>Now</u> is the time to make your choice. Are you going to live life traveling the high road or the low road, the good side or the dark side of the force, the positive or the negative, *Star Trek* or *Star Wars*? Are you going to be a killer or a protector of life?

You can't break an old dog from bad habits. The older you get, the harder it is to break the habits of your past. A bad habit you have for a year will take you a year and a day to break ... of course, unless you are smarter than the average dog!

It is possible to overcome an unhappy childhood? You have to be stronger mentally than your tormentors are, physically or emotionally. Human beings are capable of evolving in a very short time. Don't blame your parents or the bully at your school; you can overcome, and it starts by exploring, reading and watching the progressive media. You may be tempted by people who tell you that you must fight back with hate and weapons, but their agenda is power and intimidation. You can beat the dark side only by rising above it.

I am sure there must be some positive movies and TV directed toward Millennials and people under 29, but I haven't found any yet. Clue me in if you find them.

Some of you are voting now, and I hope so! Voting is one of the most powerful and decisive actions you can take in your life. Finding a mate, an occupation and a home are in that group. Vote for good people who are patriots to democracy and the Constitution and Bill of Rights, but please do not vote for those politicians who use those sacraments just to make money and gain power. It is known in the heads of most people that democracy and the U.S. Declaration of Independence, Constitution and Bill of Rights are the most beneficial documents and ideas ever conceived to protect the safety and well-being of most people in America and, ideally, the world. That would be, in my estimation, 97% of humans.

Every time I get down about something, I remember that when I do so, it brings me down further. And when I am happy, I get higher, and those around me mirror my mood, and I mirror their mood back at them. We all benefit! Breaking the downward spiral may be the best thing your brain can do.

Don't ever say never! Always question why you don't want to do something, and maybe some day you might realize your judgment was wrong.

Insecurity is acquired by allowing others to set your limitations. Arrogance is not self-confidence; it is insecurity. You can't fight your inadequacies; you can only rise above them!

The hippie definition of arrogant: Self-centered due to a feeling of deficiency and sometimes shame.

*Karma, a Sanskrit word for "action" or "deed." A form of fate inherited from former lives or accumulated from good or bad deeds committed previously. A belief held by many Eastern religions that we create our own "luck' through our actions; a form of cause and effect.* (From *The Hippie Dictionary*)

# Open Letter to Millennials
## Day Five

The discourse is getting more serious; the consequences are getting more terminal for this world! The people who are fighting human evolution and even hampering the survival of humankind are getting crazier with their arrogance and un-democratic attitude. So, in spite of my harmonious, liberal nature, I must fight them with what I have. My words will not lie, libel or incite violence against my enemies, as they would do to me. I will speak freely within the laws given us by our Founding athers. Truth and democracy are always the moral path.

Conservatives don't understand, nor do they like, good people. Good people make them feel insecure and a bit embarrassed. Conservatives like self-righteous people, but they don't like righteous people. Morality to a right-winger is a weakness. Hypocritical morality is more to their liking. Saying one thing and doing the opposite is the "Republican way."

Many computer games use humor to camouflage violence. They know the visceral impulses toward fighting attract more people than the intellectual messages toward diplomacy. Thomas Jefferson would love this discourse. Education is the great equalizer, not the divider that some say. Peace and good humor require a brain! Violence and bad humor require ignorance.

Our current president is incompetent, irreverent and obstructive. His administration is beginning to look like that of Stalin and Hitler. What he is doing is firing everybody around him who does not agree with his stupidity, so he can become our dictator. The only problem is that he is way dumber than those two other most destructive dictators of all times. We are in for a bad century if we don't get rid of him.

Advertisers, please stop raising the volume of your commercials on my TV, you scum! Someone with a capitalist mind will always shaft other people.

Many people today can't get anything of real importance done because they are too busy answering Facebook, tweeting, texting, selfie-taking and cursing "social" media. "Social" media is not really social! It may be media, but it is actually self-indulgence. It makes many people feel safe from the complexity of real human contact.

Most conservatives don't have the brain capacity to think themselves out of being wrong!

*Stranger Things* and other TV dramas and reality shows are making people think it is OK to be stupid. At least they think they are getting their 15 seconds of fame or infamy, but they are so dumb they don't realize other people think they are dumb. What value is that to your life or self-esteem? Remember, you can never live down something you do or say on the Internet; it follows you forever. One day you may want to run for office, get a good job or find a rational mate.

People who are not too smart about the realities of life will fight for their right to make lots of money from others. People who know what real life is about will fight for our environment and the right to live in harmony with others.

## Open Letter to Millennials
## Day Six

Truth and knowledge are the only things we have left that can save us. We can't hide our heads in the sand anymore because the earth is now polluted and toxic.

Everything wrong in this world today is driven by desire, fueled by advertising, paid for by corporations looking for more profits from people who don't need the product or service and who can't pay for it.

Some people say there are two sides to every argument; they say it should at least be a win-win situation. Not so! If your reason to win is immoral, against the benefit of the majority, or for your ego or pocketbook alone, then you do not deserve to win anything. We in this world have to stop following the greedy man's argument that because he is arrogant and a better liar, he deserves to win.

The Parkland shooter survived. Most shooters don't survive, and they will forever be monsters. Did you see the footage of the brother of the monster who killed the people at Parkland? The killer was crying and blubbering; he said he was sorry, that it was too late to redeem himself. He will always be a crying, spineless, monster. Yet when he planned the killings and while he was taking innocent lives, he thought he was a big man, a warrior and soon to be a famous person. No, he is not famous; he is not even a person. He is as stupid as the gun he used. If there is a hell, he will live in it for eternity, and right now he is trapped in a living hell because he forced others, the survivors and families of the dead, into a living hell.

The capitalists are just going to keep powering on getting their share, in spite of the obvious facts that capitalism is killing this world and our society. The taste for money overpowers some people's common sense and morality. Of course, these capitalists will be dead before their atrocities cause the destruction of this world. But what about the capitalists' children and their beautiful little grandchildren? Oops, they haven't thought of that!

To the real corporate thieves of the world, it is not actually about money; it is about who is on top, who is in and who is out. Ego!

The United States must be saved for democracy, not capitalism.

Maybe someday our moral and physical lives will begin to agree with each other.

Why do young people's movies and TV require such large amounts of violence and death? Normal life does not have that amount of carnage. Well, I think I know why, and that is because the producers are just trying to get attention to cover up their poor scripts. And you know what it does to young minds? It makes Millennials think violence is acceptable behavior, and that is not good for the future of our society. Also, dealing with suicide is a subject where you have to know your audience and not use killing yourself as sensational or as an alternative to life.

There are smarter people in this world than you, just as there are smarter people than I, but if you or I let our egos get in the way, we will never learn what other people know. Learning should not stop after school!

## Open Letter to Millennials
## Day Seven

Someone stole a Buddha statue, someone opened bottles in a store and spit in them, someone pet-napped someone's dog. What kind of mindless idiot would do those things? Someday when they are older and hopefully wiser, they will think about their life and contributions and sins. It will not be a happy time for them! It may destroy them; their karma will come back at them; prison, depression, drug-induced self-abuse, perhaps suicide, may be the consequences.

Millennials, if you play with bad people, cheating or stealing from others, eventually your playmates will do the same to you. A criminal usually gets burned by his closest criminal friend. Stay clean; your life will be better off for it.

We all have egos. Some people's egos exclude others; most people's egos at least recognize the value of other people.

From many years of observation, I have learned that maybe 10% of our U.S. population gets their satisfaction from being arrogant, criminal and/or frightening. They do this because they think it makes them appear to be strong, more important and decisive. Being strong and decisive is only a good human trait if you are doing it for the common good and not because you are insecure. Of course, the conservatives think common consciousness is a weakness!

People of color, diverse ethnicity, women and LGBTQIA should fight and vote against this president. That would be a majority of the population of this country, because he is threatening all of us, including many of those who voted for him the last time. Even a green, two-headed squirrel would be a better president because at least it would be passively accepting of our Constitution and America's founding ideals instead of tweeting unpatriotically.

Many younger people today think that rules, morality and compassion are old, unnecessary ideals. If I remember, I did so myself when young. Fortunately, I did not make mistakes in those areas for which I or anyone else suffered. Rules, morality and compassion can be considered to have debatable definitions, but everyone possessing common sense knows they should all be founded on the Golden Rule!

The media is dumbing you down. Look for shows and movies that challenge your mind with real life lessons, history and environmental issues.

Am I the only one, or do you agree it is getting harder to figure who or what is real?

The answer to our present socio-economic mess is to adopt the best and most humane parts of both free enterprise and socialism so we can become reasonable human beings! It comes down to this: are you a Klingon or a human?

## Open Letter to Millennials
### Day Eight

I hate locks on doors. They take up so much time and paranoia in our lives. Maybe if we fed, clothed and housed everybody on the planet, we could do away with locks, wars, guns and prisons. To do that, and we do have the ability to do so, we would have to neutralize the 1%, not kill or imprison them, just change their minds.

Fantasy is meant to remain fantasy; that is what the word means. Reaching out and making your fantasies real will teach you that the reality is not as exciting or safe as you think.

As you get older and your dreams falter into reality, the way it happens with most of us, you will begin to look more toward the progressive viewpoints, the viewpoints of our Founding Fathers and hippies. Pay your insurance premiums, or, better yet, vote for socialized medicine, because later in your life you will need it. This applies to other hot-button political and social issues, such as separation of church and state, free education, and equal tax structure. Vote liberal and save the world.

# Haiku

I am not with you
and the music of your life
with your earphones on

I hope I am wrong
this smell of burning is my
own world around me

a leg to stand on
and do I really have one
in this autumn rain

you have an answer
both he and she do as well
listen, listen too

society works
as long as we can retreat
to a coffeehouse

always be kind to
strangers who just might become
friends or enemies

## "Tweet"

War is stupid except to people who profit from it. They're smart;
they make you fight and die for them. A dead man in camo surrounded by collateral women and children shows as debit <u>and</u> credit to the
capitalists in Washington, DC. So F.Y.

Don't you just love the computer age? It saves so much frivolous time for us!

I have to hurry up and write all these things because someday soon many people won't be able to understand the words or the nuances of what I say.

Don't ever decide to take up arms against the people you despise, for then you become just as hideous as they are.

God forbid, but if you are ever confronted with a cowardly mass murderer (and all of them are wimps), run toward him. If everyone ran toward him, even without weapons, he would kill fewer; he would panic and be subdued.

The conservative, capitalist mind is like a germ or virus. I see its damage, but I don't understand why it wants to be so destructive or how it gains pleasure from or justifies what it does.

## Open Letter to Millennials
### Day Nine

You Millennials, and most likely all people born after 1980, will have to experience all the horrors that are now being predicted for this world, such as anarchy, food and water shortages, maybe global nuclear war, and hungry and desperate people killing each other just to live. The liberals and hippies have been predicting this would happen and have been trying to stop it since the 1950s. The conservatives, robber barons and capitalists have been busy working to produce the destruction of polite human society since the early 19th century. If you don't vote these people out and stop buying their junk, you, not they, will suffer, die and see the world of reason disintegrate.

What is wrong with mankind? Are we self-destructive? Are we self-absorbed? Are we insecure? Yes, yes, yes! But there is something more--an even more diabolical element to humankind that is possibly driving us to destruction. We have curiosity! We have fear! We have the sex drive! We have selfishness! Yes, yes, yes, yes! Which one of these will be our destruction? I think humankind has been through so much toil and trouble that we are tired. We would like to see some progress. We want a quick fix, but it doesn't work that way. This human evolution takes time and work.

Some people don't want to wait and work for success, so they lie, cheat and steal to see some progress. But the evolution of mankind will take time and good, rational and moral actions. It isn't going to be purchased cheaply or even with money or force. We won't be given back the Garden of Eden until we deserve it. There are some cynics, socio/economic/religious scholars, who say we can never save mankind and its home; it's too late. I tend to agree with them intellectually, but humankind is a fighter, and I have my hopes.

If I were to say I would solve all the problems of the world, I would be vilified first. Then, picking myself up, I would again try the same thing I did before to get rid of religion, greed and hatred--introduce love, art and music. Then, if they let me live, I would build a world government, open all borders, and divide all the money amongst everyone. Then, after I got out of jail, I might win accord. But then we would have to do it again in 100 years because the egotistical, greedy people would have broken down the perfect world to get it all back.

So the robber barons sucked the last penny out of the public, and that created the 1929 depression and the 2008 recession, and the capitalists wonder why the public can't buy their cars, houses and luxury items. You can't get blood out of a pickle! Let's get rid of our luxury egos, deceptive advertising and predatory profits. That is the American way to restart the American Dream.

Now corrupt and guilty politicians are creating conspiracy theories (about themselves) just to muddy the waters of truth, so that when the politicians lie, people cannot tell which is true and which is false.

From my reading, my observations and long life of critical thinking, I can see no proof that God takes sides or rewards the good over the evil. At least I have never seen, read of heard of God showing any favoritism since some things that were written in the presently acknowledged Bible back around 250 A.D. No concrete evidence has ever been recorded that God or Christ ever gave preferential treatment just because someone professed a belief in God or Christ. Job of the Old Testament was the prime example of how humans think that deities, all deities, treat both humble or rebellious human beings.

If you know the history of humankind, you will observe that "God" has let a lot of horrible people have their way and kill a lot of good people without God's interference. Even more interesting is that good people, good businesses, towns, states or countries, are not spared discomfort, pain or death. Also, Christian countries are not spared indiscriminate misfortune.

Faith in God's divinity does not give us a get-out-of-jail card, and faith in God's divinity does not prove that the god you are following is the "real God." I am leaning toward fate as the culprit in all of our happiness and/or misfortune. Along with that, I believe good or bad human choices play a big part. Just like chess. you have to look several moves ahead and also know the inclinations of your opponent and your own history.

Millennials, it's OK! Make the changes you want, yet remember, you will have to live with what you've made. My advice: be gentle, think of the rest of us poor and old folk. I'm sure that if you take some time to think, you will find the best solution for that situation and time. But then get ready; be prepared for the time when someone younger and more anxious comes to alter your creation, and in some cases destroys it or perhaps improves it.

A lot of people write off bigotry as a minor social crime, but it is one of the cancers of our world that has made all of our lives, all our ethnic and religious cultures, a living hell at one time or another. The British can attest to that, and it is possibly the real reason they will decline. But what could the alternative be? Let's all feed and love and protect all of us in the world, and then we could talk to each-other and solve the problems and live happily ever after.

Robber barons--I assume you have heard of them. It is the old name for capitalists. I am now officially reintroducing that term. Capitalists are robber barons who were feudal lords in the old countries.

Have you ever considered becoming a pervert? A pervert is someone who, being insecure and maybe unable to communicate rationally with potential mates, decides to direct their sexuality toward things such as voyeurism, pornography, stalking and rape, which usually causes them to be constantly frustrated, incarcerated and forced to register as a sex offender. Is that the way you want to live your life?

Don't use pride to make up for ignorance!

Or you just may be one of those greedy wimps who says, "I'm going to quit the human race and fend for myself; to heck with all the rest of the people! I want money and power; so fudge the rest of humankind!"

## Open Letter to Millennials
### Day Ten

Let me try get this straight for you. My definition of a Millennial is someone who is around 35 years old and younger. I believe the age of profound reasoning is something like 10 years old. Anyone who was 10 years old in 2000 would be 29 years old today. For slippage and individual education, I will say anyone 35 or younger could be called a Millennial

Of course now we the X and Y generations, but until they make a real name for themselves I cannot make any judgment or suggestions.

The Ruining Class: That is what I call the ruling class (today) because they ruin everything for all the rest of us. We now, again, have a ruling class here in the United States of America. King George of England in 1776 was the last ruler of the people of the 13 Colonies of America. We are not supposed to have a ruling class; we are a democracy. Mankind has been trying to get rid of the ruling class for thousands of years. Almost all of the colonists and immigrants to America were escaping the feudal and/or royalty systems, but the feudal lords followed, became robber barons and now we have a ruling class again.

How did we let them take over our lives again as they did in the old countries? Today we don't have monarchs, land barons and feudal lords; we have a new ruling class. They rule us not as political leaders, but through economics, profits on goods and services, not necessarily by taxes, though that is a result and a part of the problem.

The ruining class is ruling us by dividing us all, the workers against the middle class, against the intellectuals.

The majority of the people living in Germany, England, France, Russia, Italy and America leading up to the Second World War were all very much the same people. They had the same hopes, dreams and needs. It was Hitler who first divided us all on a global scale.

Both fascism and communism are totalitarian ideologies that treat and abuse the populations in the same way--badly! Many of the socioeconomic activities of fascism and communism are exactly the same. They are the lowest form of cultural evolution. The higher forms of cultural and economic evolution are free enterprise and socialism. I advocate a free enterprise/socialism society. Give those who have curiosity and vision a chance to prosper, and give those who cannot compete in this difficult world a helping hand. Let's help our young, aged, and the mentally and physically challenged. They are our families and friends. It is better for society if we don't forget them or imprison them. Bob Marley said, "A hungry man is an angry man." Don't just imprison or hospitalize those who cannot keep up.

Free enterprise and socialism can work very well with each other. Everybody can get what they need and actually what they want. It will all work except for these capitalist and communist dictators, both small-time and national. They just want to push people around and to always win at any cost.

For the sake of humankind and the earth, let's try to start acting like rational human beings. You might be from the right, and I might be from the left, but to save the planet and humankind, we need to compromise between ourselves. Anyone who doesn't compromise is either an egotist or a suppressive, undemocratic capitalist.

There are drugs that can make you feel like Superman, but you are not Superman; you cannot fly. You also do not know everything, and you are not the center of the earth, but you are you. You can do good and great things as yourself. And if you are not careful, you can do bad and horrible things. Don't ever, ever make any decisions on the spur of the moment that will change, ruin your life or the lives of others, especially if you are using alcohol or other personality-altering drugs. Many of us old folks have been guinea pigs, testers for what we humans can handle in the cornucopia of alcohol, drugs, etcetera! When we tell you something, listen; it may save your life and the lives of others.

The most wonderful realization a human can have is to admit they are wrong and then go on to find the truth!

For over fifty years the hippies were among the most denigrated people in America, along with African-Americans and any non-Christian person. Now, 2019, the hippie is beginning to look like the most patriotic, the most rational and helpful person in the United States.

Millennials and even many of you post-WWII Baby Boomers, I ask you; do you like music and know anything about music and its cultural ties? Please, please, please, watch and listen to *Monterey Pop, Woodstock, Laugh-In, TheSmothers Brothers Comedy Hour*, oh and yes, theSonny & Cher TV shows. And remember this when you see old media: it was not a reproduction or a reality show; it was real creativity speaking to you! And don't complain about the CG; that has nothing to do with the emotions of the story.

No woman has ever wanted to be a ho; it is the men who made them so.

It is poignant that in wedding protocol, you say congratulations to the groom and best wishes to the bride.

Millennials, I'm not going to get into a discussion about which of our eras is/was/will be considered the best for humankind, the hippie or the Millennial age! I am just asking, what is most important to the solutions and future of the world and human race? Are you going to step up as we did? We can't forget from where we came, or to where we are going, or else we are forever lost!

## Open Letter to Millennials
### Day Eleven

Millennials, have you ever considered what you will be doing and what you will be like when you are my age of 76? If you haven't, you should try. If you survive, your world will be very different, and it would be good for you to know that, and to make some preparations.

Try to get into my head with the changes in my life, and you may have a start on your own life changes. Time changes in history; science and philosophy are being compressed into shorter durations of evolution. Prepare yourselves to be made redundant, outmoded and unnecessary at a faster rate. But don't despair; if you help to make this world a nicer, more rational and helpful world, then you may succeed in making it a better place where you will be respected and taken care of by the society that you have created.

If you think I am a negative person, just check out the people I am warning you about. They are the negative forces that are creating my message. Don't kill the messenger.

I can't think for you and for me both! I want you to know the things I know and to see them the way I do. Yet I want you to process them through your own knowledge and experience, and maybe then we can all live in harmony.

I love the human brain, and I have such a respect for it, yet I have seen its limitations and excesses.

Again, I repeat, I have to write down and say, very soon, all the things the future generations need to know, because sometime in the near future our language will be reduced to 250 words and 2000 signs and emojis.

Accepting the reasons for laws is the first step in society. I don't like all laws, but I understand the reasons why they have been enacted.

You realize there are good laws and bad laws. There are laws for the wealthy and laws for the working class. If they benefit both, that is OK. If only the poor or rich win, then society will break down completely, and it is back to anarchy--the Dark Ages.

You can't be current in styles, computer-wise, or politically and economically current if you don't watch TV. That's sad! We used to read to learn in this country, and reading imprints knowledge more deeply and better than just the visual impression. But then, so much of our society is changing at the tick of the digital clock dial.

Short-term education is important for knowing computers, cell phones, dashboard keypads, TV remotes and the like. After you learn basic mathematics, which is that one is the small number and nine is the high one, and zero makes it all happen from there, you can skate for about six weeks until thy change the function of the keys on the computer. Then you have to educate for the next computing generation, and then you have to learn the new values, passwords, key designations and programs. Millennials think they know everything, but wait until the power goes down in their home and batteries.

And this being said and done, you can't get too excited about the other avenues of endorphin thrills: vapid entertainment, gaming, for which I can't even understand the appeal, and TV because the programs have been dumbed-down as well. TV today is so damn bad creatively and educationally that it actually suppresses your brain cells! TV and Hollywood movies, these are both titillation machines that give you only cranial interpretations or interruptions, but no deep intelligence,

That which you go and find for yourself will be with you for the rest of your life. Read and research! Go for the deep intelligence; it will eventually save you and your world.

Most blogs lie or give incorrect information because they don't rely on three respectable corroborating sources of information. Most conspiracy theories are just theories, but there is such a thing as a true conspiracy. Yet it takes research and wisdom to find it out--Watergate!

What is the one most important reason that you are given life? Mother Nature would say, "You are here to reproduce your species." God would say, "You are here to worship me and my creations." Bacchus would say, "To party." I will say, "All of them!"

Your family, your school, your looks or the color of your hair position you in your school or on the street. Don't believe in stereotypes or pigeonholes. I know you don't want to be a stereotype yourself, so do you honestly think other people want to be pigeonholed?

Some children are taught they have to fight for everything they get, including love. That education will not serve the world or its people well. If we teach children the weapons of love and war, but not the diplomacy of life, then we will all fail.

Respectful and rational are two words many people don't actually understand. Yet these two human emotions and actions will be what saves the world, if it is to be saved.

"The industries" have trapped us all into electronic gadgetries and computer configurations to the point that our lives, time and happiness are so involved that when these screens and handhelds fail us, we are thrown into chaos.

Your ancestors may be Native American, Mexican, Irish, Italian, German, African, Polish, Chinese or Japanese, but we are all Americans. Or you may come from the blood of the Middle East or Southeast Asia. We are all Americans; that is what the Declaration of Independence and Constitution are all about. That is what the United States of America stands for. Why are we still polluting ourselves with bigotry when we should be drawing together as humans of the earth?

The Electoral College: In the history of this country, there have been five presidents elected in spite of the fact they did not get more votes than their opponents. One, John Quincy Adams was a Democrat/ Republican; the other four were Republicans, including the last two Republican presidents. They know how to use the electoral college and gerrymander votes to bypass democracy and steal the presidency.

Most immigrants to America from 1600 to the present have come here to get away from the feudal systems, dictatorships and capital-ist-type systems, but the feudal lords sent their lawyers and accoun-tants over on the second boat, which was aptly named *The Fortune*!

I'm losing more and more faith in mankind all the time. This does not mean I am giving up on my crusade to help people be at least of average intelligence. It is an important endeavor, helping people to learn enough facts to be able to practice self-preservation.

Again I say to you Millennials, soon this will be your world, and it's good and bad. I hope you will soon start to solve some of the problems the generations before you and me created and the genera-tion between us did very little to solve.

We've seen the worst; now we really have something by which to judge the good!

Millennials, if you ever want to know more of the true-life, nitty gritty history of America in the 20th Century, watch *American Pickers* on TV. You will also learn a lot about human nature that will help you in the rest of your life.

For those of you who don't grasp what I just said, I wish you well!

Open Letter to Millennials
Day Twelve
Mankind has faltered again in its evolution!

*'Unlike all other creatures that we know of, human beings, alone, suffer emotionally and physically with the fear of pain, lost love, bankruptcy and death!'*
JMc 4/5/20

The stock market, with help from the robber barons, is responsi-ble for all, I say all, the economic problems in this country. As I write this, they are polluting and prostituting the rest of the world as well.

The stock market needs an overhaul and a downsizing. The original intent in creating the stock market was to provide money for companies to research and develop new products and services, to help the country's economy and all people's well-being. It was not intended to provide astronomical profits for the companies' owners, officers and executives. The market was meant to be a means to prosperity for our society, not just an end in the bank vaults of a few.

The stock exchange became corrupted when it became more important as a source of income for the stockbrokers and investors than as a stimulus to create new and better products for the economy. That is when this country started on its way toward becoming a paper, or shadow, economy rather than an economy based on the industry of its people. We must tone down, control or even neuter the stock market ego.

At this time, to be publicly traded on the stock exchange and succeed, a company must show a profit every quarter and then improve that profit each and every quarter thereafter; that is an unattainable goal. In the process, a lot of people are bankrupted, and their futures are jeopardized. Only a small number of people succeed and therefore become functionally successful, and some offensively rich. Quote me! The publishing industry is a good example of how the stock market has destroyed an originally valuable industry. Because publishing companies are now on the stock market, they cannot experiment with new writers, and therefore creativity in literature is dying. No new ideas, no new mentality. The world is dumbing down, and that means humankind will now start slipping back into the jungle. Even John Steinbeck or Mark Twain could not get published today!

It must be obvious to you by now I'm not just trying to reach Millennials. I am also trying to connect with all people of voting and purchasing age. Some people find their voices early in their lives, some struggle all their lives to be heard, and some do not know they have voices.

Having had an early career in the advertising industry, I watch it closely. I will tell you the industry is at a high point of consumer control. I have watched for years as they have gone up and down, from revolting, to obtuse, to controlling. But what are they selling now, and is it of any real value to the majority of people?

Millennials, I don't even care if there is a god; I am going to live my life as purely as I can, whether or not she, he or it exists. I don't have a religion or an ego; I have only a morality.

The media is dumbing us down, and not just about politics. Worse, they are making us insensitive to violence and teaching us to accept it as a daily part of our lives. It is not just the entertainment media that is doing this, but also the news media, which is supposed to be informing us of the truth in proportion to how it affects our lives.

This world needs a certain number of every type of person at all times in order to be whole.

Millennials, take note. The medical "industry" has taken us hostage and is blackmailing us because of our natural physical frailties. Doctors, pharmaceutical companies, hospital corporations and medical insurance companies have all broken the Hippocratic Oath. Our bodies have been kidnaped by the illusion of perfect health.

We are in a class war again. We are not just white or black or brown or yellow or Christians, Jews or Muslims. The most important battle we as humans are fighting is of the wealthy against the poor. And we all know who is right and who is in the wrong. If someone is willing to wager on human lives for the sake of profits, they do not fit in any true religion or on any moral platform.

You know, I admit it; I am ruthlessly and continually positive about humankind's abilities to become respectful and rational.

The feudal lords thought they were doing the right thing. The robber barons, the capitalists and stockbrokers continued to do what pleased themselves, while they were actually doing all the wrong things for the future of humankind. The competitive spirit often overpowers the joys of living, satisfaction of working, fulfillment of playing and ecstasy of loving! "Toxic masculinity:" my daughter, Siobhan, gave me that observation.

I am not here to entertain you; I am here to give you food for thought.

Economic realists, people who believe a good business deal is one where both sides are satisfied, know the world will not survive if we continue to accept predatory capitalism. Having to make a profit on your every profit is not a sustainable plan. Competition is fine for entertainment in sports or to let off steam, keep fit, and wager on from time to time. But to kill people, steal their land and livelihood for competition; this is insanity! Power and greed corrupt you; fight those desires. They will often end for you in bankruptcy or in being imprisoned as a dictator.

Yes, black lights and lava lamps can expand your intelligence.

During the Vietnam War, I used to hear, "Go back to Russia where you belong!" Since then, I have learned the hippies in the Soviet Union were treated even worse there than we were here. All oppressive, dictatorial and uptight governments and their followers dislike freethinkers, liberals and people of peace.

Millennials, check out some real American culture: *M\*A\*S\*H*, *Movie Night* and *1977*, and also *Two Broke Girls* and any and all *Perry Mason* reruns on TV.

I hate stupidity and ignorance because they are so destructive.

We can't do any better than the best we can do until we learn more stuff. But, God help us to learn good stuff!

## Open Letter to Millennials
## Day Thirteen

What do you have invested in this life? Is it just your ego? "I'm going to succeed and damn everyone else!" Then you are destined to fail. If you invest your soul, then you will succeed, even if, on paper, you are short.

"Whistleblower" is not a bad word; it indicates a person who is telling officials about the immoral or illegal crimes of someone. If his information is incorrect or a lie, then he is a false witness. The current administration is creating conspiracies of its own, then debunking them, saying something, then saying the opposite, lying, then saying they didn't say it, all to confuse matters. They know the mental capacity of their constituents. Thanks to Fox 'News, one-third of this country is uninformed. Don't forget anything they say; your freedom depends on it!

Most of the current conservative administration and Congress are so embarrassed or afraid of what they are doing they don't know whether to quit, change sides, or accept this B.S. I, myself, will forgive them their transgressions as long as they stop committing them and help us get rid of this guy. Let's start a "Pardon the Republicans" movement!

Fifty million years and human beings haven't learned how to stop killing each other. We haven't learned that together we are strong; individually we are divided.

There are members of the current administration who will suffer in their nightmares about what they are doing right now. Republican members of Congress will regret within their own heads and feel hatred within their own families because of their continued cheek-spreading and support of this Nazi capitalist administration's sins.

Throughout the ages, human beings have developed a pragmatic intellect. If something is deadly, dangerous or destructive to them, they have found ways to reduce the threat. Automobile transportation required laws; now tobacco, alcohol and drug use have laws. Why not gun ownership?

Catfishers are a reject of humanity because, not having real emotions of their own, they don't know the value of such a thing, and, therefore, they are willing to toy with the emotions of others. They are a snake eating its own tail.

Right now our government does not represent this country because there are not enough good people who are willing to accept the punishment of running for political office. It is difficult being a Democratic politician; it is easy being a Republican politician. Republicans can lie with immunity and get lots of money from rich people for doing so; Democrats get caught with even a hint of untruth and it means their political demise and a bad reputation. For conservatives, a bad reputation is a recommendation.

Materialism, commercialism and capitalism do promote advancements, but we must not fall prey to their shiny objects. Advertising is the trap! Our advertising industry has fooled us into thinking possessions are signs of sexual prowess and that the ability to buy them shows virility. We should consider criminalizing false representation of products and services. Lying is not constitutionally or morally acceptable! And, of course, these new luxury items and electronic diversions are also eating up natural resources, polluting our air and water and destroying the future of the whole human race. Materialism, planned obsolescence and advertising are burning up our world and dulling our senses.

What advertising actually does is lie to you about how good life is, or how much better it could be if you possessed more of the company's stuff. With smoke and mirrors and damn good psychological hypnosis, capitalist advertising convinces you that you are inferior until you own their bright, shiny objects, at which time you become just like them--rich, beautiful and self-confident.

I worked in advertising. One of my jobs was hiring models for TV commercials in Hollywood. I was choosing from the pool of beautiful people available, a young couple to represent the upper middle-class, cool people of the world. The actors I chose happened to turn out to be a girl who couldn't make it in the movies, became a junkie and a prostitute on the weekends, and a boy who was a homosexual.

No disapproval of the gay life, but this couple was a lie. What they had and how they lived was a fabrication to sell you some sugar water in a bottle. We created the Joneses, who had everything, from actors who had nothing, and told you that you must be just like them or you would never be part of the "in crowd."

Well-crafted lies by advertising agencies are part of what is wrong with this country, and they are contributing to the degradation of the moral and ethical fiber of this otherwise proud nation. Freedom of speech functions properly only if there is an agreement that the truth, or at least the truth as one knows it, is employed by all parties in the discussion. The moment lies and deception are used, freedom of speech becomes useless. We are back to communication anarchy, and our culture suffers.

Is this what our beautiful America has come to? A country driven by greed, where deception is the common practice in business and morality is reserved for Sunday?

Advertising as we know it must be altered, or our society will become the domain of cheaters, and our earth will dry up and be unable to sustain life.

One of the major problems with present-day advertising is the amount of product packaging created and the natural resources it wastes. This is a whole area that intellectuals and the creative community can help with. The possibilities for improving and saving our future are numerous if this society will listen to the intellectual voice.

Millennials, that old woman in front of you in line obstructing your life was once the sexiest, most desirable and stimulating person you can imagine. That old man in front of you in line obstructing your life was once the sexiest, most desirable, stimulating person you can imagine.

Choose your drugs, control your drugs, and don't let them use you!

## Open Letter to Millennials
### Day Fourteen

Once you find the good people who search out the sun, have their fun at no one else's expense, and let others live and let live, then you have found where you should stay. It is a dream many of us had in the counterculture of the 60s and 70s. Now Ronald Reagan's ghost, Cheney's sins and the current president's greed are dragging us down again.

All the peace and love is being sucked out of this country, and eventually the world, because of this presidency. All you folks who voted for him who wanted change are going to get it, all right. The changes are going to be harder on you who are under-employed, under-medically insured and under-educated. The rich will get richer, and you will get poorer, and it will be guaranteed that you will never reach economic stability. Sure, on the surface it may look like you are doing better, but that will not last. This man is the kind of person who sucks money and joy out of everyone over whom he gets power; just ask those who work with him in his administration and business dealings.

We are in a time of jeopardy to the peace and freedom of our world and its people. Political leaders are running amok, ignoring what is good for the earth and its population. The capitalists, dictators and several leaders of otherwise avowed democracies are thinking only of themselves, while an ignorant population is supporting the powerful and not the good.

I am not a complainer by nature, but this political climate and the world has so many criminals pretending to be our elected representatives. Now is the time to speak out! We must as U.S. citizens speak when we see something going wrong.

The Republicans are good at double talk. Do you want to be governed by people who talk out of both ends of their bodies?

Do you think a new car, the next series cellphone, or your green lawn is more important than the lives of the next generation? Well, that would make you a criminally greedy person!

If we really want to be a democratic society, we can do it with digital, computer eye-recognition voting for every person on every issue that concerns them. We can actually do without the representational form of government. It may sound radical, but it is rational, legal and possible under the Constitution. I know how to do it—ask me! Start representing yourself; you will get a much better deal that way. With my plan, nobody will suffer; even the rich or career politicians can have better, less stressful lives, and it has nothing to do with pills or psychotherapy.

To be civilized, you must be diplomatic and rational. Otherwise, you are only an animal fighting for a place to stand, food to eat and a mate to carry on your species. Only democracy and equality will take us out of the anarchy of the jungle; we have to have rational government in order for peace and freedom to exist. The battle between your own personal selfishness and the survival of the species should be a no-brainer, but because so many people have no brains, survival of humankind is in jeopardy.

Religious hypocrisy is when someone who has had an abortion for their own personal reasons, then finds "God," and then later lobbies for laws so that no one else can have an abortion for their own personal reasons. You have had your abortion when you needed it, but, now, no one else can have her's!

How can these people who call themselves Christians live with themselves when they are prejudiced against people of color, people of ethnic diversity and the poor and disenfranchised? Christ is rolling over in his "grave."

I wrote a poem years and years ago, and to paraphrase it; "If mankind is so stupid as to destroy this beautiful world, I hope that when life comes back to reside, there are only two of every other creature, but no humans to procreate their stupidity."

The battle between the stupid, the ignorant, the intelligent and the aware is ongoing. The stupid "think" they are OK, the ignorant don't know that they are, the intelligent are trying to help, and the aware are worried. Don't take sides religiously or ethnically; look at the social and geographic circumstances of the people first.

The people conservatives call "pinkos, do-gooders, ecologists, civil rights nuts, and left-leaning" are really trying to help you. Most people who are doing all these iconic things and speaking the heavy thoughts are not planning this or contriving it. They come from some people's souls to do these things for nature and humankind, and most of the time they don't get paid or appreciated for it. You can have your religion, you can have your guns, you can even hate people you don't understand, but if you ask for these rights for yourself, in this democracy you must allow others the same rights. Don't try to take other people's rights to their religion, their chosen lifestyle or their race, which they had no choice in being. If you want to get into heaven, you must be worthy, and that means you must have compassion and respect for everyone. Judge not, lest you be judged. God and Mother Nature do the judging unless your church is of the Devil.

All you people who voted for Trump, see what you have done to us? But I hope you realize he did not win the popular vote, and therefore you are losers twice!

War and many other stupid human mistakes are created by male ego. You buy a house you cannot pay for, you invade Russia, you bet on a horse, and you play Russian roulette.

We have so many wonderful people in this world working for peace, freedom and prosperity for everyone; why must they suffer all these accusations of working just for themselves?

## Open Letter to Millennials
### Day Fifteen

Learn how to follow orders and then learn how to experiment!

Do we have a race of people on this planet who thrive on war, greed and competition?

I would really like to know everything, but I know that knowing everything is impossible, so I want to know everything about one subject, and I have chosen saving the world.

Everything technical is going to be difficult for everyone at the wrong time.

I don't completely know what's going on. That must mean we are in trouble, because I know that because of my age and reading habits I am more aware than most of the people on the planet.

We are now a global society, and if we don't start thinking that way, we are all going to be toast.

It is hard not to be arrogant when you are right all the time. It is hard not to be humbled when you find you are not even right most of the time.

We have built our present modern world on magical creations of electricity and engines and sound waves, all of which sometimes fail us, and could someday disappear or become insupportable. Water, air, oil and electricity are luxuries we are over-using and abusing. Oil prices and reserves, water depletion, oxygen deprivation and possibility of electrical polarization reversal can make our lives unlivable. Greed and overuse are causing the demise of our earth's water, oxygen and oil.

The moment you become arrogant, everything falls apart! You have to be confident to do anything great, but once you let it go to your head, everything begins to short circuit.

You have to be a good liar to be a good advertiser!

I have a dream that soon the world will turn in favor of the good people instead of the capitalistic, bad people.

The unrest in Third World countries is caused by economic and political repression of the poor, working classes. It is created by capitalists' pressures on the people and their governments. It will continue to escalate throughout the world into more affluent countries because of capitalist and stock market greed. It will eventually hit Europe and the USA because, "A hungry man is an angry man," as Bob Marley said. In the United States most people are happy poor people; at least, they think they have some control of their lives. But once they realize advertised materialism has imprisoned them in an economic system from which they cannot escape, they will become like the rest of the discontented masses of the world.

Young people cannot judge me; they have never been old! I can judge them because I have been young. Believe me, I have judged my youth and myself already.

Our infrastructure is falling apart because of the stock market's concern with profits, and therefore, our society is going to deteriorate into the anarchy of everyone thinking only of themselves. Eventually, we will be back in the Dark Ages.

Why are all these 27-year-olds running one of the most valuable technologies and most important mechanisms to all our lives right now, the tech industry? They create these things and then recreate them and recreate them and don't pay attention to common sense; oh, maybe because they haven't learned common sense yet!

We have to help the good and moral people rise up, people who have never had a voice and have never been listened to. Most of the vocal people now have a selfish agenda. But those who are poor and voiceless are not greedy; all they want is a rightful share of the beauty of this world. The rich who have a voice are only asking for more, and they are taking it from all the quiet and poor people. Vote for a person who is not a capitalist.

Young people are trying to time out us older folk! Is it because they are ashamed we know things they don't know that are still important to their lives? Do they want to do it on their own, so they don't want to hear it from us? I, for one, am just trying to tell them things to help them; I have no ego about that. The separation between the old and young has always been a strange thing to me; we are all human beings, we all live on this earth and want and love a good life. We could all have such a wonderful life together if we all cooperated. I know, that sounds like hippie, New Age tripe, but if you can find something better, let me know.

I am writing about many things that should be done to improve or ensure the future of humankind and its planet. There is almost a certainty I won't be alive to benefit from these changes. Yet I, like all benevolent and future-thinking people, am concerned about the survival of humankind.

I love baseball! It is one place where you can compete but you can't cheat. A team sport where everyone is necessary. Democracy and truth while having fun.

I was not given the greed gene.

## Open Letter to All People, Including Millennials:
## Day Sixteen

Work smart! Know when you're over your depth! Ask questions! Follow rules and laws that make sense for the majority! Finish the job! Then you may become a reliable person!

Temple Mount: If we could get all the self-important religions to cooperate together on that one place, we might be able to solve the religious "problems" in this world, and then we would be 90% toward a happy future for all of us. Otherwise, it may be a sad ending for us all. The next step is getting the political leaders and dictators of the world to agree on peace as the only solution to this madness.

Don't ever ridicule someone if you have not been in their shoes. You can feel sorry for them, try to help them or commiserate, but you are ignorant if you disregard their struggles. To be an old person and not accept the struggles of young people in this time and reality is forgetting your past and being insensitive to the confusions of life. As a young person, being disrespectful of your elders is failing to realize what they have gone through, and what, some day, if you are lucky to live, you will have to endure yourself.

Don't expose your tummy; expose your heart!

Social justice, something many people don't think much about. Justice for you should mean justice for everyone, or else it is a scam that will not work for any of us. Social justice is the cement that holds society together. Social means to be equal, which means to be friendly and democratic. Justice means the Golden Rule.

Call it divine guidance if you wish, or call it creativity, or progressive thinking, pragmatism or self-preservation, but having an open mind has brought mankind this far, and it is the only thing that will save us. Human evolution has always been a constant. What does "AI" do to this? Are we going to continue to grow, stagnate, or self-destruct? From a thought I read in Dan Brown's *Origin*.

I want somebody to hack me. I hope they have the balls to print, steal or challenge what I write. Steal my words, please!

I am certain about politics! You should do the right thing for the most people.

Some people educate themselves, progress and develop to achieve their desire to dominate. Some people educate themselves, progress and develop to serve. Who are our heroes?

Please, may I say the right thing at the right time to every person when it is appropriate and they need to hear it? I don't want to be obnoxious and butt-in, but I don't want to miss the chance to help.

You are such cynical people, those of you who try to find some selfish reason why hippies, ecologists, feminists and peaceniks believe in love, peace, women's rights and world preservation. "They can't just be doing these things because they are nice. They must have a hidden agenda." Conservatives, since you think one way, you assume everyone else does too. Well, it doesn't happen that way; there are over 7.7 billion people on this earth. If you don't have the benevolent gene, you think everyone else should or must be self-centered. Well, try to think again. Not everybody has your ideas about life, economy and self-value. There are people who have other sensibilities than you, developed most often in their childhood. They love rather than hate, they look for the good, they forgive. Ignorance is never your fault, but it is a curse on the world you live in.

Strength is not as strong as knowledge; sex appeal is not as lasting as love,

In this day and age of economic disparity where "most" people are just fighting to keep their heads above the flood waters of capitalism, I am almost understanding of petty crimes, dismissive of cheating and blind to many misdemeanors. (This, of course, is a shame in a polite society, but understandable in this time of near anarchy!) When you add to impending poverty the proliferation of addictive drugs created by the pharmaceutical corporations' over-production, then "normal" people have little chance of surviving without turning to some minor crime or "social misbehavior" just to exist. The true tragedy of our time is that often the criminals are preying on people who are not their enemy, and who suffer from the same oppression or poverty as their victims do. Stealing from corporations is difficult. They protect themselves very well, whereas they can steal hundreds or thousands from you and all their "clients and consumers." You can take back only a few dollars from them.

I don't make any statement that I can't support or rationally prove. Since I no longer work in advertising, everything I say is true, unless I am joking over a drink or two or pulling your chain at a party. I am a political historian, and as an historian, lying or being adamantly wrong is a curse to me. Everybody can make a mistake, but if they learn their folly and apologize, it can be excused unless people die or suffer from the mistake. What I mean to say is that if you are sincere and lie through ignorance, it can be excused, but if you are an ac-knowledged falsifier, you are a scum and a pox on the peaceful flow of the world. And do you know the true definition of sincere? "Keeping your mouth shut if you don't really know what is going on." Sincerity is the absence of lying. A lot of people have lied and think that they can be half truthful or half sincere.

I know you're tired of this discourse by now, so start over and read it again.

### Open Letter to All People, Millennials Specifically And Those Yet Unborn: Day Seventeen

I would like to make something of myself. Not for anyone else, but just for myself. If I died without anyone knowing my name, I would not care at all.

I have been writing since I was four or five. My mother wrote down my stories and as of now I have published, written and photo-graphed three well-respected books. I have written more words than most people have read and owned more computers then most.

I am dyslexic. I can't spell. I'm not handsome, tall or muscular, and was a C student.

I built the most beautiful and fastest stock truck in L.A. when I was sixteen and have owned two other cars that are arguably the most sought-after metal sculptures ever to roll.

I took a bicycle around the world, hitchhiked across the U.S. twice and through Europe, and have been to five or maybe six continents. I helped invent beach volleyball and the California cooler in the 1960s, and I was one of the first people to perfect upside-down body surfing.

I was a real estate salesman in L.A. at nineteen, yet had trouble closing deals because I can't lie.

I was an advertising wiz, art director, and account executive at Top Ten ad agencies in L.A. at twenty-five.

I have worked in more than 44 occupations, mostly to find out what I didn't want to do with the rest of my life. I was a cowboy at 12 and first smoked a cigarette as a bowling pinsetter.

I did at least my share of psychedelics in the 60s, 70s and and 80s, but by staying away from cocaine or putting needles in ourselves, all my friends and I have survived and are living successfully.

I have built my own home with my own hands, married and am living happily with one of the most well-loved women.

I have a very fine collection of ties and an interesting and varied closet of clothing. Yes, I am trying to impress you, but only for the purpose of promoting my words.

It is well known that you should not start every sentence with "I" or "I have." But I am not self-centered; I slit my ego's wrists in the 1970s and don't have an ego anymore.

So, but, if I were to die tomorrow, I would consider my life a failure. I have no desire to be nailed to a cross, though it might be an interesting life experience. I have no desire to be a wealthy mogul, movie or music star, or a political leader. All I want to do is save the world from the wealthy moguls and political leaders. Nobody likes a thief or a dictator, so why do we accept them and their control over us?

It would be egotistical and self-delusional for me to say that I could straighten out this crazy world by myself, but I want to contribute my two-cents worth. If everybody, or at least a majority, could imagine and live the the Golden Rule, this could be the Garden of Eden for all of us. I would be stupid and naive if I thought it would be easy, but I point to *Star Trek* and hope!

You don't have to read between the lines when reading me. I am completely truthful and maybe even too straightforward for some.

In case you haven't noticed, we are living in a very predatory time. Our current president is the reason, because he is a predator, and many are just following his lead. He has made greed and ego OK in the minds of small minds. That is our most dangerous problem at this point in American history, and greed is by far a worse threat for our country and the world than "terrorism" or drugs, and much worse than undocumented laborers, farmworkers, maids and restaurant workers.

Many people cannot visualize or verbalize emotions or actions unless they are guilty of them and know those faults themselves. Don't ever ascribe or accuse other people of your own faults, because then you open your mouth and convict yourself. Don't place your hang-ups or values on others.

A cigarette butt, a full doggy bag abandoned, a plastic bottle on the beach, all left by an ignorant, stupid or selfish person. You may think this is nothing to worry about, but it is indicative of the carelessness and lack of concern of people, which will eventually kill us all and our children too.

Watch and listen to Rick Steves and Ken Burns if you want to know about the Western world's mistakes, successes and possible things that might help save us.

In this day and age, we humans should not need to be predatory to survive. That was what we needed to do to survive the other larger animals early in our existence, but now we are the top predator. Other humans are our only enemies, and they are the capitalists, dictators and to a much smaller degree, other people who are poor like us. We have to fight evil as a species of humans, or we will die. This is a challenge to you Millennials, because if you don't do this, you will probably not live your entire life in a happy ending.

The people who support, like, or "love" our current president do so only because he is the only person who is a bigger cheat or idiot than they are, so they have somebody to look up to or down on, depending on their own levels of insecurity.

The poor Republicans who support and read their crafted, lying speeches are freaked that if he is not re-elected, they will lose their seats in Congress, or if he wins and they abandoned him, they will suffer his sanctions and retribution. They are damned if they support him and damned if they don't! How many White House and Republican functionaries has "he" fired, defamed and tried to destroy? You may be next! Even as a former TV writer, if I had been asked to write the worst Presidential sitcom scenario, I could never have dreamt up this tragedy.

One of the deviously crafted speeches and Fox rhetoric is that the president is helping the middle class financially; well, he is destroying democracy at the same time. Who are the other government leaders he sides with most often? Putin and Sun Myung Moon, two of the most violent and destructive dictators in the world right now. Soon we may have three destructive dictators.

God's divine intervention can, at times, appear to go both ways. The perfect person dies, the perfect business fails. But, and this assumes that you believe in God's power, God often wakes us up with a strange, terrible or confusing event. I think what is happing right now is one of those cases. On 2016 election day-plus-one, many of us cried, but many of us also thought this might be the moment when humankind learned whom they shouldn't trust. Capitalists are not your friends, and self-centered people are to be avoided.

Let's bring some dignity and truth back into the presidency, and maybe then other countries will respect us again. I can give you the definition of ignorance and I can give you the meaning of I.Q., but stupidity is an amorphous point. Our president is stupid, and it is based on ego and insecurity. I would like to make something of myself, but not through the suffering of other people as our president does.

Oh, and Millennials and 27-year-old pipsqueak techies, please stop over-thinking cell phones, TV remotes, watches and toilet bowl flushers, etc. We don't need so many functions.

You took a perfectly good flip phone and made it unwieldy, unfriendly and unstainable. Planned obsolescent at its most expensive level. You are mucking with the ecological viability of the world by squandering our limited natural resources, and you are putting people in dangerous economic trouble that will affect the whole world, including your own families.

You have created objects that are smarter than most human beings, and what good is that to a normal human being who is just trying to use a tool? I think you have even outsmarted yourselves; even you have to go through ten or more learning curves every three months, maybe weeks. That is unsustainable for even someone your age, and remember, you are getting older.

And again, Millennials, on a lighter but still critical social level, lose the scraggly, precisely shaved beard. It is an insecure adherence to a phony popular style. Most women don't really like it. At least shave the prickly mustache so as not to irritate their delicate places.

CHAPTER 69

## Conclusion

### March 1, 2020

Human society will never be perfect, yet it could be a lot better than it is today. I hope and I think this pandemic can make us realize that we are all in this world together, and that anything that affects anyone else affects us. Poverty, illness and bigotry forces people to do things they would not do in "a perfect world"!

We are now living in a sick society, and it is because of the corruption, competition and greed that capitalism has created. We need to evolve into a free enterprise/socialistic world or else we will all die.

### December 18, 2019

97% of this book was written before the current president was elected, but most of it was written to help protect us from these three years ever happening again.

The critical problem in our country today is that the silent majority doesn't realize who their true friends are. They have been brainwashed by the conservative media into thinking that liberals want to dismantle their way of life. It is actually capitalism that is slowly destroying our democratic and free enterprise way of life.

The silent majority mistrusts the liberal's efforts to protect freedom for all and democracy for all. They misunderstand the liberal attempts to help the poor, to ensure freedom of religion for all religions and concern for the environment.

The silent majority thinks liberals have an ulterior motive. They don't realize that these crusades are made only for truth, not for money or ego.

The silent majority thinks the conservative and capitalist agenda will ensure that they will live in peace and comfort. What the average person doesn't realize is that the conservative and capitalist club is very small, and they keep it that way.

Who honestly believes a capitalist is going to help them become rich? In a society where competition is supreme, why would they reach down to help others up to their level?

Liberals are doing what they do for everyone, not just for the poor. There, but for the grace of God someday you could find yourself poor. What, then, would be your view of free enterprise? You could have been born a Jew, Muslim or Copt. What, then, would be your attitude toward freedom of all religions? Someday your government may suppress your ideas and ideals. What, then, would be your tolerance toward freedom of speech?

Liberal intellectuals step into others people's shoes in their thinking, and visualize what it would be like to be poor, disenfranchised and discriminated against. The silent majority does not realize that liberals are concerned for their well-being the same way our Founding Fathers were. The reason is that America's founders were, almost to a man, liberal intellectuals.

This country, based on tolerance for ethnicity, economic position and all religions, must not let the tyrants change our perfect union. We need to revisit the ideals of our Founding Fathers and our Gods.

It means a revolution of thought and of ideals. We must return to our passion for freedom, democracy, tolerance and compassion. What it means is that we may have to tell some people that they can no longer tread on us.

What it means is that we must re-evaluate our capitalist economy, we must reconstruct the stock market, we must rethink our policies in dealing with other countries. But most of all, we must start listening to the voices of dissent coming from among the thinking population of this country. After all, this is a free speech democracy of human beings, and human beings are supposed to be the most intelligent creatures on the face of the earth!

In this book I have outlined a number of misconceptions and errors of judgment that the American public maintains about this country and its government. These examples of misplaced loyalty and misunderstanding are killing this country, its dream of freedom and its democracy.

After reading this book, if you don't agree with what I say, give me some facts to prove I'm wrong. Don't just scream at me. Don't just mouth some propaganda spin. Come up with some facts. If you find what you think are lies or miscalculations herein, tell me. As a rational human being, send me an intelligent letter or e-mail. I'll listen, but I want you to listen to me completely first.

I am passionate about the truth, so if you want to express and help the truth, then I am your guy. If you convince me that I am wrong, then you will have a very committed and intelligent advocate, so give me your best shot.


Paine Wrote in *Common Sense*:

"These proceedings may at first appear strange and difficult; but, like all other steps which we have already passed over, will in a little time become familiar and agreeable; and, until an independence is declared, the continent will feel itself like a man who continues putting off some unpleasant business from day to day, yet knows it must be done, hates to set about it, wishes it over, and is continually haunted with the thoughts of its necessity."

As Thomas Paine said, and I also say, "Change of the magnitude I am proposing is fearful and mysterious, but it is necessary if mankind is to progress to his next advanced stage."

We must get away from greed and greedy people or we will perish.

George W. Bush, an ignorant, second-generation capitalist pig, along with his arrogant friends has done more damage to the peace and economic welfare of this country and the world than any government leaders of America before them. Even 9/11, handled properly by benevolent diplomatic gentlemen could have been a positive turning point in diplomacy and cooperation of nations.

We have to change the way of man. Our old ways are not working; they haven't worked for a long time. Change is overdue.

With population as it is growing, our old ways are even more destructive. We must abolish greed, religious intolerance and ethnic intolerance. We are all in this world together and unless we start cooperating we will all sink together in our stupidity, competition and arrogance

# CHAPTER 70

## Ending chapter: Things You Should Learn, and Poetry, and a Political Patoi's & Pastiche

Some people like lies and secrets. You may be one of those. You may be attracted to what you think is strength and independence in people who lie and are secretive. You may be someone who is a liar and secretive yourself. But do you really like dealing with other people who are lying and secretive to you? If you do, you are stupid, and you will remain stupid and ignorant twice, first of what they think of you and second of who they are. Now that makes you a very lost soul.

I do not understand a person who hates liberals, socialists and hippies, but likes flowers, social security, Medicare, free education, peace and a living wage. How can you vote for a conservative? What have they done for you? You are like a person who has one foot pointing forward and one foot pointing backward. You are going to do a lot of stumbling and falling.

Congressional Republicans, how do you live with yourselves? Some day, God forbid, your children and children's children may be in need like half the population of this country, and some other SOBs will give government money to the corporations and let your future family suffer.

Their Covid 19 reactions are a good example of how little conservatives, capitalists, Republicans and Christians care about human life.

For men, the stress creators are achievement in relationships, work and ego self-satisfaction. For women, they are relationships, the desire to procreate and work both at home and, if need be, commercially.

Like the leaf that grows on the twig is nibbled by the bug, plucked by the bird, wet by the rain, warmed by the sun, and blown by the wind, I will fall to earth someday to start life over from the gutter dirt.

I can be critical of some people's choices, but I'm not dictatorial. Make all the foolish decisions you want. I've made my own. But don't make stupid or selfish mistakes that impact other people because then you are a criminal!

$19.95, are you that stupid? It's 20 dollars and anything you buy for less than 20 bucks is not going to last for $20 worth of time! And $19.95 in three payments is only going to be the same times three, and don't forget shipping cost, plus "For an Extra Fee."

Get rid of Republicans; they are expedient and shortsighted toward their bank accounts. What will happen when the real people won't have any money to buy the rich man's shit, just like 2008 and the Corona virus stimulus "package." The government run by the Republicans will have to bail out the rich people when the poor and middle class are the ones who need to be supported. Reagan's trickle-down is a scam to get all the money and power into the hands of a few thieves!

Most Republican political representatives are out of touch with what it is like to be poor and uneducated, so they don't have any sympathy with someone who, due to birth and family circumstances, is poor and uneducated.

When are we going to realize that people are manipulating our egos? People are manipulating our egos, advertising, sports, religion; they are using our weakest emotions to sell us things and to manipulate our loyalties and affections.

For some reason, some people need a "Nigger" to hate, to make them feel better, more important, more normal or acceptable. Often, it is because, at some time in their own lives or in the lives of their family, they were somebodies else's "Nigger"! So how stupid, how insensitive is that, to hate someone else for your own insecurity?

*"I understand the ignorant person and forgive them. They sometimes look for someone with power to follow. I understand the lost person and hope for them. They sometimes look for a stimulant to help them find the way. I understand the poor person, feel for them, they sometimes take from others to make their way. I do not understand the greedy person, nor forgive them. They often take from others who are less fortunate then they, and do not care for the poor, lost or ignorant. The greedy person is responsible for most of the troubles of this world."*

So said Jesus in the temple.

Negotiating is not a loser's way. Negotiation among moral men is the solution to war, poverty and all human pain.

My target audience is you, all of you, because what I write about affects everybody. Greed, selfishness, bigotry, war and ignorance damage us all, and ironically, most of all, they destroy those who practice them as much or more!

I don't believe in God. I don't believe in the stock market. I don't believe in the American flag. I don't believe in oil. I believe in human beings and our capacity for goodness.

Our current president is a bad influence, facilitating and enabling low I.Q. people to behave badly, act irresponsibly, violently and actually unpatriotically to our democratic foundation of majority-ruled harmony.

I'm a muckraker. I did not create the muck I am raking it out so people can see it. I am the messenger.

Words have changed this world more than anything else for good or bad, except one meteorite strike 60 million years ago.

312

Often, violent people think being peaceful will make them vulnerable, and that peacefulness means weakness. But a peaceful nature requires a strength that they cannot understand. A good and realistic person is strong enough to take the chance to have faith that others will see and appreciate the spirit of peace and cooperation. And that realization is the pinnacle of human intelligence brought on by wisdom. And that is why I call violent people ignorant.

Often, greedy people think being generous will make them vulnerable, and that giving something without an alternative motive or bigger return is foolish. But unselfish giving requires a strength that they cannot understand. A good and realistic person is strong enough to defer rewards for peace of mind and a better spiritual foundation. And reaching that is the pinnacle of human culture brought on by education. And that is why I call greedy people ignorant. Watch these two movies, "Sabrina" (1995) and "Pretty Woman". P.S. Giving money to a religious evangelist is one of the most foolish things I can imagine. I have been close enough to these people to know that they are playing you. My family was in that religious "business"!

Diplomacy (being realistic) is the only thing that will solve the problems of this world. (Be kind, be open-minded.)

Non-violent protest is the most positive and successful contrast to the unpatriotic assholes who are greedy and bigoted.

People who want to save history, archeology, environment and wildlife are called greedy by greedy people who make a lot of money and want to make more by burying history and archeology, killing wildlife and destroying the environment from which they make their wealth. Some people think that everybody is selfish and greedy like themselves. But ecologists, historians and lovers of animals do not do what they do for money; they do it for self-satisfaction, joy of intelligence and the warmth of compassion.

313

Bigots, greedy, selfish people, you should be ashamed of yourselves, calling yourselves Americans and not understanding what patriotism means in this country. Our Founding Fathers were creating a country where everybody could live in freedom and safety.

I cannot argue with crazy people. They think their craziness is correct. Please stop your craziness. Please think as one person among the common sense of the majority. You creatures of selfishness, you bigots, you are a wound on mankind.

I ask myself over again how can I help people change their minds toward the truth, the good, and the peace? It seems too easy, but can I warm a heart that is cold or expand a mind that is frozen into an iceberg of untrue ideas?

As in "The Jungle Book," how many lives of other creatures will a man destroy or kill? How much rain will he stop or air will he suck from the plants or water will he foul?

Many people today have reverence for gods or deities, yet in the history of humankind most of our reverence has been toward Mother Nature, plants, birds, the stars, sun and moon.

*"Always do the right thing! Always do the right thing! Always do the right thing! There is a reason it is called the right thing! And it doesn't mean the right thing just for yourself, but do the right thing for everybody. Sometimes you may think that it conflicts with you and your family and friends, but trust the Golden Rule; it is best for everybody, even your 'enemies' who may then become your friends."* UG 500,000 BC

Stupid people are insecure people; they are afraid of what they don't know. Learning is stepping outside their comfort zone. And yet knowledge has never killed someone, but ignorance has killed millions.

I think we are going to have to give these Trump people immunity in order to get them to tell the truth and get on with the rule of our law we hold dear in this country.

I respect the poor, because I know it is usually not their choice or their fault, but I do not want to be victimized by a poor person. I would rather give more to a thief than he or she steals from me. I believe in a social system that covers the needs of the poor. Education is first, housing, basic health coverage, healthy food, birth control and respect are next.

You can be very smart but wrong, you can be moralistic but wrong, you can be kind but to the wrong people you can lie to yourself! Become right! And the only way you can is if you judge yourself, by making sure that you do everything for the people, all the people, even those that you don't know or like.

My compulsion to find the truth is like picking a scab; I cannot contain myself.

Some people confuse power with intelligence and truth. Power corrupts intelligence and truth.

Come on, people of the United States, we can do it; we are the melting pot of people the conglomeration of the whole world. If we demand cooperation between the people of the world, we can change the world to be a cooperative effort. We can create a perfect world in spite of the greedy and egotistic selfish few. It is only 1% that we have to put in their place so that the world will work

Working people don't always know who pays their salaries. It is not the companies they work for; it is other people like themselves who actually pay their salaries.

We have too many disreputable big box stores, too many car manufacturers, too many air carriers, too many gas companies. What we don't have is enough reputable schools, hospitals, home town stores. Let's stop worrying about the corporations' survival or the rich peoples net quart bottom line and start worrying about the real people and their future and children.

This coronavirus has shown people for who and what they really are. Some people are worried about the death and the human suffering, and some are worried about the capitalist world and not being able to buy a new Porsche or play more golf around the world.

Most Christians don't know who is giving them the freedom to worship as they want to, and that is the liberal separation of church and state.

Corporations have the proprietary thing down; it is the inventor, creator and artist who gets screwed.

I believe that everybody in the United State should learn their true blood line and ancestry! Too many people are prejudice against people who might just be related to them. It is important to learn where you came from so that you don't continue hating people just because you think they are different and have nothing to do with you.

> *"Don't be loud, obnoxious and rant and rave; it diminishes your message."*
> Ug 400,000 BC

Look to morality, the Golden Rule! Go back and watch 1950s, 60s and 70s TV shows and start living by the morality of M*A*S*H, Gunsmoke, Perry Mason, The Lone Ranger, and then we can start fixing this society and this world.

How do you feel about someone whose ideas, politics and voice are against your own path; are you offended by them, or are you worried they might be right? Take the time to find out which.

I think that human beings are meant for something better, like getting their shit together. You know down deep inside that we can and should do it. This is not a religion or a church; this is reality

All the best books, movies and TV shows are about freedom, against bigotry, greed and war. So how the fuck do some of you people still believe in suppressive bigotry, greed and war? Don't you feel a bit like an asshole?

316

Whistle blowers have nothing monumental to gain. In fact, most often they suffer from telling the truth. If they wanted to make money, they could blackmail the corporate and political criminals, and then they should get lots of money, but/or possibly they would be assassinated by the political and corporate thieves.

War; there are a number of different kinds of wars; Religious wars, wars of ideology, are the most damaging and least productive.

Ug, Mug and Thug, three fictitious prehistoric people.

Democracy is really the true calling for humankind. With our capable intelligence we should, can, and must create the perfect world. Rodenberry and nearly all intelligent people believe in it. Only our current president and his fellow capitalist thieves are against a perfect world and democracy, which means majority rules, majority morality and majority common sense.

Some people worry about their eternal life when they should be enjoying what is going on right here in front of them.

The Intelligence Quotient (IQ) is a measurement of a person's intelligence based on how much they know about the facts of their surroundings. It is a very important measurement, since it is an indication and prediction of your possibilities of being successful and even your survival.

There is a line on the IQ chart that is the point at which a person realizes they have to think before they speak or act on a subject. Intelligent people know what they don't know; dumb people don't know that they don't know!

A person can increase or decrease their IQ by reading or watching Fox "News."

I know that artificial intelligence is going to have its day, but I also know that a human will never challenge the machine; the machine will have to challenge the man.

The rich may have to be forced to take a cut in their greed. They can afford it, but will they become human beings and have compassion?

I recently had a conversation with several people who are opposed to poor people. They still cling to a belief that the rich, the capitalists, are correct in being greedy!

Everywhere I go, everything I see, a broken piece of plastic is following me!

Some men have a tendency to exaggerate and distort their events and abilities because of their insecure personalities.

A lack of patience, a temper and stupidity. You may think I am describing a species of monkeys, rats or snakes, but I am describing a large percentage of human beings.

There are some people who are just socially, culturally and politically insane, and the most realistic definition of insane is to be anti-social.

Common sense and common knowledge are related! People who don't have common sense don't have common knowledge, and they are outside society; beware of them. In a world where all humans and animals are related by space, time and common elements, anyone who does not know this or follow the rules of our commonality is an enemy of humankind, animal kind and this world.

How about saving the people instead of the economy!? After all, without the people there would be no economy, except for a few thousand rich people waiting around for some poor people to get some money so they can steal it.

There are people who really don't care about other people. In most cases they were made that way by the circumstances of their upbringing, or they were introduced to that selfishness by the dynamics of their family. It is sad for them, it is sad for the people that they mistreat throughout their life, and it is sad for society that has to compensate for them. Treat your children with respect and love, teach them to think, teach them to feel, teach them to be humble and teach them to vote for Democrats.

Think, think, think, don't just fall back on your old habits, false egos and outmoded actions. Mankind is better than that; we are the thinking animal. We should be able to change the world together and save humankind.

The good, hardworking people have been fighting the capitalist, feudal lords and stealers of happiness for thousands of years. We may lose the battle, but we will live in righteousness for eternity, while they will walk on hot coals forever!

"The true wisdom of a man is having power and knowing how to use it, and then not using it." Dudley Griffin 7/11/06

Money is a means to an end, not the end in itself, as some misguided people think. The love of money is a sin, as Jesus and most of the two Bibles proclaim and demonstrate.

Read this book with a skeptical mind, but with an open mind, one that is willing to be changed if the truth appears.

I am a terrorist! The definition of terrorism by Webster's Dictionary in 1987 is the policy of using acts inspiring terror as a method of ruling or of conducting political opposition. I oppose and write against capitalism and suggest the possibility of ending it, and therefore, I can be called a terrorist because my actions may frighten people who rely on capitalism for their livelihood and personality. Terrorism does not have to be violent; it only has to frighten someone.

Asked in an interview, "What is your goal?" I answered, "To learn, teach and pass along the bullshit to watch out for."

A really good person is someone who knows that they could rule those around them with their knowledge, strength, personality and spirituality, but chooses to help people instead.

*"God, is there anybody up there? Please help the good people, and we will save, eternity!" JBMc and his thoughts on "Star Trek"*

There is a God or Mother Nature, but they don't want people fawning over them they want us to take their lead and solve it ourselves.

Let's let the "no-maskers" congregate if they want and then stay away from them. Let them get sick if they wish, but I feel sorry for their families, young children who are innocent.

I don't know if there is a heaven or hell, a God or a devil. We can't see much proof down here, we are all just trying to survive, but, it seems whoever you are, you are giving all the advantages to the bad people!

Free thinkers as opposed to money thinkers!

Money is a trap because you are not getting something you need for something you don't need. Money is something you can always need and want; the thing you buy will get eaten, break or become out of fashion. The introduction of money introduced credit, and borrowing percentage, which introduced profit for doing nothing. We can thank Hamilton for introducing this travesty into our otherwise democratic landscape.

The advance of pharmaceutical and medical progress and lowered mortality rates is being slowed down and suppressed by the capitalists and the stock market. The capitalists and stock market should be promoting free enterprise and democracy, if they call themselves patriotic Americans.

*"I want to go in reverse on the treadmill and stationary bike."*
JBMc 1/2/20

*"Species, race, breed, religion, national patriotism, all things that separate living creatures... We must overcome the urge to be exclusive, or we will fight each other into extinction! We have the intelligence, and I believe God gave us that knowing that we should be able to think our way out of killing ourselves. Our ultimate rejection of God would be if we failed to use what he has given us to maintain life on this beautiful planet He has given us."*
Dudley Griffin 2019

God has a different kind of wisdom then we ascribe to "IT". Guidance instead of force.

We all knew this stuff after the Dark Ages and then again in 1776. Apparently, we must learn it once more. We don't have much more time; this may be our last chance to learn it and act appropriately.

My liberal friends, colleagues, teachers and I keep shaking the truth tree, hoping that a leaf, branch or coconut will fall on the right people or the wrong people and make them solve this life-threatening problem.

I don't ever want to get to the place where I have to be aggressive.

Watch M*A*S*H, "Mail Call", 1974 and learn to be a man!

Watch M*A*S*H, "A Smattering of Intelligence", 1974 and stop being a fake patriot.

There is no magic, there are no gods, it is only hard work.

In war there is nothing more honorable than victory! Avoid it if you can!

Love is devotion; it is not, "I want to fuck you"!
I am not a well man I am twisted, and observing the straight people today, I see I am twisted in the right way.

Some people think that peace is something you have to fight for. No, it is like a small child you must nurture.

I am of the age, location of birth and gene pool that make me cognizant of all the social changes, political and technical activity that have happened from 1955 to this moment, 2020. John Bassett Mc-Cleary, b. 3/5/43 San Francisco, CA, USA

Without dreamers there would be no dreams come true!

There are some people who are able to forward think, to foretell the future or know what is going to happen in the days to come. This is not clairvoyance, fortune telling, oracle, hocus pocus, or magic. This is because some people watch, listen and read about our society.

What's right is right: it is time for truth, or else we will all die clinging to our lies and delusions!

Two things that conservatives do regularly that make them un-American and un-patriotic are that they censor other people's free speech and make threats that suggest violence. These are both illegal and immoral, and so if they consider themselves Christian then they will not make it to heaven unless they ask forgiveness, and if they do it again, then they are also hypocrites. A bumper sticker during Clinton's presidency read, "Where is Oswald when we need him most?" This is wrong in so many ways! Advocating the killing of another person is wrong by American standards and Christian standards.

I am a terrorist because I frighten some people by accusing them of being immoral and illegal.

I am a patriot because I frighten some people by accusing them of being immoral and illegal.

I want to scare people into being better with other people. After all, this is a society that is getting more and more crowded, and we must be more diplomatic and understanding if we don't want more road rage, parking rage, breathing rage.

I would never try to frighten someone into changing who they are. First, because I am not that stupid as to thinking that I could do so, and second, because I appreciate individuality. Again, I just think that they, and we, and me would be better off if we just cut each other some slack.

I am a patriotic American, and because I am, I would never advocate censoring a person's words or thoughts, and I never advocate violence! But I am frightening to some people because I ask people to change their bigoted or corrupt ways. And this is because I know they are only hurting themselves and all the world around them.

People of privilege don't know what it is like to be the people they enslave.

I hate keys, door locks, fences, and Internet site passwords, I hate them because they waste the time of us good guys. I wish we didn't have to be worried about someone stealing from us. If they come to me and are in need, I will give to them. But please don't steal from someone you don't know; they might be in worse economic shape than you are. Stealing from rich people is a bit different, but I don't like that either. I hope you can find some satisfying occupation.

If you can't, I hope our society will give you a helping hand to reach self-sufficiency and satisfaction.

Everyone has to do something good more than half the time, or else the world is going to fall apart in greed and corruption. And then, sadly, some of us will have to work to do more than our share in order to make up for you slackers, cheats and greedy people!

There is nothing you can do about a human dildo. If a person is a dildo, they will not listen or contemplate; they just continue to act dildoish. Our current pretender to the presidency of the United States is a dildo, and so we just have to put up with him until we are able to legally retire him to the dildo's hospices.

You can't cut out somebody's ego as you can tonsils or adenoids. If the ego is developed in a person's youth, it may take a lifetime for them to repent.

Nobody knows what the ego is; it is like defining God or Devil. All I know is that it takes mind expansion to find your own ego and then to stop your ego from persecuting other people.

Recently, the CEO of Delta Airlines supported the current president's Tweet or suggestion or brain fart, to privatize the Air Traffic Control system, the ATC. And then and then, the Delta CEO, complained about the disarray within the Air Traffic Controllers, which by the way was initially caused when Reagan dismantled it by killing the Air Traffic Controller's union in 1981. I wonder if the CEO is a champion of Ronald's trickle-down theory of government bureaucracy?

And what happens to every essential agency of our government when it is privatized? You get less sincere service at more expense!

First, Reagan (a Republican president) killed the Air Traffic Controller's Union, and now our current Republican president wants to privatize the ATC. We all know how this is going to work out---poor service at more cost to the public! And when you are in that airplane, do you want to know that the person with your life in their hands is a happy person proud of their job and who actually cares whether you get home safely no matter what the cost!?

The true money givers of this society are the consumers. All the money flows up from them, and so the capitalists have learned to control the flow. And we are letting the capitalists lead us on into our own slavery to them.

I can't believe that these Republican voters, congresspersons, and capitalists can be so naïve as to perpetuate this current president's lies! They must know that eventually it will not look good on their resumes.

People of stolen or fabricated privilege don't know what it is like to be the people they enslave.

If you are so much of an individual that you don't care about the difficulties of others, in the long run, in the end, you and they will all suffer. Society is a good thing for everyone. Anarchy, hyper-individuality is going to take us back to the Dark Ages.

2020: People today are so used to being exposed to fantasy in movies, TV and advertising that they are not appalled, as they should be, by getting fantasy from the White House and Washington D.C., Right now we are very close to a rebellion by the rational people of this country. It will, and must, be won at the voting booth as Jefferson and our Founding Fathers wanted.

There are good maniac and bad maniacs, crazy, but not stupid, exciting, but not death defying, Russian roulette players and drunk drivers… "woops, he didn't defy that!" Wise up, you are not the chosen, the indestructible, don't have "Died by Misadventure" on your gravestone.

Teaching your children to hate a different race of people is a mortal sin. Teaching your children to hate people from a different country is the curse of death to this world. Teaching your children to hate other people's religion is a sin against God. God and Mother Nature put us all on this earth, and you will be a damned person if you do not except their choices.

Again I state, since supporters of our current president ignore the facts: The current pretender to the presidency's statements that he beat Hillary is really fake news, fake truth, and a lie. She beat him by around three million votes. It was the Electoral College who "determined" that D. J. T. won!

Again I ask, since his supporters ignore the facts, did you know that five presidents have been elected even though they lost the popular vote?
Again:
John Quincy Adams, in 1824 as a Democrat/Republican
Rutherford B. Hayes, 1876 as a Republican
Benjamin Harrison, 1888 as a Republican
George W. Bush, 2000 as a Republican
D. J. T. 2016 as a Republican
What this means is that the Republicans are very good at stealing elections, which is un-American and un-patriotic. Are you proud of that, all you cheaters who are always calling Democrats un-American and un-patriotic?

Ug, Mug and Thug were walking around on the earth 400,000 years ago. Ug, a female, was a feminist, Mug was a man with a spiritual and creative mind, and Thug was a capitalist who raped Ug and stole ideas from Mug.

Thug had sat in the back of the cave and watched Ug and Mug invent, create and make all kinds of things to make the cave more comfortable and safe for the whole tribe.

One day Thug patented all of the things Ug and Mug had created, the fire, a log to sit on, wall paintings, and the bowl to hold their food and water.

Then Thug started charging all the tribe members, as well as, Ug and Mug, for using all these inventions. Thug was the first accountant/ robber baron/capitalist.

## Acknowledgment

This book was edited by Joan Jeffers McCleary, with able hands and a loving heart.

I want to thank Thomas Paine for his inspiration. Artists and photographers are Kenton Hoppas, Shepard Fairey (Obey).

My advisers were Tom Berg, David Cloutier, Karl Dobbratz, Steve Forker, David Glover, David Grubbs, Patricia Hamilton, Joyce Krieg, John and Richard Miller, Bill Minor, Kerry Sissim, Gordon Terry, John Thompson.

## Suggested Books to Read

*Fugitive Days,* Bill Ayers
*Big Lies,* Joe Conason
*Lies And the Lying Liars Who Tell Them,* Al Franken
*Stupid White Men and Dude, Where's My Country,*
    Michael Moore
*Too Much and Never Enough,* Mary L. Trump. PH.D.
*The Bible,* both books

People to read: Lenny Bruce, George Carlin, Dr. Martin Luther King, Jr. and, and, the list is so lengthy, just read anything as long as it tells you something new.

# Glossary of Words and Author's Definition or Opinion

**Abuse:** A form of physical, emotional or sexual mistreatment by an authority figure toward a person in their charge, employ or control. It is one of the most detestable human acts because it assumes that you are a person of respectability who breaks your moral obligation to those you oversee. Noblesse oblige; look this up.

Examples of detestable people are those who abuse women and children in their care. My most hated are sexually abusive church pastors and priests and leaders of Cubs and Boy Scouts. These abusers have a destiny to live in torment in their older lives and then for eternity.

I would like to see a support system for the grown men who were abused emotionally and physically by their fathers.

**Advertising Industry**: Advertising agencies are in the business to lie. This industry should change its morality and start stimulating sales by advocating quality and creativity of the product, not the presentation of the product.

**Bigotry**: Bigotry is the mistrust, fear, and/or hatred of other people. In America, a continent of such ethnic diversity, bigotry is one of the most stupid, self-defeating and damaging of all national mistakes. Bigotry to me means ignorance! As human beings, other people are the most important elements of our lives. The Lone Ranger, in 1956 TV show, "There is no room for bigotry in this country; there never has been!"

**Birth Control**: Birth control and real sex education, not abstinence or abortion, are the solution to overpopulation. By the way, anyone with a drop of brains and any knowledge of mankind's history knows abstinence is a hoax. Religion will be the real cause of humankind's death and destruction.

**Capitalism**: The most destructive force in the world today.

**Conservatives**: A group of folks who always try to control everyone and everything! Where's the democracy in that? Conservatives may help administer our government if they wish, but they should never be allowed to make the laws in a democracy, because they always tend to change the rules in their own favor.

**Cowboy Mentality, Violence, and Arrogance**: It served us well in our efforts to rape and pillage the American continent, but I don't think the rest of the world is going to stand for it. We better expect more terrorism unless we can start using our intellect and tolerance to become a partner in this world.

**Democracy**: Democracy is the only form of government that can actually create peace on earth. Humans will always rebel against dictators, tyrants, monarchs and leaders. That is why our Founding fathers devised this form of self-rule. Self-government is theoretically capable of producing a satisfied population. It remains to be seen whether the greedy capitalists and conservatives will allow that to happen. Democracy is a salad; politics is the lettuce, religion, economics and ego are the condiments.

**Depression or Recession:** It is a point at which the money people stop paying the poor people enough to buy the products that the money people are selling, so the money people have to get the government to bail them out. The stock market and usurious moneylenders figure into that as well. And then the CEOs of the market and lending institutions go off to the Bahamas to play golf.

**Ecology and Environment**: A simple definition is the air you breathe, the water, plants and animals that feed you! We can't live without them, yet capitalists cannot seem to live peacefully with them.

329

This is your world and their world too. Fight for it or die when it dies! It is a sad commentary, but most people on this earth are so busy worrying about their own existence and survival that they can't take the time to do anything about the world that keeps them alive.

**Foreign Policy**: Our present "government" does not have a foreign policy. Its involvement with other governments would best be described as an economic arrangement. The United States now economically supports "governments" that allow US businesses to harvest natural resources and exploit their cheap labor forces. Often, we support the leaders of these "governments" against their own people to ensure that we have the freedom to take advantage of that country's resources.

**Freedom**: Freedom is the inner drive for individuality, which is one of the most basic human traits. It is not a gift given by others, but a right that comes with being human. To take away a person's freedom is to deny them their basic human instincts of curiosity and exploration, which in turn produce our most valuable trait, that of creativity.

**Free Enterprise**: Free enterprise, not capitalism, is the economic system our forefathers chose for this country. Capitalists do not believe in free enterprise; they believe in a monopoly.

**Freethinkers**: liberals, radicals, creative people. Those people who believe in freedom not

**Government**: The US Government is now run by businessmen, lawyers and accountants. What do they know of democracy? Our government is supposed to be, of the people, for the people and by the people. And if those who run our government do not champion our best interests, then we must, as good Americans, vote them out of office and replace them with others who will.

**Ignorance:** One of the most destructive forces in the world to-day. (If you can't, don't.?)

**Law Profession:** We all need, at times, someone with a better knowledge of the law we live within. And let me add here that without laws there would be no human society; it would be the jungle, anarchy.

**Left wing:** is someone or something that is connected with socialist philosophy. The association of the word left with socialism refers to the fact that the Left Bank of the River Seine was the socialist part of Paris in the 1920s and '30s. (From *The Hippie Dictionary* by John Bassett McCleary)

**Liberals:** The people who would like to see everything run smoothly for everyone, not just for themselves. And they're not doing it for money. Liberals and intellectuals think right between capitalism and communism, taking the good parts from each and emphasizing freedom of the individual. For this, they are feared and despised by both capitalists and communists.

**Materialism:** One of the most destructive forces in the world today. To buy something just because you can, in order to enhance your image, that shatters all the moral laws!

**Media:** The law giving us freedom of speech also expects us to tell the truth when exercising that right. To knowingly lie while using your freedom of speech is to admit that you are not worthy of possessing it.

**Monopoly:** It's a cute little board game we play at home. But it is not all that much fun when confronted out in the real world. It brings out the worst personalities of mankind, and, in the end, it may destroy this world. It is no fluke that monopolies and interest rate usury were regulated by our founding fathers, and it is no surprise that capitalist politicians have been dismantling the regulations ever since.

**Patriotism**: True and real American patriotism is toward the ideals of the Declaration of Independence, Constitution and Bill of Rights. Patriotism is not meant to be directed at a flag, a president or an army. You are not a patriot if you persecute others just because they are not Americans, or for what they think, or for their religion.

**Planned Obsolescence**: Should be a crime punishable by long prison terms. It is not only a crime against mankind, but a sin against Mother Nature.

**Pride**: Is the first sin, because it begets all others! Jesus, 33 years A.B. and JBMc 2/1/20 A.D..

**Religion**: Religion is man's desire for unity, but organized religion is divisive! In God We Trust, does not mean in Buddha we trust, or in Christ, Muhammad or Confucius. It means in God. God is bigger than all our petty religious divisions and squabbles! If your religion is not directed toward enhancing the harmony of this world then God will have nothing to do with it. You are not smarter than God so don't try to put his motive's into your words.

**Silent Majority and Middle Class**: Their only flaw is trust, their only misunderstanding is faith, and their mistake is not seeing who their real enemies are.

**Socialism**: What is wrong with good will? What is wrong with taking care of your fellow man? The Bible tells us to support the poor, children, widows and the aged. It is not a crime to want to help others in need. It is a sin if we don't.

**Stock Market**: A pyramid scheme, which I define as a social and economic system where by a small number of people rise to wealth and prominence on the backs of all the other people. Society in the shape of a pyramid. And the stock market is also a legalized Ponzi scheme, where people borrow money to support their illegal and wasteful lifestyles and then borrow more money from others to <u>almost</u> pay back the people they first borrowed from. If you were to explain it to someone who had never heard of such a pox before, they would think you were crazy. But don't stop dumping your money into the stock market, or we might have a recession and get rid of all the capitalists.

## Apology

### If The Wingtips Fit, Wear Them

In this book I have generalized about the personalities and actions of several occupations and ideologies. If I have offended anyone, I apologize to you unless the characterization fits. If you feel that I have wrongly accused you just because you happen to be a lawyer, accountant, capitalist or conservative, I will admit that there are righteous folks among those groups of individuals, I personally know a few. But I don't know you and therefore, I must, by default, lump you in with the 1% who are scoundrels. And before you embarrass yourself and vehemently deny your guilt in front of your friends who know the truth, please look in the mirror and ask yourself, "Am I really an OK guy or am I actually a snake as the author of Common Sense depicts?" If you realize through this self-examination that you really are a snake, don't slither off. Stand up, admit your faults, take it like a man "or woman," change and evolve as all good humans do.

Paine Wrote in Closing:

"The sun never shined on a cause of greater worth. 'Tis not the affair of a City, a Country, a Province or a Kingdom; but a continent (*and a World)--... 'Tis not the concern of a day, a year, or an age; posterity are virtually involved in the contest, and will be more or less affected even to the end of time, by the proceedings now. Now is the seed time of Continental (*World) union, faith and honor. The least fracture now will be like a name engraved with the point of a pin on the tender find of a young oak; the wound would enlarge with the tree, and posterity read in full grown characters...."

I write in ending and paraphrase from Thomas Paine:

"Volumes have been written on the subject of the struggle between greed and intellect. Men of all ranks have embarked in the controversy, from different motives, and with various designs; but all have been ineffectual, and the period of debate is closed. Morality, truth, is the last resource and will decide the contest; the appeal was the choice of selfish men, and the selfless hath accepted the challenge."

At this point again you may be thinking, this guy is a dammed idealist! He is proposing humans become perfect, and that is a dubious possibility. I know we will never be perfect, but I hear from a reliable source that it is possible we could succeed with our humanity here on our lovely planet home if we just get smart.

*"Straighten up, you assholes!"*
Message from God 1/2/20


*"I am only the messenger!"*
JBMc

# About the Author

## John Bassett McCleary

Mr. John Bassett McCleary has worked as a writer, art director and photographer in the newspaper, music, publishing and advertising industries for the last fifty-three years.

He is a third-generation journalist. His father and grandfather were muckrakers, newspaper owners and political speechwriters. John's grandfather, J. M. Bassett, owned The Golden Era, Oakland Tribune and Los Angeles Herald in California and was the secretary/advisor and speech writer for California Governor Leland Stanford. John's father, W. K. Bassett, owned, wrote and edited newspapers papers in Massachusetts, California and Hawaii. In the 1940s and 50s W. K. was also the secretary/advisor to Honolulu Mayor John Wilson.

During the 1960s and 70s, John McCleary was a music industry photographer in Los Angeles and was on stage and in the dressing rooms with The Doors, Jimi Hendrix, The Stones, Tina Turner and others. In the early 1970s, he produced a series of twelve posters and *The People's Book*, a photographic essay of the counterculture of the era.

*"Why is it that the most important songs are written during the bad Republican administrations"?*
Dudley Griffin 4/5/2020

John participated in and photographed many civil rights and anti-war demonstrations across the United States during the 1960s and 70s. His photographic essay of the 1960s counterculture was published in 1972 by Celestial Arts in San Francisco, and in 1998, he self-published *Monterey Peninsula People* a book of photographs and bios of Peninsula residents. John is also the author of *The Hippie Dictionary: A Cultural Encyclopedia of the 1960s and 1970s*, published by Ten Speed Press in 2002, revised in 2004, and now published by Crown Publishing Group, division of Random House.

Mr. McCleary is considered "The Authority on the generation that questioned authority." John is soon to publish two other books on the hippie counterculture entitled *Mother's Heart, Father's Mind; The Sexual Revolution of A Young Man: 1955 to 1985,* and *Common Sense and Reason Again.* These two books and the Hippie Dictionary will complete the *Hippie Trilogy!*

In his own words: John says, "I have been asked who my 'target audience' is? My target audience is you, all of you, because what I write about affects everybody. Greed, selfishness, bigotry, war and ignorance damage us all, and ironically, most of all, they destroy those who practice them!

I make no excuses for speaking the truth, though it may incite, offend or convict some people. I am not responsible for their flaws; I just discover or expose them.   I say what I say so that hopefully someone will find solutions to the problems and then pass them on to the next generations."

I think it is time for us to stop going through all this differences shit. It is time that we start thinking about our similarities, and how important it is for our survival that we all become the same!